DEATH
IN A
LONELY LAND

PETER CAPSTICK'S VIDEOS

Capstick/Botswana Safari
Capstick/Hunting the African Lion
Capstick/Hunting the Cape Buffalo
Capstick/Hunting the White Rhino
Capstick/Hunting the African Elephant

Peter Capstick's *books* are available from St. Martin's Press.

His *videos* may be obtained by writing to:

Sportsmen on Film
5038 North Parkway Calabasas
Calabasas, CA 91302

BY THE SAME AUTHOR

Death in the Long Grass
Death in the Silent Places
Death in the Dark Continent
Safari: The Last Adventure
Peter Capstick's Africa: A Return to the Long Grass
The Last Ivory Hunter: The Saga of Wally Johnson
Maneaters
Last Horizons: Hunting, Fishing, and Shooting on Five
  Continents

THE PETER CAPSTICK LIBRARY

Peter Capstick, Series Editor

The Man-Eaters of Tsavo Lt. Col. J. H. Patterson, D.S.O.
Hunting the Elephant in Africa Capt. C. H. Stigand
African Hunter Baron Bror von Blixen-Finecke
The Book of the Lion Sir Alfred E. Pease
Big Game Hunting in North-Eastern Rhodesia Owen Letcher
Memories of an African Hunter Denis D. Lyell
African Game Trails Theodore Roosevelt
African Adventures Denis D. Lyell
Big Game Hunting in Central Africa William Buckley
Kill: or Be Killed Major W. Robert Foran
After Big Game in Central Africa Edouard Foà
Big Game Hunting and Collecting in East Africa, 1903–1926
  Kálmán Kittenberger

DEATH
IN A
LONELY LAND

PETER HATHAWAY CAPSTICK

Illustrated by Dino Paravano

FOREWORD BY DON CAUSEY

More Hunting, Fishing, and Shooting on Five Continents

ST. MARTIN'S PRESS

NEW YORK

Library of Congress Cataloging-in-Publication Data

Capstick, Peter Hathaway.
    Death in a lonely land / Peter Hathaway Capstick.
        p.   cm.
    ISBN 0-312-03810-0
    1. Hunting. 2. Fishing. 3. Shooting. I. Title.
SK33.C339   1990
799—dc20   89-24092
                                                                CIP

10

Contents

CONTENTS

x

FOREWORD

Being asked to write this introduction to Peter Capstick's latest volume sets my mind to wandering back over the years I have known the man and his writing. A somewhat late-starter, I didn't really know how well Peter could write until his first book, *Death in the Long Grass,* hit the outdoor publishing world like a hurricane in 1977. I was Executive Editor of *Outdoor Life* magazine at the time and I can still remember Hunting Editor, George Haas, coming into my office with a copy of the book and suggesting that I "dip into it most anywhere and see what I thought."

Lo these many years later, I can still remember the pleasant surprise I felt when I cracked open that copy of *Death in the Long Grass.* Here was writing that reached out and grabbed you. Right there on the page were dawns that "hemorrhaged in the east" creating an awful sense of dread, and unbelievably wild African rivers that "slid beneath the trees like molten grease."

The stories that unfolded before my eyes had all those small details that make a yarn come alive—the feel of dew on the gunwales of a boat, the sound of wind in the trees. More important, these stories captured the primeval excitement of being outdoors again . . . of hunting and fishing . . . of strange things b-r-e-a-t-h-i-n-g in the dark.

I was sold on the spot and *Outdoor Life* agreed to hire Capstick to write a column—which immediately became the most popular feature in the magazine. Coincidentally, some of the columns he wrote for *Outdoor Life* at the time appear in this second volume of his collected magazine articles.

It's no secret to most of you how Capstick's writing career has taken off since then. To his credit now are nine books, each one more popular than the one before it. Interestingly, Capstick is one of the very few outdoor writers who has transcended the narrow outdoor field and won favorable comment from the likes of *The New York Times, Sports Illustrated,* and other mainstream media. And, Lord, have his books been selling. When the dust clears around Peter Capstick, he is certain to be the biggest seller of outdoor books ever.

Why? . . . What is there about the works of Peter Capstick that makes them so addictive to so many people? I think I know but the quality I want to describe is hard to pin down. Perhaps I can sneak up on the answer by way of an anecdote.

A half dozen years ago, I met Peter in Botswana where he wanted me to see and possibly report on the game-rich hunting concession a friend of his hoped to be awarded from the government. The concession was down in a remote corner of the Kalahari Desert that had never been commercially hunted before.

"The area is crawling with lions," Peter told me over the crackling static of a transatlantic phone call when the idea for this trip first came up.

"Oh, really," I said.

There was an ominous pause before Peter answered. Yes, the lions were quite large and, unfortunately, hunting season was going to be closed during our visit, which meant we would not be allowed to carry any guns with us, he said.

But not to worry, Peter added. The trip would be "fun."

The appointed day arrived and Peter and I boarded a small plane in Gaborone. The four-hour flight to our rendezvous point in the middle of the desert was bumpy but uneventful. Peter's friend was waiting for us with a Land Cruiser packed with tents, food, and other paraphernalia. Off we went into the lion-infested wilderness without a gun between us.

That night after our tents were up and the sun had gone down we sat for a while around a campfire, listening to night sounds. At one point, way out there in the distance somewhere, there was a faint "uuum-umph" sound.

"Listen!" Peter said, holding his hand up. "A lion . . . !"

We all held our breath and listened. And sure enough, there it was again . . .

"Uuum-umph . . ."

The sparks from the campfire whirled up into the pitch-black sky. The surrounding desert was definitely quieter than it had been a minute before.

We all pushed up a little closer to the campfire and listened. When no more sounds were forthcoming, Peter was moved to tell a hair-raising story about some man-killing lions in Tanzania. The backdrop for his story was perfect. And so was his sense of timing. At dramatic moments in his tale, he would pause just long enough for us to start listening beyond his fictional lions for the real lion out there in the desert that just might come in the camp that night and e-a-t u-s! He was having a ball, scaring the living daylights out of us.

When we turned in that night, I'll never forget how Peter made a big point of wedging a chair in between my tent and the Land Cruiser parked nearby. He did that, he said, to make sure that any lions that came in camp that night would not be able to walk right by my tent, where they might get my scent and be inspired to do something . . . well, you know, unspeakable.

This last was delivered with a raised eyebrow and a meaningful, sidelong look.

Old Africa hands will smile at the drama Peter created that night in the Kalahari. And they would be right, in a way, because there was truly a very small chance that a lion, or anything else, would come in the camp and take one of us. But small chance does not mean no chance.

Regularly, all across Africa, people are indeed taken by lions and other dangerous animals. On the most fundamental level, down where children and good writers live, life is dangerous no matter where you live, and full of wonder, too. One of the functions of the good storyteller is to remind us of that.

And boy does Capstick do that! He makes your skin crawl and your head reel. And, in between, he riles you up about the earthshaking importance of everything from Cape buffalo to BB guns.

With admirable self-insight, Peter has described himself

as a "full-time professional small boy." And he is, the lucky devil! While the rest of us have crusted over with grown-up-ness, Capstick has managed to keep himself hard-wired into that place where feelings, fears, and perceptions incandesce.

And that is precisely why hundreds of thousands of us can't get enough of Peter Capstick. Keep a chair wedged between the tents, pal. And keep on writing . . . !

Don Causey
Editor, *The Hunting Report*
New York City
September 25, 1989

INTRODUCTION

It was the late Robert Chester Ruark who once observed that writers were not *actually* people. Further, it is common knowledge that writers don't really work for a living. Not many people would disagree with the Ruarkian Hypothesis, and to my financial astonishment some years ago, a divorce judge didn't reckon that tapping a typewriter constituted gainful employment, no matter by how much lucre it swelled the marital coffers of what I had always naively thought of as joint tenancy.

However, as I was to discover in the fullness of time, there are lots of ways to get paid, many far juicier than cash. Certainly, the joy, nostalgia, and sheer memories of reliving the years of accumulated adventure that added up to *Death in a Lonely Land* and its brother book, *Last Horizons,* lumped up into a duke's stipend of psychic payday every time I wrote a new introduction to these old pieces.

That these books exist is really thanks to my wife, Fiona, who, sniffing through much-shipped odd boxes in the garage and wading through trunks, ancient manila folders, and even *my* filing system, hopefully without developing some disease new to science, accummulated a tattered, evil smelling, yellowed and brittle pile of theoretical prose about as attractive as used mummy wrappings.

But, the stuff was there! And, so were my memories.

Perhaps I had spent too many of the last years working on contemporary African books. Maybe there were just so many more aspects to earning a living that I had lost touch with my own past while writing about others'. The point is, I had for-

gotten so much of what I had considered important. But, here
it all was!

I had forgotten the searing shock of a half-frozen foot
regretfully immersed in a hot tub after a day hunting ruffed
grouse in the January New Jersey snow. I had forgotten Opening Day 1955, when my father, my brother, and I had all taken
limits of grouse, woodcock, and ducks. The thrill of shooting
dragon flies with the Mini-Menacer BB submachine gun had
been usurped by such ho-hum fare as wounded lions and
mambas. And, my war with the Vlackfontein baboon troop
was almost fifteen years ago! How could I forget the Everglades dawns with Ray? Or the incomparable mud of Brazil?
Or that first leopard? Or his last victim? Or the hordes of
snipe in Morocco?

Hell, it was all here. The wet-dog smell, the bite of nitro
solvent, the mopane smoke, the gut-glow of Highland anti-
corrosive, the dead grass and dust smell, and the elephant
dung. The brilliant yellow Ethiopian butterflies clustered on
the glazing pool of oryx blood. The chanting Brazilian boatmen over the slithering mercury of the Araguaia by moonlight.
The soft gabbles of KiSwahili, Amharic, Sindebele, Awiza, or
pure Texan over dying campfires. The wrinkled wink of Paddy
Golden as he closed the schoolhouse, took a swig of *soomthin'*
agin' the dew, and instructed his pupils, in Gaelic, how to
properly retrieve a gentleman's wood pigeons, provided His
Honesty hit any, of course.

Old memories. Old friends. I wouldn't walk across the
street to catch the new world record brown trout or collect the
greatest kudu that ever spanned a spiral without one of those
old pals to tell me I was doing it impossibly, irretrievable
wrong. Of course, they were without exception always correct.
Trouble is, like most things in life, including grand sunsets, if
they're any good they just don't seem to last long enough.
They die. I don't like to hunt, fish, tell lies, enjoy campfires, or
drink alone. So, if the title of this book seems a bit puzzling,
just take it from me that the great sporting lands are a bit
lonely without Silent, Invisible, Tom, Dean, Ray, Mahlon, and
the rest of the good ones.

As in *Last Horizons,* these pieces are roughly grouped through the peversity of my nature. That Ye Loyal made that book a best-seller is a charming gesture to the concept of nostalgia as a commodity. To so many of you, this will be our ninth trip together. Loyal companions make for a smooth journey. Not having had an appropriate chance to do so before, may I simply say, "Thank you." Your consistent courtesies and kindnesses speak well in an ever-shrinking world that oft seems overrun with misconceptions of sportsmanship and the true nobility of fair play.

Before leaving you to the world of the professional small boy once again, I would like to incorporate the Acknowledgments as offered in *Last Horizons* into this Introduction. All those who provided their graciousness and generosity are well recorded there, and I feel it unnecessary to repeat them here, but to reiterate my respect, gratitude, and appreciation.

One important change would be to express my professional esteem and personal thanks to the man who wrote the Foreword to this book, *Death in a Lonely Land,* Don Causey, whom you will remember as my editor at *Outdoor Life Magazine* frosting the glass on a decade ago. Don, for the best of reasons—ability and talent—is the publisher and editor of the ever more prestigious *Hunting Report,* a monthly synopsis of *exactly* what is going on in the world of hunting. Thank you, Don, but I wonder if anybody ever believed you that it was pouring icy rain on our last trip to the Kalahari Desert? I know. Another trip with Capstick. . . .

Thus, I abandon you to the Lonely Lands. Of course, I hope you enjoy the old prices and "period" concepts as much as I have in reassembling them.

PETER HATHAWAY CAPSTICK
On Safari, Namibia
September 1989

DEATH
IN A
LONELY LAND

ROLL BACK THE YEARS!

GUNS & AMMO —
MARCH 1980

The Crosman Model 760XL.

AUTHOR'S INTRODUCTION

It is my personal belief that if a man forsakes the great days and "toys" that brought him a wonderful childhood, he would be foolish to start taking himself seriously and forget those same things that brought him the joy of youth as he grows a bit longer in the fangs. Of course, we have to contend with the Bible, which suggests that a man must do away with childish things, but I really don't think BB guns were part of the message. The joy of shooting and teaching the shooting arts must be eternal. After all, who taught David to use his sling?

I'll not bother to give the source of the idea that the only difference between men and boys is the cost of their toys. But if you show me a man who takes himself seriously, you will usually find that he's missing a great deal of his own heritage.

So many times now, I have said that shooting is a state of mind, whether with a $50,000 Holland & Holland Royal grade double rifle or the Daisy or the Crosman. To sneer and be "above" such juvenile pleasures comes right off the limit of your moral credit card. What, after all, is the shooting life all about? I believe it is to have fun. So, go on. Take a couple of shots. I'll bet you remember things gladly that were long forgotten. . . .

It was just the other day, a bright, clear Southwest Florida morning replete with dueling mockingbirds, soft, rising sea breezes and loafing, poison-green chameleons in the hybiscus when my wife wearily asked me what I wanted to be when—and if—I grew up. Possibly the fact that I had just spilled half a pack of BBs with improved cylinder distribution over the kitchen vinyl had something to do with her query, but then you never really know about women's motives.

She gave me one of those sideways looks (probably searching for an artery near the surface) and held the dustpan, all the while observing that she has three children: her son, daughter, and me. I wasn't really listening, struck by the curious fact that neither Daisy Super Accurate Precision Ground Bullseye BBs nor Crosman Perfectly Round Micrometer Tested Super BBs tend to make the apparently simple transition between broom and dustpan edge without slickly rolling at right angles to pour back under the dishwasher. The *other* dishwasher, that is. I am applying the empirical processes to this phenomenon, possibly a matter of sectional density or, conceivably, an aberrant ballistic coefficient. Then, it could be that my broom handle needs one-quarter inch more drop at the heel or that the dustpan has a poor wood-to-metal fit and should be glass-bedded.

Despite being six foot eight and having a sense of humor like Irving R. Levine, my wife is really a good woman at heart. She never beats me where it shows in public, sees to my nourishment with astounding zeal, and has seen to it that I am never guilty of Ring Around the Collar. Yet she is a woman and, by genetic selection and sexual definition, suspicious as a low-water brown trout anytime she catches me edging out the back door with a BB gun, muttering and woe-is-me-ing under my breath that I am not really going out to have a crashing good time playing Rover Boys but am, in fact, a serious firearms journalist on a bona fide research project. I flash my press card at her and stand firm. At least reasonably firm. I am working. Employed. Assaying the dizzy heights of semi-solvency.

I don't wander around all morning plinking at things and shooting up the new phone book for penetration tests because I *like* it. God forbid! It's dirty, dangerous work. I would infinitely prefer cleaning out the garage or playing human fly washing the upstairs windows for the party next Friday. But, A Man Sees What Must Be Done and Does It. Like all gun writers, I have a very deep-seated sense of professional responsibility. I am also completely bananas over BB guns of any description, the affliction being known, dependent upon your choice of clinical nomenclature, as either the Red Ryder Syndrome or Crosman's Disease.

Like most of you Faithful, my first frontal assault on the world of shooting was with a Daisy. If I'd gotten a nickel an hour for the time spent stalking mastodons and king cobras down by the frog pond and wandering the nomadic, after-school woods aglow with the sense of satisfaction that only the dry rattle of a full BB reservoir can bring, I'd likely now be living off a stable of municipal bonds on my private Greek island.

There have been a lot of vodka martinis over my inlays since that first lever-action Daisy, yet I can still remember every nick in its authentic hardwood stock, including the magnificent hand work I did engraving my initials in bas-relief with a Christmas-new X-acto woodcarving knife kit. When I was finished, halfway through the crossbar on the H, they were able to wire up the tendon of my left thumb quite neatly, although it played hell for years with my flipper reflex on the pinball machines. That rifle, after spitting what must have been a half-ton of BBs, somehow got laid aside and is undoubtedly resting, fossil-like, somewhere in the primeval plasto-metallic sludge spawned by the debris of the culture of Montville, New Jersey. Helluva shame. If you can find it, I'll trade you even for a new Holland & Holland Royal.

When I was nine, I graduated to the Daisy pump gun, a real magnum after the old lever action. But I never liked it that much because all the trajectories and Kentucky windage wired into my circuits were negated by its greater power. It was also trickier to load and didn't have the vast magazine capacity of the lever gun. I went back to the saddle gun with its loop of gen-u-wine rawhide knotted about the ring on the side of the receiver, the purpose of which accoutrement I never did fathom, except that Red Ryder and Little Beaver both thought highly of it. Later, about the time I was paroled from reform school for conspiring to overthrow the School Board by force, I got one of the fancy hammer versions, the Buffalo Bill Scout. Zowie! I still shoot it in fits of beloved melancholy.

Actually, the use of a BB gun on a regular basis is one of the best possible ways to keep sharp the hand-eye coordination necessary when hunting with either a rifle or a shotgun. Just as snow skiing transfers to water skiing, so does the BB gun transfer many talents to firearms use. Want to teach your son or daughter the elements of lead for wing shooting? Have them spend a few hours popping away at dragonflies or firing at chips of wood in a fast-flowing stream. Even the U.S. Army has found the little guns a valuable training aid for the instinctual act of combat firing, teaching recruits to hit thrown lead washers and smaller items in the air with BB guns that have had the front and rear sights removed.

BB guns have come a long way, baby, since the early push-pull, click-click models of my wasted youth, let alone since their introduction by Daisy back in the 1880s. Recently, I got stuck into the subject again after combing through the sleek new offerings in the rear sections of the *Guns & Ammo Annual,* and decided to pick an example of the newer developments in the field for evaluation. Completely disregarding the ultra-sophisticated grouping of match and high-performance pellet guns, I settled almost arbitrarily on a new air gun by Crosman, the multi-stroke Model 760XL. Oops! I do beg your collective pardon, Messrs. Crosman; I meant the Model 760XL Deluxe Powermaster with "Deluxe Styling!" and even "Deluxe Features," no less.

Wow! I'll give you this, boys: if you're used to a double beef Whopper, hold the onions, extra cheese, the creature that lay before me was a double helping of larks' tongues on Beluga caviar with Tasmanian leatherwood honey sauce. If *that* was what BB guns have come to, then I may have been naive about the relationship between Red Ryder and Li'l Beaver. If I'd had that gun when I was fourteen, I would have been the first kid on the block to rule the earth.

No two ways about it, the 760 is a mean, sexy-looking machine that is really far more than a BB gun in the sense I normally think of one. First off, it's a hybrid between a repeating BB rifle (Imagine! Rifling! Ten lands!) and a single-shot pellet rifle offering a wide choice of power selections, depending upon how many times you pump it, between a minimum of two strokes and a maximum of ten. Why not eleven, or for those of you who strike without closing cover, even twelve?

Well, I've put it off long enough. If you're a gun writer, you just have to take the terrible dangers inherent in the profession as part of the price of earning the tremendous fees we command for these high-risk articles. I picked up the gun in my bare hands and hefted it. (Incidentally, there is a common misconception among anti-gun folk that guns are "slimy." This is not true. They are simply smooth and cool to the touch.) Having determined from the owner's manual precisely which was the "barrel" and which the "stock," I located the Reservoir Loading Port, which, for the sake of keeping this whole thing professional, I shall call the RLP. Having cleverly decided to try the repeating BB action first, I cracked the milk carton of 1,500 Crosman Super BB Perfectly Round Micrometer Tested ammo (SBBPRMT). I took their word for it that it was not just 1,499. Careful not to point the muzzle at anybody I did not want to shoot, I put the gun on "SAFE" and attempted to pour 180 SBBPRMTs through the 5/16-inch RLP. After several minutes and the application of some language our younger readers might think unsporting, I got enough in to at least cause some trouble. Ah, but if you think that's all there is to foddering the 760XL, you didn't read the manual. Next, you must transfer, untouched by human hands, eighteen SBBPRMTs to the Visual Magazine (VM), from the R of the RLP. At this I proved expert. The VM is a space that runs along the top of the receiver and acts as the receptacle for the immediate shots to follow, if, of course, I don't screw this thing up. To get the BBs into the VM, you must find the BB Retainer Button (BBRB) and pull it rearward. You then, even if it seems a bit inconsistent, point the gun downward (watch those feet) and shake and twist the rifle as if stirring a super Saturday night bucket of thirty-to-one martinis (Stolichnaya vodka, of course). To discourse openly on just why I found this simple would not be seemly. You then push forward the BBRB, which locks in its load of eighteen SBBPRMTs. It's like being halfway to paradise.

You are now, and please don't be overanxious, ready to pump. I'm not going to tell you again how many times because we need you here at *G&A,* and those subscription cancellations don't do much for my rates. I will advise you, however, that Crosman lists three Shooting Safety Zones, cleverly, A through C. Two to four pumps will throw a pellet or BB 250 yards, which is Zone A. The B Zone is 450 yards, which requires five to ten pumps and, right, I didn't believe it either. Zone C doesn't exist because you can't pump more than ten times. Don't you just love it?

I decided that five pumps would be sufficient to qualify for hazardous-duty rates, which I accomplished with only one, though large, blood blister. Now, carefully avoiding Gramps, the big dog, the suburban split-level, and Mom's new Aspen, I gently worked the bolt. Nope. No BB. Checking page six, I discovered that the rifle must be pointed downward for the magnetized bolt tip to contact a BB in the VM and pull it forward into the chamber. Giddy with accomplishment, I was now ready to fire away!

Laying my firm jaw against the poly-god-knows-what plastic Monte Carlo stock with the "cheek piece that gives the XL a distinctive sporty look," I focused steely, unwavering eyes over the adjustable-for-elevation-and-windage rear sight and centered the hooded (presumably for jungle conditions) front post in its proper notch. Off went the safety as I eased into the creepy 2¾-pound pull. FFFap! barked the 760XL Deluxe Powermaster. Clank! went the center of a Coke can on a log ten yards away, twisting on its axis and toppling to the forest floor. I picked it up and whistled. Right through. In one side and out the other. Pretty impressive, considering this is not an article about the .600 Nitro Express. Up went some paper for grouping, and on went the shooting glasses in case of a ricochet. If you pooh-pooh this, drop a BB from shoulder height on a piece of stone tile and you will find it more lively than a golf ball.

Through the afternoon, I found that the pellets, which are loaded singly through the bolt, gave better performances accuracy-wise, but I preferred the ease of loading the BBs. I've had the gun for a week at this writing, and must give it full marks for what it is supposed to be, a fun gun, but with vastly expanded potential for circumstances requiring greater range and power. Perhaps I have been overly cruel, kidding about the literature, which would be unfair to the gun itself. I think it's a real beaut—accurate, handsome with its spacers and brass-plated receiver—and personally endorse it to the extent of my experience with it, which would include no malfunction at all when instructions were followed. On the Tepeco Speed-Meter sky-screen chronograph, alternating between BBs and pellets, varying the number of pumps from two through ten, muzzle velocities ranged from 202 fps through a very impressive 671. The suggested list price for the 760XL (what do you suppose XL stands for?) is about $43, although in the couple of months before you read this, it may be quoted in Krugerrands.

After looking over the current crop of air guns of all types, it's pretty obvious that there is still no shortage of small boys of all ages in this country, and that's fine by me. Backyards and camping trips just wouldn't be the same without the BB gun, as far as I'm concerned. I know that just as soon as I get to be a real fireman, I'm going to carry my Crosman 760XL right on the truck with me. If my wife will let me.

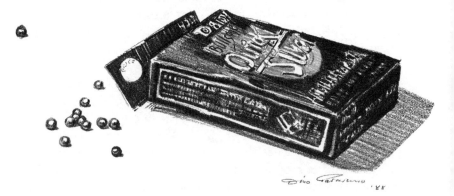

BB ammunition for the Crosman rifle.

THE MINI-MENACER

GUNS & AMMO — MAY 1976

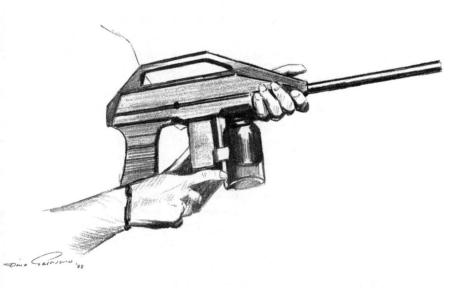

The Mini-Menacer BB submachine gun.

AUTHOR'S INTRODUCTION

What can I say of the first fully-automatic-fire BB gun? Either you yearned for one as a kid or you didn't. I did.

Back in the days when I lived in a Venetian-style town house on pilings over Moorings Bay at the north end of Naples, Florida, I had a Mini-Menacer hooked up to a $600 air compressor that enabled me to spray the bay at will. My then-wife said it was a lovely view; I maintained it to be a great field of fire. No, no nuns, preachers, or other taxpayers suffered, but I for sure found out how many bottled-up, frustrated bankers, real-estate moguls, and assorted chaps there were who still loved the sorts of things that gave them a kick many decades before. When I tell you that in a period of two hours before the Gulf sunset, these people blew away $200 in BBs, you can get a grasp of how emotionally landlocked many professional people are.

Of course, I am an escapist in the extreme. I never felt I had a professional act I had to live up to. I dangle participles and mix metaphors as I see fit. No senior vice-president looks over my purchases of BBs. If I want a compressor for my BB machine gun, I damn well buy one. And I take it off my taxes because I write about it. It's legitimate. Yes, I think many would pronounce me guilty of poaching female dragonflies out of season, but I haven't had the first complaint from the Audubon Society, of which I was a member when I lived in America. Thus, get thee hence; get an M-19A squirter and take a psychological skinny-dip into the old swimming hole. If you regret it, they'll give you your money back. I haven't heard of any refunds as of this writing. . . .

He came out of the sun, the golden light of late afternoon blurred along his wings and gleaming from the metallic blue of his fuselage as he swept over the water, straight at my position in the palms. I watched him narrow the range, shifting slightly, the weapon with its full magazine heavy in my sweaty hands. The seconds ticked off as he bore in on me until seemingly at point-blank and I could stand it no longer. I swung the weapon up, leading him over the glassiness of water with the thick, black barrel. There was a cold, rattling hiss, like sleet on an icy morning, as I touched off a short burst of twenty rounds that churned the surface in a frothy string just behind him.

But he was an old hand. As the metal string of tracers reached out to intercept him like an orange cord, he pulled up sharply, clawing for altitude, rising at a sharp angle. By feel, I increased lead and touched off another burst above and ahead of him, watching the necklace of racing steel snake behind his tail, the optical illusion of my full-auto rounds seeming to bend in flight as they edged closer and the first strike registered on his tail assembly. He was full in the pattern now, and I knew I had him. I held the trigger back, watching chunks of his fuselage tear off and flip away into his slipstream. The deadly burst moved into his wing roots and he was finished as flashing steel cannoned through the delicate surfaces, rupturing their magnificent mechanisms. The near wing tore completely away, spiraling slowly as his heavier wreckage plummeted to the still water below. Scratch one DF-4-B.

I lowered the M-19A Annihilator and let the trigger flip up into the safety position. The cheers of my shock troops, two small neighborhood boys, echoed through the jungle of my Florida backyard. While one fished out the defunct DF-4-B with a long stick, I sent the other, a mere colonel, on a covert mission to the fridge for another beer. Aerial gunnery is thirsty work, and this had been my fifth confirmed kill of the afternoon, not counting the two probables that likely ran out of juice somewhere out over the bay on their way back to base. There had been others, but then, even Von Richthofen didn't get 'em all.

A DF-4-B, for the benefit of you nonmilitary types, is an official designation of the Walter Mitty Aerial Gunnery Brigade, a small (very small) but proud unit commanded by this writer. In civvie talk it refers to a dragonfly with four wings and a blue body, one of our most common predators in the Southwest Florida Everglades country. And our principal weapon against this dreaded foe, the M-19A Annihilator, is the greatest shooting kick for children of all ages over eighteen that's come down the pike since I used to have to cock my Red Ryder carbine with one foot through the lever. Imagine! The first kid on the block with a fully automatic BB submachine gun!

Such heady dreams have haunted me for thirty years, but my love affair with the M-19A Annihilator didn't begin until about a year ago when I started flirting with its radically primitive forerunner, the M-19, after seeing an ad in *Guns & Ammo* I was unable to resist. After three weeks of what I recall as actually undeserved comments to the postperson, it really did arrive and my disappointment was as great as three decades of anticipation could have made it. I've had the same thing happen with girlfriends, but you expect, well, something trustworthy about guns. It was a clumsy affair utilizing a length of plastic tubing folded up inside the forestock, and was coupled with some more plastic hose to a twenty-pound canister of Freon 12, the air-conditioning gas. Loading the Paris Railway Gun surely couldn't have more involved than this affair, but when you finished the procedure of putting BBs one at a time into the tubing, and if they didn't all fall out the other end, and you got both ends properly connected to the nipples and the tubing folded just right and the lead tubing didn't rupture, you got a nice, one-and-a-half second burst of automatic fire. But there were just too many problems of weight, awkwardness (ever go plinking with a twenty-pound steel canister under one arm?), and inconvenience to make my great dream of ruling the world with the M-19 practical. There had to be a better way. I got on the phone with its inventor, Russ Clifford, and, to greatly shave a saga, found him at my front door two days later, refund check in hand, his eyes agleam with near-religious fervor with plans for the M-19A, a totally incorporated and completely new version of the auto BB gun principle. Ve haff veapons of vich you haff never dreamed!

It was another six months before I saw Russ again, after I had returned from a safari season in Central Africa. This time, he was so excited he had a pal fly him across the state from Miami to my home hangout of Naples. I met him at the airport with his lovely wife, wondering if in his enthusiasm he had forgotten the gun back home on the piano. All he carried was a small attaché case and the look of a genius.

As in many towns, the Naples City Dump is located just upwind of the airport, and we drove a mile or so for a test firing. On the back deck of my station wagon, he opened the case and WOW! It lay in its fitted Samsonite oozing more sex than a *Playboy* centerfold, black as death and smooth as a snake against the red plush of its case. It was pure Buck Rogers and then some. If Ian Fleming had ever seen it, you can absolutely bet that 007 would have been using it in one of his escapades with arsenic-coated BBs. As I stepped aside to keep my drool off the lining, Russ assembled the Annihilator. He removed the main firing mechanism, a stockless, snubbed-off creature with a topside carrying handle and stuck on the barrel, which was fitted next to it. He selected one of a pair of black cans, sort of like over-caloried tins of spray gun oil, and a subtle *phhhht* sounded as Clifford punched one over the hypodermic-shaped Freon 12 piercing valve. Reversing the gun belly-up, he loosened the magazine and dumped in about a thousand BBs, resealed the mag, and handed it to me. I have seen more interesting things on a dance floor, but not many.

We walked over to an area not being bulldozed, and Russ stuck up a series of old glass bottles, this being pardonable as we were, after all, in a dump, where broken glass would not be a hazard. He pointed his chin at the rank and suggested I let 'er rip. I held the Annihilator at the hip in the classic position Combat Kelly always used, swung the muzzle at the left edge of the line of ketchup and cider containers and eased down on the trigger, which controlled the release valve of the propellant. Halfway through the smooth pull, I felt the pressure as

Stream of full automatic fire from Mini-Menacer destroying glass bottle.

the trigger tang bore against the firing spring. There was a whispering, rather nasty, low sound as a stream of BBs tore out in a burst that chewed the heavy bottles into a shower of glass, almost a rope of solid metal, so rapid was the rate of fire.

Over the next hour, I went happily, legally, through the four canisters of Freon that Russ had brought along, not to mention several pounds of BBs. I could not have been more delighted if a nearly extinct alligator caught up with Cleveland Amory. No question about it, I decided in a cloud of flying plastic, glass, and beer cans, this one's as good as the other model was bad.

But it wasn't quite.

That was six months ago, and over the extensive test period I fired the gun in preparation for this piece, I found that there were still a few little bugs to be rooted out. A problem developed with the sealant glue used somewhere in the gun's innards, perhaps the gall bladder, that permitted a minute leakage of the propellant. No problem. Clifford switched to a much stronger and more pressure-impervious compound that corrected the fault immediately. There was another snag with the detachable barrel (the Annihilator can be fired with or without the barrel extension) shooting loose from the main firing group after heavy use. Russ solved that one with a small wire tang that slides under the barrel housing and protrudes through a small hole, locking the two parts in perfect alignment. The latest model, with the aforementioned modifications, reached me about twelve canisters of Freon and God knows how many thousand BBs ago, and I finally feel that the problems have been worked out, at least to my personal satisfaction, to call the gun practical. Sometimes minor jams do occur, mostly due to the BBs simply clumping up in the magazine, yet I haven't had one that hasn't cleared up with a light tap of the hand on the stock. The only fully automatic gun you can buy without a federal permit is here! And it works.

The Annihilator is sold by mail at a price tag of $29 including postage, handling, and the usual garbage in states where BB guns are not prohibited and the buyer certifies his age to be eighteen or over. With a shipping weight of five pounds, the actual weight with a full can of Freon 12 and about a thousand BBs is probably closer to seven. The main assembly of the M-19A is one-piece molded WEP—water-extended polyester to you and me. It comes with a removable wire butt-stock, which I found unnecessary and a bit of a nuisance to fool with. The Annihilator is strictly a pointer, lacking a front sight, the sheer volume of BBs blasted through the eighteen-inch detachable seamless aluminum barrel making fire by correction easy and fairly accurate. In daylight, even average eyes can follow the BB stream in flight, and failing that, correction may be made by bullet strike. Carefully timed one-second bursts at 75 degrees Fahrenheit, with a more or less full canister of Freon 12, consistently yielded over sixty BBs in a patterning target. This figures to an incredible rate of 3,600 rounds per minute, well over the inventor's claim of 2,000 per minute.

Freon 12, or if you want to be cute, *dichlorodifluoromethane,* is interesting stuff. Russ Clifford has taken a new tack on the old principle of propelling a missile by the harnessed, rapid expansion of gases, such as created by the confined burning of gunpowder or the release of CO_2 as utilized by many BB guns and pellet guns. Yet the Annihilator can also be operated from any source of compressed air *not exceeding 60 PSI* by attaching a supply hose to the piercing valve with a vinyl-type glue; however, as it comes from the shipping carton, the Annihilator is geared up for use with the ordinary one-pound canister of automobile air-conditioning Freon 12 available from your hardware or auto-supply store at somewhere around a buck and a half a copy. Depending upon the length of your bursts, you'll get a bit over a single thousand-BB magazine from a single can. It's not really cheap to shoot, but in comparison to the cost of modern firearms cartridges, it's certainly far from exorbitant.

Loading the M-19A the first few times is a bit tricky, and you'll probably have some loss of Freon from your first couple of cans until you get the knack of it. Even though the trigger design of the gun, which is partially withdrawn into the stock, makes accidental discharge unlikely in the extreme, you'd better be sure to load it out of doors and without BBs in the magazine. If you somehow triggered a burst in your living room, the place would look like that garage after those wonderful folks brought us the St. Valentine's Day Massacre. Anybody in the remote area of an Annihilator should also wear protective glasses, preferably the shooting type. Steel BBs tend to ricochet, and a direct burst in the face would ruin your day, I guarantee.

Although, of course, complete loading and safety instructions are enclosed with each gun *and should be carefully read and obeyed,* here is the general procedure for priming the Annihilator: Place the canister of Freon 12 at the edge of a tabletop and center the hypo piercing valve over the metal wafer sealing the can. Clifford recommends wearing a glove on the hand holding the Freon, because, should it somehow slip out of the valve, the fast loss of pressure created as the liquid turns to a gas creates an instantaneous and very impressive drop in temperature that will cause the can to freeze anything it comes in contact with. I've never had one slip out, but I presume it's conceivable. Carefully push the piercing valve through the seal and hold tightly. Above the receiver and beneath the carrying handle is a tension screw with a thumb-tightener that activates the propellant retaining clip, a long, hooked rod that holds the canister in place. Tighten the wheel until the canister is sealed against the soft, poly-plastic gasket above the piercing valve and listen to determine whether any Freon is escaping the seal. If there is any hiss of leaking gas, tighten further or slightly shift the angle of the canister to the valve until it stops. Now you're ready for BBs.

Keeping the muzzle safely pointed away, turn the M-19A upside down and unscrew the magazine cover plate, a rectangular metal slab lined with a rubber gasket. Pour BBs into the magazine until three-quarters full. Don't fill it completely, as the BBs need a little elbow room to flow freely when being fired. Carefully center the gasket back over the magazine so it evenly seals all edges, retighten the retaining plate, and you're ready to play Elliot Ness.

How powerful is the Annihilator? Depends. Although power is fairly constant through the life of a container, there is a tendency for the release of the liquid through the mechanism, where it becomes the propellant gas, to cool the can considerably. A long, extended burst causes pressure to drop a great deal, yet as is the case for all hand-held automatic weapons, short bursts are the best utilization. It's curious. With firearms, the problem is overheating; with the M-19A, it's over-cooling. Still, the Annihilator has a scary rate of fire and the basic rule of thumb is that the warmer the Freon canister is, and it should always be kept *under 100 degrees Farenheit,* the more powerful the expanding gases and the faster the BBs will shoot. Since, obviously, you won't be firing constantly, the best method of keeping the can warm enough to give proper results is to carry and shoot the gun with one hand on the can, using it as a fore-grip or carrier, the heat of your hand keeping it warm. Incidentally, always plan to use a can of Freon completely and make sure it's empty before removing it. To store the gun under pressure could, in time, damage the valves.

Ideally, I find my Annihilators throw a BB about 125 to 150 yards which, if you consider that a light steel sphere is the worst possible velocity-retaining missile, ain't bad at all. I spray paint my Freon cans black because they look better and warm faster under sunlight after heavy firing, although you must take care not to let them overheat in direct sunlight past the hundred-degree pressure safety point or they could rupture. The M-19A is not a hunting arm by the wildest stretch of imagination. It's simply a fun gun, an extraordinary plinker with a very low noise level and a very high rate of fire. It's ideal for such make-believe shooting fun as dragonfly hunting, which really is the best wing shooting on a perfectly reduced scale. Certainly it would be great for "pest control," and I wouldn't want to be the rat that caught a burst of Annihilator fire.

There is one factor you must be very careful of when out shooting or just carrying the M-19A: It looks too real.

I usually take the Annihilator along just for jollies, when fishing in the Gulf of Mexico in my small boat. Unfortunately, we have had a lot of "pot drops" from aircraft from the Islands to enterprising boatmen, and the area is heavily patrolled. A police helicopter happened low over me one afternoon and spotted what must have looked like the latest from the KGB lying across the seat. Within ten minutes, a police launch was alongside and I was looking into two .357s, which were not the batting averages of the pair of nervous-looking boys in blue who held them. They told me to "hold it," and you may take my word for it that I did. I held it like nobody's ever held it. I was getting an idea how the guys on the *Pueblo* must have felt.

When we finally established that I was not running slaves or dope and that the Annihilator was actually a BB gun, the two much-relieved representatives of law and order had a ball with the gun, happily shooting up a couple of canisters at flotsam. My treat. Anytime. Both asked me for the address of the manufacturer, LARC International (P.O. Box 340007, Coral Gables, FL 33134) so they could order their own Annihilators.

Still, you'd better not forget that the M-19A looks real enough to get you perforated if you act funny with it around somebody who might have reason to suspect a genuine automatic firearm; if, for example, somebody's called the authorities in the belief that you're carrying a submachine gun and most likely up to no good. Being human, approaching a chopper-toting suspect has been known to make police a touch skittish. It's an identification problem that could have very dire consequences if you play it wrong. My rule, and I've been stopped three times now, is to lay the thing on the ground, step away, and raise my hands until it's established that I'm not really out to knock over Brinks. Incredible as it sounds, there may be as many as ten law-enforcement officers in this country who will not have read this issue of *Guns & Ammo*.

The deadly DF-4-B dragonfly.

THE KILLER BABOONS OF VLACKFONTEIN

THE AMERICAN HUNTER —
OCTOBER–NOVEMBER 1979

Vlackfontein killer baboon.

AUTHOR'S INTRODUCTION

This is the only piece I have ever written that has drawn questionable reaction from my reading audience. I can only suggest that this comeback results from the lack of exposure to the civilized world of the many African species of baboon and their very real threat to human life, most particularly in rural regions.

This chapter, which comprises a two-part article, is not a piece of pulp. Any professional hunter of reasonable experience will confirm this, especially in southern and central Africa. I care not for the insipidity and unreality of those who espouse the concept of no wild animal being dangerous. It is simply and most demonstrably incorrect.

Space does not permit a thoroughgoing investigation of the matter of aggressive baboons in this volume, but I can offer to the researcher the following pieces that have appeared in the various newspapers cited. I did not write them, and you may draw your own conclusions.

- **Pretoria News** *(SA), Oct. 6, 1983: "Monkey Business Just Didn't Pay." Deals with increasing aggression of baboons because of drought.*
- **Natal Mercury** *(SA), Dec. 29, 1983: "Baboons on Rampage." Deals with baboons of Nyanza District of Kenya, near Lake Victoria. Baboons in hordes invading homes, attacking livestock, ransacking houses, stealing food. Mrs. Abondo Agwavo just manages to save her baby.*
- **Pretoria News** *(SA), Sept. 21, 1984: "Baboons Accused of Kidnapping Child." In Harare, Zimbabwe, a two-year-old boy was taken by baboons, but was recovered unharmed the next day.*

- **Natal Witness** *(SA), Oct. 18, 1984: "Cape Man Attacked by Baboon." Mr. Spiros Germanis swallowed his terror and fought his way out.*
- **Pretoria News Foreign Service** *(SA), April 4, 1985: "Five in Hospital After Baboon Hunt." In Harare, Zimbabwe, a rampaging baboon was the source of at least eight wounded Zimbabweans after it ran amok through a densely populated area. The baboon was killed.*
- **Pretoria News** *(SA), April 19, 1987: "Baboon Attacks Mum on Road." In Cape Town, Joyce van Schalkwyk was badly bitten by a baboon when she tried to protect her nine-year-old daughter. The victim was monitoring a cycle race. After attacking the woman, the baboon looted her car. Two days later, on April 21, 1987, it was reported in the press from the same source that a marathon runner on the same cycle course was severely stoned by baboons in the same area of Chapman's Peak. It took twenty-nine stitches to close the runner's wound in his upper arm. He dislikes baboons.*

This chapter is no joke. It happened. And my actions were necessary.

The image of the old baboon was surprisingly clear through the Bushnell 2.5X-8X scope. Even the brown of his sharp, hard eyes gleaming through the slight waver of heat haze was distinct as I steadied the crosshairs about twenty inches over his savage face.

As softly as possible, I raised the bolt handle and lowered it, cocking the action on a 270-grain Kynoch .375 H&H Magnum round in the old Model 70. With the scope at full power and the Pachmayr Lo-Swing snug, the 450 yards between the baboon and me seemed like a few feet in the laser-like sunshine of the Rhodesian [Zimbabwe] afternoon. Sweat sheeting down my dirty face after the long stalk, I paused to get my shooting breath, watching him through the scope.

He surveyed the area, alert and cautious, an aloof but lonely figure among his clan, which he disdainfully ignored. The silver edges of his hair ruffled in a light swirl of wind, and I removed my finger from the trigger to see how the gust would flow. The Winchester was zeroed at two hundred yards, and I knew the holdover at four hundred would be about twenty-seven inches. So, at an estimated 450 yards, I had better allow a good thirty inches to drop that big, soft-point surprise smack into the boiler room.

I watched the grass stalks and dull mopane leaves, deciding on a three-quarter breeze of about five miles per hour, and shifted my hold a whisker left. The rifle was propped against the edge of an old termite hill—solid as a benchrest—with my crushed beret for insulation. Revenge would now be mine.

I started my squeeze and was startled when the big rifle roared. After what seemed a very long time, I saw the big baboon slam backward from his perch atop a rock. A glimpse of his face showed the purest astonishment. He rolled over once and lay on his side in the short grass.

Bedlam rocked the hillside with the arrival of the bullet's sonic crack. I quickly worked the bolt and lined up on another huge male that had paused in flight, confused by the echoes of the muzzle blast. As he looked over his shoulder, I sent him an Air Mail Special COD that passed through his back and continued on to throw a cloud of topsoil from beyond him. He threw up his arms and rolled down the hill like a bad guy in a grade-B Western movie. The crosshairs swung past a female with a baby clutched to her chest, and pulled ahead of another male. The hurried shot landed just short, showering him with high-velocity dirt and gravel. He gave a shriek that was piercingly loud even at my distance as he jumped an easy ten feet into the air and cleared the ridge before I could jack another round up the spout.

I kept perfectly still, scanning the hill for movement, but nothing showed after a full five minutes. I opened the action and clicked in fresh rounds. With the rifle at the ready position, I cautiously started across the low valley and up the little hill, which was snaggled with boulders and tangles of grassy cover.

The old baboon lay where he had fallen, the exit hole of the bullet through his spine. His terrible madman eyes were still open and staring unglazed at my feet. Lordy, but he was huge—at least ninety pounds of iron muscle and tent-peg fangs that could disembowel a tom leopard as easily as a man opens a Ziploc bag.

"Tag, you're it," I muttered softly, rolling him over with my foot, an odd feeling of ancestral murder running through the dark back of my brain.

A chorus of outrage erupted from the trees, well out of range. I went to inspect the other big male farther up the slope. He lay in a huddled lump. I prayed he was dead; finishing off wounded *mabobojan* was spooky. They are just too bloody human—nasty as the creatures are.

As I walked toward him, I had to pass a large jumble of boulders about six feet high that formed a shadowy cave of solid rock. When I was fifteen yards away and just even with it off my right elbow, I chanced to glance into the dark corner. I got the absolute fright of my misspent life.

In a blur of hairy motion, the shade exploded with an earsplitting series of screams and assorted intensely unpleasant sounds as a gigantic male baboon launched himself at me. He was a terrifying, nightmare creature, bounding with amazing speed straight at my sweet young body. His lips were pulled back from the black mask of his Doberman muzzle, displaying his awful fighting fangs. Nearly two inches of switchblade ivory displayed in that manner is not likely to go unnoticed. I'd be lying if I said I wasn't downright spooked. But I'll promise you one thing, brother, I wasn't having any of *him*!

If I'd passed five yards closer, it would have likely been the ball game—no hits, no runs, one major error. I reflex-shot him from the hip at about ten feet. The big slug lucked into his left eye and took out everything west of his teeth. The impetus of his final leap brought his corpse almost to my feet, in spite of the impact of the .357 Mag's bullet. I jumped aside and swatted him again, no matter how unnecessarily. When they try to bite you, you can't make them *too* dead.

I lit a cigarette and got my heart restarted on the third try. I promise you faithfully that I approached the other male on the slope with one eye on the rest of the rocks. The bullet had taken him dead-on, and he was dead-off when I turned back down the hill. Watching the vultures volplane lower, I wondered what bright day they would be stopping off to visit what might be left of me. Africa has a very effective way of stifling any ideas one may entertain of immortality.

Well, I thought, trudging back toward my temporary camp, I'd finally won a skirmish with the Vlackfontein baboons. But the war was still very much in question. At the rate I was going, I'd be tripping over my beard before I could induce the huge troop to pack up and change territories.

In 1975, when things got a bit sticky for palefaces in Zambia, and extremes of weather and overhunting had made Botswana less than it used to be, I had entered into a deal to conduct client safaris in Rhodesia. The area I was to work in was the Matetsi Wildlife Area Safari Unit No. 4, about fifty miles south of Victoria Falls and the Zambezi River. I had chosen as headquarters an abandoned house originally built in 1902 by a chap who had actually driven an ox wagon all the way from Capetown. (The feat was, in those days, the same as flying a single-engine aircraft to the moon and back would be today.) I preferred canvas or grass huts for most safari work, but the solid, plaster-covered adobe walls of Vlackfontein (Flack-fohn-tain, from the Afrikaans term meaning "Fountain on a Plain") offered excellent cover from surprise machine-gun fire and mortar bomb fragments. They were the rage in that area of the world during the bush war.

The land surrounding Vlackfontein is like a coral reef in the open sea or an oasis in the Sahara. Deep, cool springs, alive with delicious tilapia bream, were bearded with ancient groves of fig, acacia, and fruit trees planted when the place was a going concern. The trees were now in poor shape, but still offered a gigantic smorgasbord for a baboon troop. Lions roared, rattling the remnants of windows from what I brazenly called "the lawn," a grassy *vlei* with the tall grass crushed flat by buffalo herds in the dry season. Leopards lurked in the rocky hills, singing their love and territorial songs anytime they felt like it. Herds of sable and zebra ghosted the edge of the bush off the veranda, and bull kudu drank daily at the nearest springs, with the brassy early light accentuating their ivory-tipped corkscrew horns.

Heavily enlaced by deteriorating barbed wire was an enclosure fifty yards from the back door, containing the grave of the last owner of Vlackfontein. The man had killed more than 150 lions here in a single year to protect his cattle herds, and still failed. Vlackfontein, you see, borders the Wankie National Park, which supplied beef-hungry lions a lot faster than he and his men could kill them.

One day, when he was prepared to call it quits anyway, he walked out into the backyard, smack into a bull buffalo that didn't like the way he parted his hair. They buried what was left where the hyenas had tired of him.

But, if Vlackfontein was a miniature paradise for other game, it was pure, undiluted heaven for the yellow baboon. The creatures had procreated until I estimated the local troop had more than one hundred members. They foraged in close company that discouraged all but the most occasional attack by marauding leopards, which normally keep their numbers down more than any other animal. The bloody baboons were everywhere, and to make matters worse, they had chosen a magnificent grove of *mfuti* or Prince of Wales feather trees as their sleeping place. They had been living about half a mile from the ramshackle house for most of the years the place had been uninhabited.

The first notification I had of the location of their dormitory was an odoriferous waft of wind that would haunt the dreams of a sewer cleaner. Their accumulated dung beneath the trees was inches thick, the smell hitting you like a wet blanket. Their night-long screeching and whooping insomnia, as well as their constant raiding of the papaya trees next to the house, soon made it clear that somebody was going to have to find new digs. It wasn't going to be me.

On numerous instances previously, I had had nuisance problems with baboon troops becoming overbold, but killing a couple usually solved the problem, at least for a span of time. Unfortunately, and fatally for one of my staff, I was to find the Vlackfontein troop very different indeed.

From the outset, I can tell you that, despite my general revulsion of them as some sort of human parody, I greatly dislike killing baboons. The problem lies in the fact that the baboon, if unchecked, can be one of the worst scourges of agriculture, game, and young livestock on earth. They are the epitome of savage, calculating, cruel, and extraordinarily intelligent varmints. I have twice been in leopard blinds and witnessed baboons catch doves that came to drink at nearby waterholes, only to completely pluck them for the sheer fun of it, leaving the bird alive. Through a career never noted for great doses of boredom, I have been in on the demise of some of my own species with, strangely, less regret than I felt at having to kill a baboon. After all, they're only trying to make a living as best they can, although often at the expense and risk of man.

Perhaps it will make little sense to you, but baboons, especially frightened or wounded ones, can sometimes seem even more human than man himself. They can sometimes offer heartrending gestures of supplication I'd as soon not get into here. The idea of arbitrarily shooting even a big, murderous "dog" baboon gives me a case of the ancestral creeps.

It may be that there's a very good reason for the creepy regret I feel when I have to destroy a baboon: Man and old *bobojan,* as he's called locally, go back a long way together in Africa. We probably share some misty common ancestor, the baboon taking one evolutionary road while we took another. If you doubt this, feel the size of the sockets of your eyeteeth or canines. Notice how immense they are in comparison to your bicuspids; we once had fangs like the baboon. But according to some of the best conjecture of our time, we lost them through evolution as we transferred our fighting weapons from dental to hand-held sticks and rocks. In short, the size of our fighting teeth has diminished because we didn't need them.

Well over a million years ago, a very nasty, though efficient, little chap dubbed *Australopithecus africanus* or "southern ape-man" did his thing, among other places, around three cave sites in South Africa. In one of his caves he left forty-two baboon skulls—just the heads, no bodies. Most clearly show that the animals were killed by right-handed blows from the hand-held leg bone of an antelope. All forty-two skulls had had the brains extracted and, with macabre certainty, eaten. Nice family we share, cousin!

At least one baboon partially squared the score in the first half of this century in what is now Tanzania, East Africa. According to the highly reliable hunter, soldier, and traveler Major P. J. Pretorius, a tremendous, man-eating baboon operated from a six-mile-wide mangrove swamp on the Ruvuma River. The swamp was threaded by a footpath used by the natives to cross the swamp to higher ground. In his classic book *Jungle Man,* Pretorius wrote:

> Here this ferocious baboon had taken up its quarters, and when an isolated native came past it would attack and tear open the stomach of its victim. It would then *break the skull, tear out the brains, which it devoured, and leave the rest of the body* [my emphasis]. The natives were unable to catch it and were so terrified of the brute that eventually they left their village.

Pretorius does not record the number of victims of the Ruvuma man-eater. However, for a lone, homicidal baboon to drive an entire village of armed Africans to leave their home, he must have had a pretty respectable score.

The quickest of glances will convince you that baboons are nothing to fool around with, despite the impish charm of the juveniles. Their primate intelligence and attack behavior, coupled with their strength, agility, fangs, and powerful hands, make them among the most dangerous close-quarters animals in Africa's formidable collection of bad news for the stupid, over-brave, or unlucky. I'd have to have a couple of long ones and a half-pack of smokes before deciding between the unpleasant choice of tangling hand-to-hand with a baboon or a leopard.

All things considered, I just might choose the leopard, despite the claws. That's because of the baboon's terrible biting technique. He anchors his great fangs in your meat and, keeping his jaws locked, uses his steel-strong arms and legs to push himself away. This maneuver rips out a chunk of meat that would just about fit into a one-pound dog-food tin. A big male's muzzle may be eight inches long, and, pound for pound, he's three times as strong as a human wrestler. I know of no wrestlers who ever had teeth that big, either!

The relationship between the leopard and the baboon as predator and prey depends upon the terrain, the baboons, leopard populations, and other factors. No leopard that had not been overdoing the catnip would dream of trying to take a member of a troop that was not incapacitated or on the very fringes of the group. Even trying for an isolated or vulnerable small or female baboon can be the equivalent of Russian roulette for a leopard.

Three times I have found the bodies of baboon-killed leopards, caught by the sentinel males. In one case, the deed had been done to a full-grown tom by two old males, both of which had taken something of a lacing themselves. I didn't witness the actual fight, but I sure heard it!

Many humans are mauled in African parks, often severely, by baboons that have become overly familiar with man. At Khwai Lodge in Botswana, which I once ran between safaris, I had to snipe about ten members of a troop that were becoming cheeky enough to charge right into the open dining area to beg or steal food. They were a real threat to the guests. I used a .22 long rifle in this case, taking only head shots from chalet windows before they caught on and kept their distance.

In 1963, a large baboon of the *chacma* subspecies, very similar to the yellow baboons of Rhodesia, was killed by South

African police. It had harassed natives for two years by throwing rocks at them! It was later discovered that this was the
same old male that had forced two African girls, aged five and
thirteen, over a hundred-foot cliff to their deaths in 1961.

Three years later, a farm laborer was terribly mauled by a
baboon while looking for strayed sheep in the Cape Province.
He survived, but not by much, oddly reporting that the rest of
the troop had just sat around and watched while he was attacked. Lucky for him, as baboons often mass-attack in a
screeching gang of flashing fangs. Only two months later, also
on the Cape, a pair of baboons terrified a mother and her two
children by trying to break into their home. The baboons
banged on the doors and windows, until police, who arrived
just in time, shot them in the garden.

Although baboons can be quite cheeky and downright
bold when they know a person to be unarmed (they have relia-
bly stolen many children throughout Africa), unprovoked, flat-
out attacks are rare. The male that tried to take me apart on
the hillside near Vlackfontein clearly was cornered. He had
ducked into the rock grotto while I was firing. Probably because he could still see the troop leader, the first dead male, he
had remained confused until I surprised him.

Just as man has evolved socially, the baboon is doing the
same thing at an accelerated pace right now, and in a very
spooky way. Since the turn of the century, he has greatly expanded his predatory carnivore instincts, shifting faster and
faster from a voracious herbivore to an accomplished killer and
meat-eater. Looking through my collection of antique African
books, I cannot find a single reference to baboons killing
smaller antelope, sheep, goats, or other livestock as they so
commonly do today.

In the tsetse fly–free regions of southern and central Africa, where livestock may be kept, baboons commonly rank
near the hyena and leopard as stock killers. Considering the
relative helplessness of women and children in the African
bush, it doesn't seem unreasonable to me that one troop or
another may finally get the same idea as that one-baboon horror show of Pretorius's on the Ruvuma Swamp. Then Africa is

going to have a problem that will make the "killer bees" seem like gnats.

My first real brush with the enemy at Vlackfontein took place near dusk the second day I was camped there. Like most of the jams I get into, this one was my own damn-fool fault. I broke a rule learned over years the hard way: don't wander around the bush unarmed, no matter how safe the real estate appears.

On an impulse, I grabbed a small hand-line and a few scraps of eland meat, intent on catching a bream or two before dark. With only my hunting knife, I wandered down the *vlei* toward the water, two hundred yards from the ruined house. A narrow trail led through the higher grass to the water's edge.

Still fifty yards from the springs, I looked up smack into the face of a huge male baboon, the leader of a string of a great many. To say that we were both startled would be tantamount to observing that Cheryl Tiegs ain't bad looking for a girl. His surprised *"Waughh"* of warning mingled with my own strangled shout. Two more males leaped up to join him as he reared on his hind legs, ten feet away. As he gave an unforgettable display of his dental work, the grass around us went crazy with sound and motion as the rest of the troop fled the unseen threat. I yelled back at them as one bounced forward in a feint, barking so loud my ears hurt. Remembering the Randall skinner at my belt, I dropped the fishing line and whipped it out in the best Alan Ladd tradition.

I knew we were too close to count on the baboon's natural fear of man to scare them off, and with the rest of the troop to protect, any one of them might try something heroic. I stood perfectly still, my attention on the biggest, as he demonstrated, snapping jaws and tearing up grass. My eyes were locked with his in the weirdest feeling of communication. Remembering the old adage about the best defense being a good offense, I brandished the knife and took a very reluctant and slow step toward them. I shouldn't have done that.

For a second I was sure they would call my bluff, all three going insane, snapping and roaring. Still facing them, I took a step backward with equal care and that seemed to calm them down a touch. Another step to the rear, and, to my immense relief, they turned and were gone.

I had been hunting the troop of apes with rising irritation and frustration. I carefully stalked them, only to have one of their binocular-eyed sentinels catch a glimpse of motion or be tipped off by birds like the gray lourie whose warning cry of *"Go-Waaaaay"* would cause a scampering exodus of the feeding troop. By sheer persistence, I had killed eight of the gang of marauders, including the three males on the hillside. Yet, if on one hand they had become more cautious of me, on the other they had become even bolder around the house and native huts. When they saw me leave in the vintage Land Rover, they brazenly raided the fruit trees and even entered the camp itself, much to the distress of my personnel. Then, six days ago, it had happened while I was off at Matetsi for supplies.

A small garden had been planted in a plot of rough earth fifty yards from the huts thrown up by my temporary laborers. It was being weeded that morning by the wife of one of my bricklayers, a bright MaShona woman of twenty-six named Wedu. On her back, as is the custom, she supported a four-month-old infant boy in a length of cloth. She was completely unarmed, not even carrying a digging stick.

She was pulling weeds by hand, when she had the strange feeling of being watched. As she paused in her work to look around, she was startled to see four big male baboons stalk out of the nearby bush. They began to advance on her, demonstrating very aggressive behavior, grunting and bouncing stiffly on knuckles and feet. With remarkable presence of mind, she threatened them back and threw a stone. This, instead of having the normal effect of sending them packing, seemed to infuriate them more. They drew closer to the now thoroughly frightened woman, surrounding her as she began to scream for help.

As she tried to wrestle the baby from the hammock on her back to protect it with her arms, one of the baboons raced in from behind and, with a ferocious tug, pulled the child free.

He immediately gripped it with his jaws. The woman, panicked to madness by the sight, charged the baboon, only to have one of his mates snap viciously at her leg. The male who had the child shook the pathetic bundle and dropped it, turning on the mother.

It happened at that moment that Amos and Rota, respectively my gunbearer and tracker, were returning from the spring when they heard the woman's cries. They came upon the scene at a sprint. Both were armed with spears, and they immediately attacked the baboons, shouting at the top of their lungs. Seeing the determined, armed men bearing down on them, the baboons broke off their harassment of the poor woman and began to stalk reluctantly back toward the bush.

Their retreat was sufficiently grudging that Rota, who was younger and faster, got within range and was able to plant a thrown assegai through the thigh of one of the males. While he bit and fought the steel blade, Amos was able to spear him to death as the other three turned tail and left.

The woman was hysterical and had several nasty lacerations. When I treated these, I concluded that the baboons' fangs had cut across her skinny shin bones. There was no hope for the child. A set of massive fang holes had punctured him through the chest, and, although he lived a few minutes, he was dead by the time he could be carried to the huts. We buried him deeply that night, as custom dictates—on his right side, knees drawn up, facing the rising sun he would never see again.

That was enough. It had not taken ten minutes for the entire labor camp to agree that these baboons were, in reality, vengeful witches and warlocks. This is a common belief among bush Africans about any man-eaters or marauders.

Was the *Inkosi* a blind man, they asked themselves in whispers, that he could not see the *mabobojan* wanted revenge for their dead and would strike any time they had an opportunity? Disgusted, I paid off those who wanted to leave and called a conference with my hunting staff for that evening. They, no matter how personally spooked by the strange attacks of the baboons, never would have dreamed of inviting the stigma of cowardice by quitting. They were *madoda*, warriors, not *mafazi* to run from danger, skirts flapping.

In the manner of any formal discussion with African natives, there is a great deal of bush-beating before getting down to the meat of the matter. But I knew custom well enough never to interrupt, so I listened to them speak for hours. I would occasionally interject polite questions as speakers gave their ideas starting with their lowest-ranked and ending with my most senior man, Gladstone. He is a *madalla* or elder of the Amandebele Zulu, who was referred to by the honored title of *Baba* (Father) by all my staff. He finally distilled the best of the arguments. After a somewhat windy appraisal in Fanagalo/Sindebele, a local form of the common language of southern Africa, he observed that the baboons did not relate my sniping them to their residence in the area. Also, since the baboons were no longer a nuisance but a full-blown menace, we would have to concentrate them for a quick and decisive slaughter. He recommended the classic buffalo assault formation of his grandfather's regiments. Finally, he said, piercing me with a bloodshot eye, if we were not able to do this, the baboons surely would kill me.

I sat alone long into the night in the canvas camp chair, watching the sparks streak upward like tracers at each addition of a fresh mopane log. Gladstone was undoubtedly correct on his first two points. I had used the wrong tactic in picking them off piecemeal because they did not relate the harassment to their presence in my area. To them I was just some big, white ape killing them for the hell of it. Further, he was right that the troop had to be maneuvered into some position where I could get their attention with some real firepower. What bothered me was his last observation.

After well over a decade in the bush, I was sufficiently Africanized to feel my hackles getting a bit of involuntary exercise when I considered this revenge motive. What if they really *were* trying to get even? They could easily have enough intelligence; that I knew from observation. Where would they be likely to strike next? And at whom? I kept getting flashes of the end of the film *Sands of the Kalahari* and what happened to Stuart Whitman when he ran out of ammo for his Weatherby, after severely picking on a troop of yellow baboons.

Slowly, as the ember of a new cigarette began to glow

deeply with a drag, an idea began to form and kindle brighter. I reached over for the web-belt holster of the MAC-10 submachine gun I always kept near me in camp in case of uninvited two-legged unpleasantries. I unrolled the lumpy, home-stitched, buffalo-hide bandolier carrying ten double-stick magazines of 9-mm ammo, carefully taped together for quick reloading. I had purchased the little gun with gold sovereigns, (very handy coins to someone in a hurry and faced with currency restrictions) from a farmer who had decided to pack it in. I had also been able to pick up his suppressor attachment or silencer, 1,800 rounds of hard-nosed military ammo, and twenty extra thirty-six-round stick clips. With its wire stock retracted, it was not much larger than a good-sized pistol, and it had a rate of fire of about seven hundred rounds per minute. I preferred it vastly to the standard FN assault rifle in 7.62 mm that most people carried in their bush cars. I thoughtfully examined the little brute and extracted the overlapped magazines. As the firelight licked silently at its dull finish, my idea formed more solidly with each throb of my thoughts.

I slept rather late the following morning, until the sun was high and I was sure the entire baboon troop was off foraging. After a leisurely breakfast, I whistled up the eight men on my hunting staff, leaving two spearmen to guard the work area, and went with the rest to reconnoiter the feather tree grove where the troop roosted.

The impossible stink of the place soon permeated our very clothes and skins. We determined which of the trees were most heavily used, deciding on four or five about in the center of the grove. Their bark was worn as smooth as Venetian crystal from the repeated touch of thousands of paws, and the dung was thick at their bases. It was not my intention to annihilate the whole troop. That would have been impossible on a practical basis without high explosives. But I did want to give them a severe enough mauling for them to be forced into changing their range entirely. They must be made to understand that they could no longer use this roost, and after the terrible affair of the dead baby and the potentially dead mother, I had absolutely no regrets about showing them the

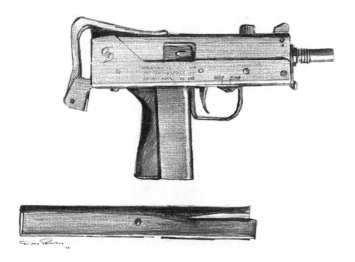

The MAC-10 9-mm submachine pistol with stick magazine.

hard way. With my battle plan firmly in mind, I walked back to camp to make preparations for my personal version of the Entebbe Raid.

Being a professional small boy at heart, my camp was never short of wondrous and fascinating paraphernalia, which included six magnesium aerial flares and a dozen or so nifty little monsters called "thunderflashes." These are really super firecrackers made to simulate grenades for training exercises. But they're no joke and easily could blow most of your throwing arm from here to the Carpathian Alps if you didn't get rid of one in time.

The sun looked like a giant red balloon as it finally began

to slip down behind the trees, leaving the sky with thick varicose veins of gold and orange. Through my binoculars, I watched the first of the troop file into the grove and disappear into the murk of shadow, their hoots and barks threatening as they vocally sneered at us. I decided to go ahead and dine, waiting for full darkness. That should give the baboons time to settle down and doze off.

We took our positions about fifty yards from the trees. Amos stood to my right with the heavy bandolier of double magazines for the MAC-10. I had removed the submachine gun's silencer for more noise confusion. With several clips in position to hand to me, Amos was ready for the attack. On my left was Rota, holding the cocked flare launcher, another cartridge ready in his hand. Flanking us were my six other men. Three on the right carried spears, and three on the left, who blew casually on embers of campfire wood, carried the slingshots so common among Rhodesian tribesmen for knocking off doves or francolin. These slingshots were loaded with thunderflashes ready for lighting and launching.

"Lungile manje," I whispered up and down the line— "All set!"

Amos gave the low hoot of an owl. I caught the small flash of a match flaring at the far side of the thickness of the grove. The tiny spark roared and grew, racing in a two-hundred-yard semicircle around the far side of the grove, where we had scratched a shallow trench. We had soaked the trench with a mixture of more than one hundred gallons of gasoline, kerosene, and old crank case oil. The fire cut off the escape of the troop effectively. No baboon, even with courage born of desperation, would try to pass through that five-foot wall of hell. I watched the flitting form of the boy Amos had sent to light the trench fire dashing closer, until he was panting beside us. It was time to go to work.

At that moment, Rota fired the first flare on my command. It arched like a giant firefly over the trees. I signaled the slingshot men and watched the sparkle of three thunderflash fuses in a high trajectory. A second later, they exploded in a ragged procession of perfect airbursts on a far side of the grove.

Rota's flare then burst under its parachute, lighting the area brighter than midday. For an instant there was silence, then the baboons went berserk. I've never been in a riot in a madhouse, but this couldn't have been much different. Instantly, dark forms began to drop and scamper from the trees, most racing in terrified panic straight for us, their eyes half-blinded by the flare. Some very icy second thoughts scampered up my spine as they poured down on us. Could I stop them with the little gun, or had we bitten off a bit too much?

I fired three quick squirts into a group of ten headed right at us. It may have been the best of dumb luck that I had removed the muzzle-flash-hiding suppressor as the two baboons not caught in the sleet of slugs veered off to the left. I let them go because one was young, and the other was a female.

The sight of Wedu's mutilated baby flashed through my mind as I ripped a long burst into a scrambling group of seven, sweeping the gun in a long arc that chopped all but the last as my magazine ran dry. Certainly, one thing was obvious: there were a lot more than a hundred baboons in that grove. More than that had already run the gamut of my selective automatic fire. About a third of their number was killed as I punched out short, accurate bursts at no more than twenty-five yards.

Again the magazine was empty, and my eyes were down, changing the clip when I heard Amos shout, *"Basopa, madoda!"*

I glanced up just in time to see two males skewered in midair by the spearmen on my right flank as the baboons bore down on us in a desperate charge. There was no need to finish either of them as my men decapitated each with a single slice of their *pangas*.

Finally, the screeching and grunting died down and the movement lessened. The tabloid of death was pinned like some great diorama in the sterile light of a new flare. Another twenty or so baboons remained alive in the grove, scampering and dodging as they sought to break our deadly ring of flame and lead. I killed two more big males, but let another six or eight go, spurred on by a couple of bursts behind them. To have left the troop completely shattered, without any of the leadership and protection that are the duty of the adult males, probably would have meant their complete extinction.

Exhausted, back at my temporary camp, I poured a nightcap while cleaning the MAC-10. I sat beside Amos, who was reloading the emptied magazines, each with thirty-six staggered rounds.

Frankly, I was having a lousy bout of depression over the slaughter, wishing it had not been necessary. Amos, quietly clicking in the gleaming rounds, seemed to catch my mood.

"*Haya kataza, Inkosi,*" he said, pausing to roll a cigarette of newspaper and black shag tobacco. "Don't worry about it. They would have killed you if they could. It is just the way of things that a man must fight his enemies to hold his kraal and his women."

I thought about what he had said for a long time, and realized his wisdom. The troop simply had to be moved, and, after killing the baby, there was no choice left to me as to means. They would settle again, perhaps twenty miles away, maybe along the Bemba. They would build their tribe again, until they had reached a natural balance with the leopards and disease. Africa would go on again as it had for the baboon since the days of the South African caveman.

GOOFS THAT
COST GAME

GUNS & AMMO —
OCTOBER 1975

Target illustrating the perils of an oiled barrel.

AUTHOR'S INTRODUCTION

*Every hunter knows that the more game he takes or
tries to take with the classic one-shot, no matter how careful
the stalk and the shot, there will be the presence of the
greatest hunter of all, Mr. Murphy. Murph—as I call him
through long association—is uncannily adept at knocking
scope sights, fouling up ammo, leaving gunbarrels full of oil
fit to arouse the attention of any sheik, and secretly jerking
trigger squeezes. He is a master at misrepresenting range,
and, should it come to simple bad ammo, he probably
reloaded the stuff behind your back.*

*Beware of my close associate, Mr. Murphy. His law
knows no politics, no latitude or longitude. He doesn't exist,
but somehow he's always there.*

*If you are to know the cause of unexplained ballistic
perfidy, then you should be acquainted with the cure.
Perhaps this chapter will help.*

There is the smell of snow in the pearl-gray dawn air.
Through the layers of thermal underwear, the frozen wood of
the fallen tree radiates a steely chill that seeps like ice water
along your spine and into your kidneys as you sit waiting, motionless as death, for the movement to reappear. It was only a
flicker, two hundred yards down the old logging road, but you
are sure you saw it, a tiny flash of grizzled brown through the

hardwoods and low, catbriar tangles. There is the tiniest sound of sliding metal as your gloved thumb snicks the safety forward and your index finger crawls reluctantly out of the slit in your shooting mittens.

The cold is forgotten. The long hours of wind-whipped waiting vanish as through frost-teared eyes you see the first doe step onto the road. She stands, daintily and nervously blowing soft plumes of breath as she looks up and down the overgrown trail. Another appears magically beside her, then a third, heavier female. With the slightest, imperceptible movement, you slide your face down to the stock, feeling the three-day growth scratching on the walnut. The scope lines up. He'll be following them—you can feel it—sneaking like smoke behind the does. You probe the trees and undergrowth, your heart jumping as he materializes between two weather-worn maples. He is enormous, his neck as thick as a rusty fireplug, the whitish tines of his rack as smooth and sharp as a thicket of frog-gigs. Your breath catches as you count them off through the scope. Keerist! There are twelve! The crosshairs are doing the tarantella as you take your shooting breath, let some out, and watch the deadly reticule slip lower on his chest. Right. Now just a touch over. Squeeze, stupid, squeeze! Hold it! The buck steps forward three quick paces, standing openly in the road now. You realign the sight, swallow down the buck fever stamping through your stomach, and start the release again. He holds as still as bronze, looking straight ahead as the thin lines settle. The shot surprises you, impossibly loud in the stillness of the early forest. The huge buck gives a single, tremendous bound and evaporates among the trees and shadows. Even at this distance you can hear him crashing away, the sound dimming, then gone. Cursing and praying, you fumble back the bolt and chamber another round, a tiny curl of smoke writhing from the spent brass at your feet. Did you hit him? You *must* have. The crosshairs were right on the money. But where was that thump of 180 grains of soft-point? It takes forever to reach the spot where he stood. Anxiously, your eyes comb the dark leaves for a slick of crimson. Here's where he leaped, long scars in the frozen dirt. You bend down, picking up the small clump of hollow hair. Your stomach hits bottom as you realize it was shaved from his withers by your bullet, a simple crease across the back that didn't even draw blood. The walk back to camp is much longer and colder than you remember it. Maybe it would be best not to mention the blown shot to the rest of the boys when they come in for supper. Who'd believe a twelve-pointer, anyway?

I know just how that man felt. Nineteen years ago, on a frosty November morning in New England, I was the man. That incredible tableau is still engraved in my brain, that fantastic animal standing wide open for a shot that was blown. As the condemned man was reported to say while on the scaffold, "This whole thing has sure been a lesson to me." And over those nineteen years, as my interest and experience have grown, I figured that missing that buck had nothing to do with my rifle. It was my fault for expecting it to shoot the same way with a clean, oiled barrel as it would with a dry, slightly dirty bore, which was how I had zeroed it.

Somebody who had a lot more sense than I do once observed that there are more ways to do a thing wrong than right. When it comes to riflery under hunting conditions, those are the facts in spades. There are at least a half-dozen common reasons why each season thousands of hunters who are fair-to-good shots blow their chances at all types of game because of simple, commonsense physical factors that affect their rifles. One of the most usual causes of failure to connect is that of not having fired a fouling shot.

For many of America's hunters, the old Winchester '94 or Remington 700 hangs on pegs over the fireplace or is entombed in a gun case for fifty-one out of fifty-two weeks a year. A fine and reliable rifle being even rarer than a woman of equal qualities, we tend to take better care of the former than the latter. The Hoppe's No. 9 and the 3-in-One go on about the same time the venison hits the hanging rack. How a hunter can drive a couple of hundred miles and spend several times that number of dollars to spend a week of soul therapy in a deer camp, yet jeopardize the whole point by not firing a fouling shot is beyond the pale. Of course, many believe that "a clean rifle shoots clean." You and I know this ain't so, but you'd be amazed how many people there are wandering around the boonies with rifle bores full of Greasy Kid Stuff.

Interior ballistics is a subject only slightly less mystifying than the Theory of Relativity (which, incidentally I have never found to be relative at all). However, a hunter who can't tie his own boots has to realize that there are different forces working on a bullet forced through immense pressures down a greased or oiled tube compared to one fired from a dry bore, from which previous shots have been fired without cleaning. A clean, lightly oiled barrel will throw a bullet generally higher, just how much so depending upon any one of a thousand factors such as amount and type of lubricant residue, bullet weight, caliber, velocity, humidity, altitude, and, I sometimes suspect, tides, moon phase, and the Dow Jones averages. Depending upon the particular rifle, even if it was zeroed-in properly, the tendency of the first shot to go high from a clean bore can be sufficient to cause wounding or complete misses at longer ranges, even on bigger game. Unless you are afield with a rifle bore in the same condition as that under which it was zeroed, you can hardly expect it to place its bullet at the exact point of zero.

Speaking of zeroing, the mind boggles at the number of casual shooters who believe that once their rifle has been sighted in, it will stay that way. The existence of the Easter Bunny might be a safer assumption. We have some really excellent sights, both iron and optical, these days. We also have good, solid mounts that can even defy the orangutans who handle airline luggage. We do not, however, have anything that will stand up with complete reliability to a really heavy blow on a sighting system. If you drop your rifle or otherwise bang it up, for heaven's sake check the zero before hunting. Besides blows, there are rafts of other things that can affect the point of zero of the finest rifle. A few years back, when slated for an extended Ethiopian safari, I was consigned two rifles from a major manufacturer, in caliber .458 Winchester Magnum. That they were not scoped doesn't change the principle. I shot them both "in" here in the States, and both were giving on-the-money groups worth writing home about. But somewhere between New York and Sidamo Province, bordering Kenya's NFD, both guns caught a dose of gremlins. I'm mighty pleased I bothered to try them again before taking on something that bites back, since both were shooting about two feet high at fifty yards! They were so out of whack, in fact, that the sights could not be adjusted to the degree necessary to compensate, and they spent the safari as excess baggage. What happened? Lord only knows the whole of it, but certainly the combination of thinner air at the Ethiopian altitudes and drying of the stock in the very low humidity in comparison to the place where they had been zeroed in the States were partly responsible.

Even if you have meticulously zeroed your rifle, it will shoot to a different point of impact on a high-mountain sheep or goat hunt than it will on an Everglades deer or pig hunt. Thin air produces less friction than air at sea level, and retained velocities are better, trajectories flatter, all else being equal. Because wood is a fibrous vegetable substance, it tends to contract or expand in atmospheres of different temperatures and humidities. Remember that as your bullet is blasted through the bore at incredible speeds and pressures, the passage imparts an oscillation to the muzzle that is hard to believe. Any change that affects the wood that touches the rifle along the areas of bedding may affect this oscillation or "barrel whip," releasing the slug at a different point of the circular motion, which will result in the bullet strike being other than at the point of original zero. The only accurate way to overcome such changes of pressure to the wood-to-metal fit is to re-zero the rifle under the exact conditions under which you will be hunting.

It is also worth remembering that when a rifle is field-stripped, the stock removed from the barrel and action, it should be carefully rechecked on the range to ensure that the zero has not been disturbed. The tightening and loosening of the master screw in the bottom of the forepiece directly affects the tension and contact of the wood-to-metal fit, and rarely is it retightened to the same precise pressure.

Many of us tend to forget that when we are hunting, the

first and most important shot will come from a cold barrel. If you finish your zeroing string with a hot barrel, not having waited for it to cool between shots, your point of zero with the cold barrel will probably be a bit off from your last paper group.

A lesser but still common cause of hunting inaccuracy from otherwise well-tuned rifles is the position used for zeroing. In the field, I tend to shoot with a so-called "hasty sling," the strap leading down over my left forearm and under the arm just above the elbow. This does produce, through the sling's tension, particularly in rifles that have the front sling swivel attached to the barrel rather than to the stock wood, a tendency for the bullet to print more to the left than if it were fired without the sling tension. In zeroing for hunting, be sure to duplicate as closely as possible the pressures on barrel and stock that you will normally use in a hunting situation. I have seen men at benchrests with the last eight or so inches of the barrel resting on sandbags. This, to be sure, relieved the barrel of its slight, natural droop, caused by its own weight. Consequently, when the rifle is fired offhand or without the barrel support, the shots will strike up to several inches lower, a critical consideration at longer ranges. If you doubt this, fire a series of three-shot groups from your favorite pill-pusher with the front rest at increasing distances along the barrel. They will group higher and higher the farther the rest is extended toward the muzzle.

In the heat of buck fever, many an otherwise good rifleman has made the goof of resting his rifle on a hard, unyielding substance such as a rock or tree stump, without insulating the rifle with his hand or folded hat. In the normal offhand shot, the flesh of the hand has a dampening effect on barrel oscillation, which, although far from completely modifying the effect, at least acts as a constant factor permitting the bullet to pass from the muzzle at the same point of the whip at each shot. When this dampening effect is lost through resting the barrel on an unyielding surface, the consistency of oscillation is also lost because of the vibrations that bounce back rather than being absorbed. I have run some fairly conclusive tests on this phenomenon over the years, and in almost all cases, using calibers from .243 through .338, the bullet strike has been high. It is very likely the bounce effect that throws the muzzle up before the bullet has cleared the barrel.

I was down at our local gunmonger's emporium the other day, up to nothing constructive, when a man in his middle forties came in and asked for a box of '06 fodder. The sage in charge of such matters asked him what brand and grain weight or bullet type he wanted, and the guy said, "I don't care; just want some deer bullets." I inquired what load his rifle was zeroed for, a fool's errand of the first water. He, a grown man, probably even without a record by the look of his Gucci loafers, didn't know or, more's the shame, care. He tucked a box of 180-grainers into a well-manicured fist, paid the tab, and left. If he got his deer, I suspect it was one who had tried to fool Mother Nature.

Actually, the amazing thing is how many deer and other game really end up in the Great Bambiland in the Sky each season, considering how many hunters swap back and forth without any adjustment between grain weights and brands of ammunition. Every manufacturer seems to have some little difference in the performance of its wares, and the fact is that most rifles will handle one company's load better than any other factory fodder. I had a .357 H&H on a Mauser action that thought Winchester 300-grain solids were ice cream. Yet it would hardly print on the paper with the same bullet from another manufacturer. It didn't mean that the Winchester stuff was necessarily a better load; just that that individual rifle preferred it. An Italian safari client I once had brought along a Ferlach over/under double rifle in .458 Magnum. The only cartridges that could even be chambered in it were of Remington manufacture, which, although theoretically identical with all .458 Magnum cases everywhere, were apparently just a hair smaller in diameter and had been used in regulating the barrels of the Ferlach. Nothing's ever simple, it seems. Perhaps it's the individual characteristics of firearms that make them so fascinating. Certainly, the ability to tailor a load for a particular rifle is the mainstay reason for the hand-loading industry's growth.

If I had to pick a single reason for game being missed—or not even fired at—during my years as a professional in Africa, besides just awful shooting, it would have to be difficulty of finding game in the scope. What many inexperienced hunters tend to do is spot the animal, look it over, glance down, then raise the rifle and try to find it all over again through the lens. Usually, in heavy cover at least, they can't do it. It sounds weird, but it's the biggest single hangup I know of. The trick to mastering this optical phenomenon is never to take your focus from your target. Keep staring at your game, raise your rifle, and simply insert the scope between your eye and the animal you are looking at. Don't look *at* the eyepiece but *through* it. Your left eye will hold the target in focus while the right is making the adjustment, and the animal should be right in the center of your field of view. If it isn't, remove the lens caps.

FILL THAT TAG

GUNS & AMMO —
OCTOBER 1976

Hand fingering a stalk of grass showing blood stains.

Author's Introduction

Ummmmmh. Sometimes old Murph gets away with it, as neat and free as a paroled parakeet. Still, there are a few booby traps that may be sown in his path, no matter how lightly he glides. Should you encounter the erudite Mr. Murphy in company, you might as well forget it. But if he's bending over, caught in paroxysms of laughter at you, you just might clean his clock with some of the following advice. . . .

If you're a rifleman, there's no need to tell you that evil spirits have become one of the major plagues of hunting accuracy in this country. In fact, there has been such an increase in their activity in recent years that hardly anybody shoots as well as he used to. Whether these malevolent djinns are the fault of improper screening at banana ports or a direct result of Soviet subterfuge is immaterial. What does matter is that every now and then a good rifleman with properly tuned equipment and optimum conditions doesn't kill instantly with a single, humane shot and produces a wounded game animal that, by the most ancient law of hunting morality, must not be allowed to escape and be wasted. I know you never wounded anything and I hardly ever did, but just in case one of us gets crossed up by a free-lance hex, let's take a look at some of the problems of following up and finishing off an injured animal under a variety of conditions.

For the sake of consistency, how's about we confine our investigation to the medium and larger North American species, especially deer, antelope, and kindred critters. With the screaming-hot loads used for varmints, nonfatal hits are rare because of the immense tissue damage of even "scratch" hits. In the case of our fine feathered friends in the waterfowl and upland categories, clearly the shooter who values and respects his prey uses a dog whenever possible to retrieve crippled birds.

It has been my conclusion over the years, based upon observation both here and abroad, that the largest percentage of animals wounded and lost were never realized by the hunter to be wounded in the first place.

Despite your interpretation of those impressive velocities and foot-poundages printed in the ballistic charts, any game may show almost no reaction to bullet impact, which might well lead the hunter to believe he has made a clean miss when in fact his quarry may be as dead as free lunch a hundred yards away. Therefore, the first inviolable rule is to make *absolutely* certain that game has not been hit before declaring a miss. If you are not completely positive of a miss, assume a hit and follow up for at least a few hundred yards, and I'll wager that 25 percent of the time you will find you scored.

Besides the obvious test of a follow-up to look for blood spoor or other bullet strike evidence, there are other indications of a hit that may be interpreted from the firing point. The first of these is the animal's reaction to bullet impact, *if any*. Different game reacts in different ways to hits on various parts of the body, no indications of which are entirely reliable because of the immense number of variables that may influence bullet reaction or lack of it. Still, some are at least helpful as a possible indicator of hit location and severity. Most heart-shot animals will immediately burst into a frantic, headlong run, sometimes preceded by a high leap, although a creased animal may also leap. A few will "fall" to bullet strike, but many do not at all. Lung- and chest-shot game often hunches up momentarily before running, while shots too far back in the gut area may produce a pronounced hunching and mincing of the rear legs. Tail signals may also be reliable indicators of bullet hits, since many species tend to run with the tail down after a bullet hit rather than in the more usual upward alarm position. Beware the animal that falls "stone dead" to the shot, as very often this is an indication of a crease or near bullet passage that has disrupted communications of large nerve bundles in head, neck, or spine. When the effect has worn off in what may be a few seconds to several minutes, the animal will bounce off like the proverbial pinstriped primate, likely not stopping until it reaches the Tien Shan Mountains. Bone-breaking shots are very hard to detect, and I have seen few animals that couldn't get along nearly as well on three legs as with one in each corner. In fact, they may show no sign of limping at all, despite terrible wounds.

Perhaps the best test of whether an animal was hit is the sound of bullet strike. If wind and distance conditions are correct (often close shots do not permit the shooter to hear bullet impact because of blending with muzzle report), the sound of impact can tell a practiced ear as much about the location and extent of a wound as a firsthand inspection. I blush to recall how many times in Africa over the seasons I have watched through binoculars while my client shot, and was completely unable to tell by bullet reaction if the shot was a hit or a miss, and would have bet money on a miss. Only when my radar-eared gunbearers insisted they had heard the *thug!* of metal on meat was I forced to change my opinion, and I cannot recall one instance when they were wrong. One old man who tracked for me in Botswana would not even look at the game to be shot, but to better concentrate would close his eyes, plug his ear nearest the gun with a finger, and cup the other hand around the opposite ear. If he said, *"Shayile,"* then you knew it was *shayiled* but good.

Different calibers and types of cartridges as well as bullet styles make different characteristic sounds on contact with flesh, but a common resonance runs through them all. The sound produced by a bullet in the shoulder/chest area is a solid, meaty thump that, once heard, cannot be mistaken. A paunch shot sounds much more hollow, something like a bass *whock!* whereas a bullet hitting a leg bone will crack without much resonance and is hardest to hear at a distance.

The next category of bullet-hit evidence is that of the on-site variety, at or somewhere near the position of the animal when shot at. The most classic interpretation of wound location or existence, for that matter, is by the reading of blood sign. Yet one of the greatest mistakes of the inexperienced hunter is the presumption that if there is no blood at the spot, there was likely no hit. Go to your tent! Five demerits! Very often, blood may not be found within fifty or more yards of the hit for several reasons. First, almost all game has flexible, loose-fitting skin that slides across the muscle structure to facilitate movement. If an animal begins to run after receiving the bullet, the skin entrance hole and the underlying channel in tissue will be lined up, permitting blood to exit only a small fraction of the time. Second, in animals with heavy or stiff hair or fur that are not arterially wounded, blood may be absorbed into the coat for a good while before it becomes thick enough to drip on the track. Third, in the case of an intestinal or paunch hit, internal organs or intestines may shift to plug the entrance hole as effectively as a finger in a dike.

With a bit of common sense, blood can tell you more about a wound than anything else. It can show how fast an animal is moving, his direction, where he is hit and how hard. But, like everything else, there's blood and then there's blood. The biggest giveaway in determining where blood is coming from, and therefore in determining wound extent, is its color and consistency. Heart or arterial blood is darkly colored and, after short exposure to air, becomes lumpy or ropy. It's dark because it has circulated through the body giving off oxygen and has not yet been recharged. Lung blood, on the other hand, is impossibly pink and bright, and when fresh usually is frothy with bubbles. Muscle blood, of which there is normally some, because a bullet must pass through some muscle tissue to reach underlying organs, is that nice Hollywood color you get when you creep the scope on your featherweight .338 Magnum or try trimming your mustache with the camp hatchet.

The actual follow-up of wounded game is the greatest test of a hunter's fieldcraft, skill, patience, and endurance. It can also be a pretty fair test of character when the going gets tedious and dangerous. The quarry is already alerted, senses sharp, his system filled with adrenaline. The opportunity of the first shot might have involved a pinch of luck more than good management, but to close to within range a second time without the element of surprise will be ten times harder than with an uninjured animal, especially if it is not badly wounded or partially disabled.

What many hunters do not realize is that the most crucial moments that will determine whether or not a wounded animal is ever brought to bag are those immediately after firing the first shot. Under most conditions, a deer, bear, or elk has no idea of your presence, or you'd never get a shot in the first place. Some, which live in heavily hunted areas or have been shot at before, will make more tracks at the sound of your shot than a bantam on barbiturates, but most will not directly relate the numbing impact of a slug to the presence of man. If you can keep calm and not show yourself, he will probably not go far past his first run. If, however, he sees you and figures out the score, he will likely shift into overdrive and keep moving until he feels safe and unpursued. Adrenaline is an excellent high-performance additive. That's the most important factor, being careful not to further alarm the target animal that he's being pursued or pushed.

There have been no shortages of opinions of the proper conduct of a hunter after wounding with the first shot, and I must stand up and be counted with the group that maintains that the best behavior is none at all until at least fifteen or twenty minutes have passed. If the wound is of a fatal type, then your buck will probably be down and out by the time you take up the track. If not, an even lightly hit animal will usually lie down to rest and gather strength, while in reality the wound will stiffen and make escape more difficult.

Most animals tend to move and feed into the wind when undisturbed. But when they are hurt, most shift and run away downwind so they cannot be surprised from their rear trail. I don't care if you're a purebred Bushman and can track sparrows across granite blindfolded, you're just wasting your time if you're forced to track downwind. The best tactic to follow up wounded game under this situation is to attempt to parallel

the course of flight, if possible from the position of best visibility available such as the side of a wooded hill if the track is
below.

In the case of wounding a herd animal such as a pronghorn antelope, remember that almost without exception the
wounded one will split off from his fellows, and even though
there may be no blood or sign, a track that obviously departs
from the herd is a solid indication of a hit. Further, if he does
break off on his own, it's a good sign he's hard-hit enough to
lie down as soon as he finds a "safe" place.

The value of a second shot immediately following a
wounding first bullet is questionable and highly dependent
upon the skill of the rifleman and conditions peculiar to the
situation. Again, the tactic of not betraying one's location can
be extremely worthwhile, as often a hit animal may stop in
confusion after a few yards, allowing a solid second shot. In
instances such as wide-open pronghorn hunting, where the target may be in sight far longer than when one is hunting white-
tailed deer in the wooded East, a second shot may be more
feasible.

Surely, no factor in the hunting process has as close a
correlation to missing or wounding as distance from muzzle to
target. Past, let's say, 150 yards or so, the odds of wounding or
missing (isn't a wound a miss, really?) probably square with
each additional fifty yards of distance as the disruptive forces
of wind, reduced velocity, and bullet performance, elevation,
and misinterpretation of range come into play. Still, it happens
to all of us even at easy ranges through human, mechanical, or
sight errors. There's nothing more exciting that's legal than
outfoxing a monster buck or several square yards of bear, but
if you do happen to wound him, better play it cool.

FOUR FANGS IN A TREETOP

SAGA—JUNE 1974

Male jaguar.

AUTHOR'S INTRODUCTION

British Honduras—since 1973 officially called the Colony of Belize—is one of those odd little British Crown emeralds somehow mislaid by the surgings and ebbings of the tides of Empire.

Sort of lurking quietly in a niche between southeastern Mexico and eastern Guatemala, it has never been known for a great deal besides natural wild beauty, grand fishing, and jaguars.

Before this trip, I had been mostly in the remote Turneffe Islands, fishing tarpon and snook, and diving on possible treasure wrecks. From offshore the jungle looked far, far more hospitable than it was. However, jungle seems to be jungle wherever it is found in the rainy tropics.

Essentially, it bites. . . .

At first, it was very hard to decide where the sound had come from. The blackness, which hung as thick as the million years of decay in the night, made my eyes useless. I was only aware of the dampness under my shriveled fingertips on the slick, oiled barrel of the shotgun, the penetrating musk of the ancient jungle on the back of my tongue, and the squeaks, chirps, grates, and whistles that blended into the dark symphony of the British Honduras rain forest at two in the morning.

Two A.M.? Maybe. I had left my wristwatch back in camp so its ticking wouldn't betray my hiding place. I gently shifted my numbed backside on the rack of hardwood poles that formed the floor of the twelve-foot-tall *machan,* and felt my spine grind into the rough bark of the tree that was the central support for the frail blind. I closed my eyes and began to filter the many sounds through my brain like cards through a computer. I sifted the hum and drone of mosquitoes from the whisper of other, smaller bloodsuckers about my head and wrists; the howl of tree frogs from the rasp of the big, brown forest crickets in the humus below, and the pat of raindrops slapping the broad leaves from the liquid rustle of the river. Each tiny reverberation was identified and rejected. Then I heard it again.

At my left, I could faintly hear still another sound— Blackbeard breathing. I thought about the big, lean hunter on the platform with me. Although he was clean-shaven, what else could you call a man named William Teach—surely one of the fierce pirate's many descendants on the British Honduras coast? I could imagine his rugged face straining into the murk, registering the same apprehension that plucked at my stomach. Then his hand touched my leg in warning, and I could feel the fear in his hard grip. He was telling me that death was close by in the darkness.

Below and in front of us, I heard the pig scuffle lightly on the ground, straining hard at the thong of green tapir skin that fettered him to a stake driven deep into the scabby forest floor. He knew better than to cry out, but moved restlessly in the shallow depression he had rooted out. Jaguar? I listened harder.

It was the tiniest scraping sound, familiar but, like a long forgotten face, somehow misplaced in my brain. It seemed to edge nearer, then stopped. Blackbeard's spring-steel fingers tightened on my leg like a trap and I could smell his fear— acrid terror in the moist blackness. A horrible sound like the hiss of a pressure cooker stood my hackles up like an icy wind as the realization struck my brain: *Snake! There's a snake on the* machan *with us!*

I jumped from the blind, struggling to keep upright, but preparing to roll if I hit the ground off balance. I felt myself turn in midair and land on my shoulder in a blaze of pain, the breath wheezing out of me. A cry of hurt and horror whipped from above to thump wetly on the ground nearby. I thrashed for the switch to my headlamp, torn off by the jump, but attached by the battery cord in my bush jacket pocket. I found it and punched the toggle, dragging the downturned reflector to me by the cord. I flashed it at Blackbeard. What I saw in the pale beam will be engraved in my mind forever.

He lay on his back, motionless in the amber flood of the light, his eyes like those of a wild animal. Less than a yard from his body was a thick olive-brown coil covered with rough triangles of scaly hide. My mind struggled to identify the creature—and sagged with hopelessness. Barba Amarilla. Yellow Beard. Seven feet of *Bothrops atrox,* the deadly tree-climbing night snake of Central America.

I felt a dry, cotton-alum taste in my mouth as I stared at the snake's heavy head, the tongue flashing beneath bright chips of sapphire blue. Think! Where's the shotgun? You dropped it when you jumped. I saw the dull glint of the barrels between Blackbeard and the snake, no way to reach it. A stick. There must be a stick. I glanced around and saw a half-rotted limb on the fern-covered river-bank and edged toward it, keeping the beam steadily on the snake, hoping the light would partly dazzle it. It didn't. It gave a great, dry, angry hiss—a sound as threatening and cold as sleet on a dark morning. Should I keep moving for the stick? Wait? Indecision coursed through me. Goddammit. If I had the pistol, we wouldn't be in this spot. . . .

I had to reach the stick. Sooner or later that snake would hit Teach if I didn't try to do something—most likely sooner. Blackbeard's drained face implored me to action. Ignoring the snake's threatening hisses, I was at the branch in three slow strides. I winced as pain lanced through my right shoulder when I tried to lift the branch. Gripping the wood in my left hand, I edged back toward the snake, the makeshift club held high. Too late! Like an arrow whipping from a bow, the triangular head lashed out and latched onto Blackbeard's arm, thrashing and chewing yellow venom deep through the long fangs.

With a strangled scream of pain and revulsion, Teach grabbed the thick snake behind the head and ripped it loose. I dashed for the shotgun and blew it in two with the first barrel as it reared up to strike again. The second load of buckshot exploded the head completely. Quick! Tourniquet and incisions! I undid the shotgun sling and fastened it tightly just above Teach's elbow, just loosely enough to permit arterial flow, then took my skinning knife and cut four incisions through the swelling fang wounds. The hunter was calm, his face the color of flour. If we spoke, I don't remember it. He knew better than to panic, but he also knew he'd gotten a full bite from a big snake—almost a death sentence, this far from a hospital.

I sucked the wound for five minutes, tasting the acidity of the venom mixed with the saltiness of his blood. I knew I had gotten some out of the arm, but how much more might have entered his system before I got the tourniquet on was impossible to tell. The wound was starting to swell badly, turning blue and purple. Blackbeard's expression showed that the pain must have been considerable. I knew the only thing to do was to get him back to camp and to the antivenin in the cooler. I also knew I had to get him there fast!

By the time I had carried the big hunter back to the dugout, he was bleeding from the gums and spitting weakly. I knew that bleeding from the mouth, and sometimes from the eyes, was a typical symptom of the hemotoxic *Bothrops* venom. I also knew that a mist of blood could develop over large areas of the skin in severe, untreated cases. Blackbeard complained of a raging thirst, headache, and difficulty in breathing. I didn't know whether to give him water or not, but decided it probably couldn't hurt. I got him into the canoe with some difficulty because of my painful shoulder, and arranged his headlamp as a beacon to light our way down the eight black miles of jungle river. Except for pauses to loosen and retighten his tourniquet, I paddled like a man obsessed until the jungle camp loomed into sight just at false dawn. José, the mestizo cook, was puttering around the fire when he saw something was wrong and came running to help me move the delirious Blackbeard to his hammock.

There were three kits of antivenin in the foam cooler. The serum, which is made by injecting horses with ever-increasing doses of venom, could produce a deadly reaction in anyone sensitive to it, so I conducted the sensitivity test advised by the instructions. I injected a ten-to-one solution of the antivenin under the skin of Teach's unbitten right forearm, where it raised a small, white weal. If there was no allergic reaction within twenty minutes, I knew it would then be all right to give him the life-saving serum.

But within eight minutes, the injection had turned his right arm flaming red and it had begun to swell. Blackbeard would die more surely from the serum than from the bite if I injected him—although it looked as if he would anyway.

Beautiful, I thought, just nifty. There I was thirty miles up a jungle river, in jungle that makes the Everglades look like Central Park, with a guy who's got less than a half-chance of pulling through. And no way to help him. Each minute Teach looked more like he was ready to give up the ghost, struggling for breath in the hammock, his mouth crusted with drying blood from his oozing gums. I splashed some cool water over his face from the bag hanging on the hammock, and had another look at the bite. Godawful. His arm was swollen to the size of his thigh, the tissue around the fang wounds the color of Concord grapes. Unless somebody did something, and pretty quick, he was going to be one very long-gone goose.

In my business, I get to see a lot of screwball things, particularly concerning human life and death. I have seen bush Africans lie down and just die a couple of days after being told they were bewitched. I've seen others—the Masai—heal without infection from lion maulings that had deposited enough bacteria in the gashes to wipe out most of Manhattan. In Haiti and India, I've seen men push steel rods through their bodies without a sign of blood, yet watched Ethiopians die from the old custom of packing a thorn wound with camel dung. I've seen most of the folk-medicine of at least three continents, but

I wasn't prepared for what I saw that day on Monkey River.

José, the Mayan-English cook, didn't look much like Dr. Schweitzer, so when he showed up with his "snake fixin's," I was a bit skeptical. He had been missing for about fifteen minutes, but I hadn't paid much attention. I had other things to think about.

"My pappy was a snake doctor, Sah," he told me, "an' I can fix up the Tommygoff bite good's new." I looked at the little pile of paraphernalia in his thick hands with a raised eyebrow.

"Just what is all that stuff, José?" It looked more like salad seasonings than a snakebite cure. He continued in his unusual brand of English, a blend of accents that included West Indian, Mississippi, and Cockney:

"This here's armadillo fat, nice 'n hot." He displayed a black-lidded marmalade jar. "An' dis is bark, I dunno what kind 'cause my pappy give 'em to me long time ago. He call it nyoka bark." I wondered if there was any connection between José's nyoka bark and the identical Swahili word for snake. It seemed likely, but only heaven knew where his father might have gotten the word. José completed the inventory of his "fixin's" by shaking a small manilla envelope, full, he said, of fresh peppercorns.

"Look, José, Teach here is in big trouble," I said, gesturing to the stricken hunter. "If we don't figure out some way to help him, he's going to cash in, go west, know what I mean?" He nodded. "This is not the time to go fooling around with some damn-fool recipe for snakebite. Get me?"

"Sah, these fixin's'll save his life . . . make him well in a couple of days. My pappy famous in B.H. for bein' snake doctor; saved all kind o' folk what got bit by Tommygoffs. Even helped a few bit by bushmasters, but then he lost a lot of those, too." He paused in thought, craftiness gleaming in his dark eyes. "Anyway, just what you goin' to do to fix him up? He can't take that needle, and unless we tries somethin', he's sure proper gonna up and die."

I looked over at Teach and realized José had a point. There was nothing more I could do, so what the hell!

José reheated the armadillo fat until it looked like rancid

bacon drippings, and smeared a dollop over and around the area of the bite. I could see Teach's grim face tighten with the added pain, but he made no sound. José made a thick poultice of soaked tobacco leaves, bound them into place over the wound, and added more fat to the top of the mess that hung on Teach's arm like a giant leech. Bringing the teapot and water, he spooned in four measures of the strange, dried bark and added half a handful of crushed peppercorns. Pouring the foul-looking concoction into a battered enamel mug, he forced the whole mess down the sick man's throat.

"Got to get de poison out'a his stomach for him to live," said José. "At least, that's what my pappy always say." Teach gagged down the last of the brew.

For ten minutes, nothing happened. Except, perhaps, that Blackbeard began to look even worse, if that was possible. I thought we'd really done it this time—killed the poor bastard trying to cure him with some medieval brew that Merlin would have scoffed at. Then Blackbeard began to vomit, great gouts of black blood and fluids from deep in his chest staining the ground under his hammock. For five minutes he retched until too weak to continue, then closed his bloodshot eyes and lay back. I thought he was dead, but he began to breath more deeply and easily until he passed into what seemed a strong, natural sleep.

"The poison get all gathered up in the stomach," said José as he checked the poultice. "I think we got most of it out . . . anyway, he do look better." He did, too, to my surprise. I began to realize how tired and hungry I was. Cracking a bottle of sweat-beaded ale from the evaporation bag, I poured it straight down my throat, then opened another to enjoy more slowly. Gratefully, I sank down in the canvas camp chair and asked José to rustle up some grub.

He walked over to a slow fire that wafted a pale cloud of smoke up to a pile of green banana leaves on a wooden platform four feet above the coals. He removed the leaves and I recognized the paca I had popped with the .22 the previous afternoon. Sort of a giant, striped woodchuck, it lay whole and uncleaned on the makeshift grill, shriveled and scorched by the heat. A tarantula would have been more appetizing.

José gutted the half-smoked rodent and began slicing off flat slabs of whitish meat that resembled lean pork. He carried them to the cooking fire and began to fry them in bacon fat. The aroma was a lot more promising than the look of the big rat. He added some hash brown potatoes to the heavy iron skillet and served the whole thing with a flourish. By golly, it *did* look pretty good!

I have never had a more delicious meal than that paca, once I stopped thinking about what I was eating. The flavor was more delicate than veal, the texture something like breast of quail. Three times José refilled the skillet, until I felt like an anaconda that had engulfed a pig just a little too large. In the shade of the big, orchid-covered mahogany tree that formed an umbrella over our camp, I fell asleep.

The dying sun was a blotch of soft orange and pink over Monkey River as I awoke to the gentle nudging. It was Teach standing over me. I blinked, then blinked again. He looked tired and weak, but I could see in his eyes that he was very much recovered. I knew it was impossible, unthinkable, that José's snake fixin's had cured him, but there he stood in the twilight, smiling slightly.

"I'm gonna be okay," he said slowly in the soft, local Creole dialect. "Thanks a lot, mon, for helpin' me . . . bad chaps, those Tommygoffs."

"Not me, Teach," I corrected him. "It was José that fixed you up. I thought you were dead meat." He smiled a little wider, his face still wan, but the look of death gone from his eyes. If there was ever a man reprieved from the dead, it was, I decided, William Teach.

He sat down next to me, still shaky as hell but able to navigate. "Let's rest up for a day or so, then go back and get that jaguar for you. Is the pig still out there?" I had forgotten all about the tethered pig bait when Blackbeard was bitten by the snake. Teach reckoned that by now it would have been found and killed by the big cat we had been waiting for. Figuring on the small size of the pig, he concluded that the cat would be ready to kill again the following night.

"By the look of you, you've lost a lot of blood," I told him. "It'll take more than a couple of days before you're ready to go tangling with any *tigres*. Stick around and rest up; if José can handle a paddle, I should be able to sort that jag out myself."

"That's big jungle out there, Yank. You sure you know what you're doing?" he asked.

I gave it some thought. I knew what I was doing elsewhere, at least. I'd guided fifteen safaris into the Central Xingu Basin in Brazil and had a half-dozen years under my belt as a white hunter in Africa. But this cruddy piece of real estate was something else. It was tougher than the Ituri Forest and Xingu rolled into one . . . not as wet or thorny as the green hell of Marajo Island on the Amazon delta, I decided, but thicker and with more *ofensivos*—snakes, centipedes, spiders, and the rest of the roster of local talent that can put you into a nice, aromatic pine box long before you're due. As my old *bwana* buddy, Chris Pollet, used to say, "Death is nature's way of saying 'slow down.'" I would have to take it very slow indeed if I was going into the Monkey River jungle alone.

We loafed the next day, lying in our hammocks and relaxing in the sun. I continually soaked my aching shoulder with rags dipped into hot water, and gradually the pain lessened and the bruised tendons became more pliable. I knew I would need full use of the arm that night.

Again, the golden sun began to creep lower in the sky until it fell over the distant Pacific across Guatemala. I lit up a cigarette and watched the blue smoke thread upward in the still air. Teach was having a bowl of soup, drinking from the lip and softly cursing as the hot liquid burned his mouth. I walked over to have a look at his arm. The swelling was dramatically down, although the discoloration of the poisoned tissue was still vivid. There was no apparent infection. I could only shake my head in wonder. The more you travel in remote areas, the less you find you really do know. . . .

The *bichos*, the night creatures, were beginning to sound off as José brought me a fine iguana casserole at the camp table. After finishing the excellent dish, much like white breast of chicken garnished with the hard-boiled eggs taken from the females, I poured a short brandy, propped up my feet, and waited for heavy darkness to fall. Sitting there with Teach before the fire, I thought back to how this whole hunt had started.

It was at a cocktail party in Sutton Place in New York City, a few weeks before. The chic apartment was well appointed with some reasonable trophies, mostly African and Asian, but with one fine jaguar skin fresh on its scalloped felt backing. I asked my host where he had gotten it, not knowing the man before being introduced that evening.

"British Honduras," he told me, and mentioned the name of his outfitter. I cringed inwardly. His pro hunter was infamous for his so-called guaranteed hunts. High fee, jaguar guaranteed, only one stipulation: when you got your jaguar, your hunt was over. Professional hunters are a small fraternity, and I knew that this man was actually buying his jaguars from animal dealers in the States, many of them having been born in captivity in zoos and circuses. He would have the cats shipped to British Honduras and would drive them out of their cages a few minutes before a client's plane was due at his jungle strip. A pack of hounds would tree the bewildered jaguar and hold it until the plane landed. Greeting the visiting hunter, he would announce: "You sure are some lucky man, Mr. Smith. I was just bringing the pack over to the strip when they hit a real hot trail. Got a fine jaguar treed only a half-mile from here. Yup, sure some piece of luck."

The client would then saunter over to the treed cat, peering down from the branches in terror, pop him like a duck in a shooting gallery, and go back to the still-waiting aircraft for his flight home. Once back in civilization, he would beat his chest, smell like leather, and crow hairy tales of his conquest of the jungle. The whole affair was completely stomach-turning, and the few real sportsmen who did know it was a setup got back into the airplane and forfeited their fees rather than commit murder. Sadly, there were lots who didn't.

As the party wore on, I availed myself of the man's ample supply of fine scotch whiskey and stepped over to hear him tell his feats to a pair of wide-eyed women who gushed over a plot more exciting than any Jungle Jim adventure. It got to be just a little *too* thick, and, not noted for my cocktail-party tact, I opened my big mouth. I said I didn't think awfully much of assassination and equated the use of dogs on jaguar with their use on bongo in Africa; it simply wasn't *done,* old boy, at least not by gentlemen and sportsmen.

The party quieted down in a hurry. The man, taken aback, blustered and raged that there was no other possible way to hunt such difficult terrain.

Ridiculous, I said, pouring another long belt of scotch. I was in too deep to back out. Any good hunter could go down to B.H. and, using nothing but his wits and some live bait, collect a big cat on sporting terms—at night. And, it could be done in ten days.

"I've got five grand that says *you* can't do it, my big shot *bwana,*" he answered coldly. "Want to put your money where your mouth is?"

I had just gotten back from a pretty good season in Zambia and had a fair wad nestled in the bank. I wrote a check and handed it to a neutral party, and my host did the same. We didn't shake hands.

A week later, I was ensconced in the Fort George Hotel in Belize, the capital city of the sleepy little country, lying just below the remote Mexican province of Quintana Roo in the western Caribbean. A few discreet questions put me onto one William Teach, fisherman and hunting guide to the wild areas of the southeast coast; something of a pro hunter dealing in everything from live animals to orchids to cat skins. A half-bottle of local rum later, I knew he was my man.

The following morning Blackbeard picked me up, and we shoved off in his twenty-foot sailboat for Monkey River, the area he felt would be best to collect my bet. I had explained the wager and offered him a straight 10 percent on a win-or-lose basis. He didn't hesitate a second in accepting. That was a good piece of hard cash to Teach.

We tacked along the inside of the barrier reef (second largest in the world next to the Great Barrier Reef of Australia), spending the night in the southern Turneffes, a fairy-tale string of islands that swing down in a long arc off the

coast. Laughing Bird Cay was our first stop. It would have
been all right with me if we were to spend a month there. It
was a tiny paradise that you could fit in your back pocket:
sugary beaches, coconut palms, and shoals of hungry bonefish.
Mayan potsherds showed that in ancient times it was heavily
visited by Indian sailors who must have found it as charming
as I did. I was sorry to see it slip behind the horizon in the
morning as José, Blackbeard's employee and companion,
grilled up some fresh kingfish I had caught with a hand-line
from the sailboat, as we cut back southwest toward the mouth
of Monkey River.

As we entered the river, Teach and José lowered the mast
so we could pass under the overhanging vegetation and lashed
it along the deck. With some effort, they kicked over the old
engine and we swung into the slow current, reminiscent of the
movie *The African Queen*. As we chugged with wheezy headway up the greasy, green highway of water, I came to the conclusion that anybody lost in that tangle of vegetation wasn't
going to be seen in a hurry again. It was nearly impenetrable,
from low, snarled greenery to great, reaching, liana-covered
hardwoods green with moss and bright with tropical birds.
Huge jacarés (or were they really alligators?) slithered with
hardly a ripple into the quiet pools, and brilliant clouds of
butterflies rose from the banks in alarm at our passing. Mosquitoes began to whine, their dartlike sound blending with the
buzz of fat horseflies and tiny, razor-fanged gnats. Twice we
saw snakes in the water. First a Tommygoff, as José told me
the Yellow Beard was locally called, cut the water with his flat
head aggressively a foot above the surface. I took my little .22
Browning auto from its waterproof case and was ready when
we later passed a thick-bodied bushmaster crossing a few yards
upstream. I hit him just behind his neck with a hollow-point.
He erupted into a snarl of tortured, bicep-thick coils at the
shot, then sank weakly into the dark water.

It might have been twenty, maybe even thirty miles up the
river before we finally dropped anchor and set up camp on a
sandy spit. I had lost all sense of distance with the thick jungle
pushing down on me like a heavy, green shroud, one giant

river bend looking much like another. I was impressed with the little camp Teach put up, the tents of good-quality canvas with snakeproof ground sheets and zippered fronts. Hordes of pumpkin-colored land crabs scuttled about in the under-growth, and I vaguely wondered what they could all find to eat to support their great numbers. They were incredibly repulsive little creatures, brazenly scampering through the camp; but there were far too many to kill and we just had to put up with them.

The next dawn, Teach and I launched the dugout we had towed behind the sailboat and began paddling upriver. Occasionally, we would beach the craft and scout the sandy banks for jaguar spoor. We found plenty along the sides of the stream, a natural pathway for hungry cats that would intercept drinking animals in the relative open, trapping them along the water. We inspected and rejected four sets of pug marks as not being big enough to bother with, and finally settled on a spoor that fetched a whistle even from Teach. It was a very big *tigre* for Central America, by the depth of his prints probably around 250 pounds, twice the size of a spanking good tom leopard. He was a solitary male with a well-carved-out territory, just what we were looking for. Only he was probably looking at us right now from one of the deep forest shadows.

Teach drew his scalpel-sharp, stained machete and began to cut saplings in a small clearing a few yards from the water's edge. When he had trimmed four to about twelve feet, he sank them into the soft ground around a foot-thick tree that would act as a central support for the *machan* or blind. He then cut others into six-foot lengths to act as the planking for the platform. Agile for his bulk, he lashed the whole frame together with the inner bark of a slender, dark tree and finished by building a ladder of the same materials. We were in business.

Returning to camp, we napped the afternoon away until twilight began to fall. José literally hog-tied one of the two small pigs we had bought at a coastal settlement north of the river for five British Honduras dollars and loaded it into the middle of the dugout. I checked over the shotgun and stuck a half-dozen Magnum buckshot shells into my pockets (twelve pellets of 00). In the veteran Beretta over/under, it was a great short-range combination for the big, thin-skinned cats, particularly at night when the niceties of aiming weren't always available. It had settled a half-dozen leopards and three lions back in Africa, so I reckoned it was just right for this situation.

I adjusted the miner's lamp around the crown of my soft hat and stuck the battery pack in my pocket, the switch just up the wire and in easy reach. Afraid the heavy smell of insect repellent might foul up the *machan* area, I decided to leave it behind. After all, you can take a pretty good mauling from mosquitoes for $5,000!

Slowly the jungle slid past us in the gathering darkness until it appeared a shadowy blur. With both of us paddling, the light craft made good headway against the current until the eight miles were past and we beached softly on the sandy river edge. While I carried the shotgun and water to the *machan* and climbed up, Teach lugged the struggling pig into the middle of the clearing and staked it down with a length of tough, green tapir hide. With his penknife he made a small slit at the base of one ear and tied a loose loop of monofilament line through the incision. Knowing the pig would naturally lie quietly, he would jerk the cord lightly every fifteen minutes in the hope that its grunts would attract the jaguar.

Four hours later, without the first sign of the big cat, the snake hit Teach. . . .

I tossed off the rest of the brandy and let my mind snap back to the present. Blackbeard bummed one of my cigarettes and said, "Well, if you're gonna give it a try, better get a move on." I reflected a moment. "Might as well. Only have a few more days left and I'd hate to miss that five grand by sitting around in camp."

Because he really wasn't a hunter, I decided against taking José into the *machan* with me. When I was settled, he would take the canoe a few hundred yards downstream and moor it to the opposite bank to await either a shot or dawn. Knowing the *machan* was really no defense against a jaguar that could leap the dozen feet as easily as a house cat jumps to a windowsill, it would be better to be alone rather than to have somebody who might panic if things got hairy.

Teach walked down to the water's edge and gave us a

push-off at about seven o'clock. The river gurgled darkly against dead tree limbs that loomed in the headlamp like snaggled, decaying teeth. After ninety minutes of soft paddling, I was able to recognize the spot where we had landed days earlier, and directed José there with the light. As we came ashore, I had a strange feeling of timelessness that often hits me in the jungle. The sounds of night birds and insects were exactly the same as the night Teach was bitten, and I wondered if there could be another snake, too.

Checking the shotgun loads again, I walked over to where we had staked out the first pig, José carrying the second. Bingo! Except for two hooves, the porker had been taken and eaten on the spot. That meant two things to me as I examined the earth: first, by the marks of his unhesitating charge from close quarters, the big jaguar was probably unwary. Second, any jaguar that might come tonight would be he. He wouldn't have eaten the pig out in the open clearing if he was worried about another cat in his territory. I knew he would be bold—but I wouldn't find out until later that he would also be rash.

I staked out the second pig and attached the monofilament, trailing it back to the *machan*. With the light, I carefully, *very carefully,* checked the branches above for snakes. They were clear. Hearing the soft swirl of José's paddle digging into the dark water as he pulled away, I settled back to listen and wait.

One of the most difficult things about waiting for a big cat in total blackness is that, surprisingly, it's hard to concentrate. After a few hours of the tremendous mental effort necessary to constantly sort out the variety of night noises—any one of which your life might depend upon—your brain becomes as exhausted as after a long, difficult chess match. There is absolutely nothing to see in the jungle night, the sky completely hidden by the shroud of trees above, and very little to feel except for your aching backside and the smooth comfort of the gun in your hands. Your mind begins to wander, to drift, much as in road hypnosis. You wonder if maybe there really *is* something to vitamin E or who was the first person to eat a raw oyster? The sudden, icy night shower shakes you back to reality as a few drops trickle down your neck. You think about the little plastic toggle in your fist—the switch to the lamp. Get overanxious and hit the light too soon, before the jaguar is in the open, and he'll melt away like a wraith. Too late and you may find that he's noticed something besides the pig, something he may regard as even more appetizing than pork—you! It wouldn't be the first time, either. You remember what happened to young Almeida back in the Xingu—the Indians brought back the bottom halves of his boots with the feet still in them, his pistol belt, and his knife. You remember packing them in layers of plastic bags for the trip three hundred miles downriver where the trade boat would forward them to his family in São Paulo. You remember Almeida and listen harder.

How many hours have passed? One? Five? The hum of the *bichos* and the swirl of a *jacaré* snapping bear-trap teeth around a big *machaca* or *roncador* drift up from the jungle river. Nothing, absolutely nothing. Then, you know he's there. You don't know how, but you're heart-slamming sure. There has been no sound, no scent, no hint of movement. But he's there. Close. It's the same feeling you get when someone stares at the back of your head, the same sixth sense that makes your hackles rise to protect your jugular. Suddenly you realize what it is. You're actually feeling the terror of the pig, heavy waves of fear coming from below you as you know the little black porker has winded death.

The minutes creep by excruciatingly as you shut your eyes and strain your ears harder into the dark stillness. The thump, like distant, muffled drums, is your own pulse swelling in your ears, adrenaline pumping into your bloodstream. There is a hard knot somewhere below your throat, and it's hard to get your breath quietly. You realize it. For once it's all clear. You're scared. Not terrified. Healthy, honest, gut-knotted scared. The fear that will make you a better animal for what you must do. You like it, but you'll never be able to explain it later to another man. If he has experienced it, there will be no need to explain.

Where is he? Has he noticed something? Is that why he hasn't hurled himself onto the pig, killing it with one savage clamp of long fangs through the base of the skull? Does he smell a human? Can it be he also feels the fear in the air?—both yours and the pig's. You wonder which is stronger.

There is the softest sound, or perhaps the *lack* of sound, from insects near him. That's it. It's not a noise he made, but the noise the night bugs *aren't* making. He is in front of you—very close.

A thrill runs up your spine like a small, furry animal. He is looking at you—seeing you through the wet, velvet night, his hard, yellow eyes dilated to gather light you could never detect. You can feel his eyes, but he's not slinking off. He's studying you, calculating what you are and if you're good to eat. You grip the shotgun tighter, the checkering of the stock leaving its pattern in the flesh of your sweating fingers. He's going to come, and you can stand it no longer. The fear might get away and become terror, now that you know *you* are the hunted.

The light flashes on as the shotgun comes up. His body is a frozen, gold-dappled teardrop of motion in the beam as he begins his charge. In slow motion, you see divots of dead leaves and black dirt his scrabbling hind legs kick into the air. In fifteen yards of low, doglike rush he is ten feet in front of the *machan,* deep shadows outlining his thick muscles as he gathers for his spring. His front legs are pulled back along his body as he launches into the air, then they extend, each massive pad tipped with erect, yellow hooks, to hold your quivering meat. But something has happened. His face is beginning to dissolve into a growing, pink mist, chips of shattered fangs angling whitely through the light. His glowing eyes are extinguished as the massed charge of buckshot mangles his head, but the flying bulk of his body keeps irresistibly rising toward you from the power of his spring. A heavy shock hits the *machan,* shaking the structure just below your legs. You are thrown off balance and the beam on your head darts wildly skyward. A heavy, wet sound like a fallen sack of watermelons echoes off the jungle floor below, as the big cat hits the ground in a hiss of impact-exhaled breath. It is the deadest sound you have ever heard.

It is full daylight when we round the last bend of the river upstream from camp, two hours into the other jungle world of light. The smile of honest congratulation from Teach is worth more to me than the big skin rolled up in the bow. We split a half bottle of scotch before I finish off the paca and climb exhausted into the hammock. As I lie across the smooth fibers, I think about the $5,000. Maybe it wouldn't be such a bad idea to return to British Honduras to spend it.

PIGSTICKING
MADE PERSONAL

SAGA — FEBRUARY 1973

Argentine wild boar *(Sus scrofa)*.

AUTHOR'S INTRODUCTION

Having already overexposed you to the joys of pigsticking in the British Raj, it seems only fair to give Argentina her due.

Over some six years and twenty-six trips, I spent a great deal of time in Patagonia, mostly with Amadeo "Chiche" Bilo, who is to the South American blood sports what Sterling Moss was to British racing. With Chiche, I shared the incredible duck and goose shooting of the interior, took trout and landlocked salmon fit to scare me, and hunted axis, fallow, and red deer that were among the best in the world. But the wildest sport—and the scariest—was with the jabalíes, the gigantic wild boars that lived on the herds of sheep the way Russian wolves used to snack on peasants.

It was grand in those days of the 1960s, when the dollar bought more of anything you could think of and still carry. I came to love Argentina so much, especially as I spoke the language better than these chapters may reflect, that it was hard to choose between Africa and those wild pampas and desert, with the southern Andes so close with their fishing. Were those bloody mountains not covered with snow so much of the time, I might still be there.

T he pale streaks of the winter dawn were showing through the feathery *alamo* trees when Chiche Bilo reined his horse up short. He swung from the gaucho saddle and with the rolling gait of the professional horseman approached the mutilated sheep. Inserting the toe of his *alpargata* under the edge of the stiffening carcass, he flipped the carcass, exposing the massive damage to the animal's underside. Bilo's brown Basque eyes stared hard at the long, irregular wounds in the sheep's chest and at the big tear across the paunch where the internal organs had been dragged out and eaten. I saw his gaze flicker to the churned desert earth as it followed the series of deep, split grooves that led into the heavy chaparral. His jaw muscle was twitching as he spoke.

"*Jabalí,*" he said quietly. "Wild boar, and a hell of a big one."

I held in my horse as it skittered at the blood scent. "You mean it was a wild boar that killed this ram?" I asked incredulously. "What the hell, I've never heard of pigs killing animals to eat." The carcass looked like the remains of an ax murder. "I thought boars lived on acorns or truffles and that sort of stuff."

"Not in Argentina, they don't," answered Chiche as he remounted in one smooth movement. "We had one boar operating about twenty miles from here that killed over eight hundred sheep and heifers over a three-year period until I finally was called in to take care of it. This kill isn't more than three hours old," he continued, rubbing a clot of blood between his fingers. "Let's head back to the *estancia* and pick up the *Dogos.*"

I slid the shotgun back into its scabbard, all thought of hunting the sporty desert partridge called *copetonas* now far from my mind. Chiche's *estancia,* I knew, was a working ranch and nothing came before the protection of his stock—including my *Saga* assignment to investigate the rumors of fantastic bird shooting to be found here in the Patagonian region of western Argentina. Anyway, I was glad of an opportunity to see his famed *Dogos Argentinos* at work.

We rode back through the dry sage and maquis of Chiche's fifteen thousand hectares at an easy canter. Angel, a giant gaucho in balloon pants with a heavy, silver-handled knife stuck through the back of his waist sash, rode heavily behind me, a grin as wide as a watermelon slice on his weathered face. Chickens and puppies scattered as Chiche led us through the apple orchard into the dusty courtyard where the big, white boar dogs strained against their staked-down leads. They seemed to sense a hunt in our pounding hoofs, and whined with excitement as we reined up.

Chiche called for maté, the traditional herb tea of the pampas. which was brought in silver-trimmed gourds by his slender, blue-eyed wife. She handed me a gourd and spooned sugar over the dry mixture, adding enough hot water for one noisy sip through the silver straw. I inhaled mine down in approved gaucho fashion while Chiche untied three of the biggest dogs. Released, they stood silently listening to his whispers in Araucano, the ancient tongue of the fierce Patagonian Indians, the only language he would use with his fighting animals. He explained to me that in the confusion of a boar fight, men shout in Spanish. Since the dogs might misunderstand a shout between hunters, Araucano was his only language of command.

The night before, over a grilled *parrillada mixta,* the wonderful Argentinian national dish of assorted meats, Bilo had told me about his *Dogos Argentinos.* Originally developed by Dr. Nores Martines, the *Dogos* are probably the most effective breed of boar-hunting animals ever developed.

When the European wild boar, *Sus scrofa,* was imported into Argentina in the middle of the last century to provide sport on the estates of the wealthy, it was soon found that conditions in Argentina were just about perfect for wild pigs. The result was that *jabalí,* as boar are called locally, grow bigger and tougher here than anywhere else in the world. Bilo has killed several better than six hundred pounds, and there are records of boar better than seven hundred. It didn't take long to find that imported European dogs were no match for these huge pigs, particularly in the heavy bush of the western areas.

A further complication arose when it was found that boar were beginning to kill stock, an almost unheard-of thing elsewhere in their vast range. Bilo said that nobody knew if they were killing stock because the breed had gotten so big, or whether they had gotten so big by killing and eating sheep. At any rate, by 1900 they had become a major menace for ranchers throughout most of Argentina.

It took until the 1930s before Dr. Martines, a dedicated hunter and dog breeder, had developed the bloodline into what is today the standard *Dogo Argentino.* He used Spanish pointer, mastiff, pit bull, bloodhound, and a half-dozen other strains to develop the qualities necessary for a real fighting dog: tenacity, ferocity, and fearlessness. After Dr. Martines's death, the development of the *Dogo Argentino,* now a national pride, was unofficially adopted by Chiche Bilo. At his ranch on the banks of the Rio Negro near the town of Allen (pronounced locally Azzhen), Bilo has about fifty of the best *Dogos* in the world.

A full-grown *Dogo* weighs about ninety to one hundred pounds of white-sheathed muscle. Their teeth and jaws are tremendous, as they must be to grab and hold boar, but they are strangely gentle, making excellent house pets, although I doubt they'll ever replace the poodle.

Although *Dogos* have a natural instinct for boar fighting, Bilo won't let his dogs hunt without having actually fought boar in his arena, an enclosure specially constructed for young dogs to learn tactics the hard way, in the hope that experience here may save their lives later. Moderate-sized captive boar are used in these fights, but despite this, many *Dogos* are killed or disabled before they ever take up a wild scent.

The tactics of the *Dogos,* Chiche explained to me, are to follow the boar's spoor silently, and to jump the big pig as a team. One dog will grab an ear while the others take legs or flank. Since *Dogos* almost never bark when hunting, curs follow them and sound off when the fight starts, indicating the location of the struggle to the hunters.

"Then," said Bilo casually, "I kill the *jabalí* with the knife."

"You *what?*" I asked.

"The *arbolito*—the gaucho knife. I kill the boar with it."

"Now, let me get this straight. You walk up to a five-hundred-pound wild boar and stab him to death? Isn't that just a little bit tricky?"

"Oh, yes, *Pedro,* many men are killed trying it. But really, it is all in knowing when to make your attack, when to—how do you say—stab."

"Where the hell did you get this idea?" I asked him, lighting a *cigarro negro.*

"We gauchos have always considered it a man's way to hunt," he answered simply. "The object of hunting *jabalí* is not to make it as easy as possible, but as hard as possible. If I just wanted a dead pig, I would buy one."

God, I thought, these crazy cowboys . . .

Followed by the three boar hounds and a pair of scruffy-looking mutts, we rode back to the grove of *alamos* and the dead sheep. A desert eagle flapped off heavily as we reined in. Chiche dismounted and whistled the *Dogos* over to the spoor. They snuffed the pungent boar scent with low nasal snorts, milled about for a moment, then forged ahead with Bilo's lead bitch, Day, in the lead. The mongrels whined and followed at a trot.

We cantered after the pack for about a mile through the thorny scrub without a hint of sound to guide us until we came to a broad plain hemmed with gray brush. Bilo stopped, and, like an acrobat, he steadied himself and rose standing on the saddle, his eyes shaded across the desert. There was no sound but the low moan of the dry wind and the whisper of the *alamos.* Dropping back into the saddle, he told me he felt the boar would probably make for the thick stuff along the river and possibly cross the jungled islands near the north bank. We rode in the direction Chiche indicated, straining to hear the bark of the curs. Finally, like the faraway ring of a small bell, it came.

Whack! went the flat rawhide whip against the rump of Chiche's mount as he spurred off at a flat run, with Angel and me behind, eating his dust. Sharp branches slashed at us as we crashed through the scrub toward the green of the river a mile ahead. Twice I swerved my horse just in time to avoid deadly *viscacha* holes, knowing it would mean a broken leg for my animal and a possible broken neck for me if he stepped into one of the rodent's burrows at full speed. Coveys of *perdices*—

tailless Argentine quail—burst from under our hammering hoofs like brown grenade fragments, and one smashed into my face like a thrown rock, blinding me for a moment. I hung on to the pommel with white knuckles, head down against the lashing branches, until my vision cleared.

As we flashed across the pampas, a high, quivering cry cut the air like a sword. It was the ancient Basque war cry that Chiche used to encourage his dogs to fight on until he got there. Ahead, I caught a glimpse of one of the curs running toward us, his tail tucked between his legs. Chiche thundered on into the cover, and I saw the icy flicker of steel as he drew his long knife. Hauling his horse back into a skidding cascade of flying dirt, he hit the ground running and disappeared from view. I pulled the scattergun, loaded with slugs, from the scabbard and followed him on foot. When I caught up after fifty yards, he was standing in a clearing, completely still, staring at something on the ground. It was Day, the leader, and she was dying.

Chiche knelt by her and inspected her wounds. A froth of bloody pink bubbles oozed from her chest where a razor-sharp tusk had penetrated her lung. A bulge of snaky intestine protruded from a straight incision in her paunch. She whined and struggled to rise. Chiche's eyes misted over as he realized she wanted to go on with the hunt.

Angel wiped her face with a grimy fist and lifted the dying dog in his arms, placing her gently over his saddle. She feebly licked his hand. Chiche rode off and returned fifteen minutes later with the remaining two hounds, both filthy with dirt-smeared blood, but not really wounded. Taking a curved needle and gut from his wallet, Chiche began to sew them up. They never even whimpered as he sterilized their wounds with brandy. I could see the muscle in Chiche's jaw twitching again as he swung onto his horse and began the ride home. I knew better than to say anything.

The pale sun had just set when Angel patted the last spadeful of red earth into place. Chiche took the shovel and drove the head marker deeply into the dirt: *Day de Trevelin— 364 Jabalíes*. Drawing his fighting knife, he sank it hilt-deep to the right of the marker and Angel stabbed his to the left. I knew they did it for the same reason an Englishman breaks his champagne glass, so that never may a lesser toast be drunk from it.

Amadeo "Chiche" Bilo is one of the few great hunters who has become a legend in his own time, not only in his native Argentina, but anywhere strong men hoist a glass and speak of great hunting deeds. He is among the last of the most ancient line of noble sportsmen who fight the most dangerous prey on foot with hand weapons.

The entire way of life of the early warrior-nobles of northern Europe and England during medieval times was based on combat and the development of skill at arms. When there wasn't a stack of Saracens handy for an afternoon's sport, or some other target available for some good rough-and-tumble, the man of action got a few buddies together and went out boar hunting.

The oldest surviving book on hunting dates from the 1360s and is entitled *Livre de la Chasse.* Written by Gaston Phoebus, by whose name the book is more familiarly called, it provides the first and best records of hunts and killing techniques, and is guaranteed to frost the sideburns of the toughest modern Tarzan. Concerning the spearing of boar on foot with a lance fitted with a crosspiece (so the boar wouldn't come up the shaft at you), old Gaston told it like it really was:

"As soon as the point has entered the boar's body, take the heft under your armpit and press and push as hard as you can and never let go the haft, and if the boar be stronger than you then you must turn from side to side as best you can without letting go the haft until God comes to your aid or some other assistance."

Bear in mind, now, that Gaston considered spearing to be the *easy* way. By his reckoning, the killing of a charging boar from horseback with a sword was really doing it right, "a finer thing and more noble" than the methods employed by the pantywaists with the pigstickers. In a technical discussion, Phoebus mentioned that the major problem in filleting your pig from the saddle was the chance of cutting off your own arms and legs while chopping away at the boar, who was himself occupied with the vivisection of your horse. The author laments the many mounts that were killed under him by boar.

It must have been a tough and short life, being in the employ of Master Phoebus. We can only hope his staff received combat pay, as Gaston recites in an antiseptic manner that he had lost many good squires and servants at the tusks of boar that would "slit a man from the knee to the breast and slay him all stark dead at one stroke so that he never spoke thereafter."

Presumably, Phoebus must have figured the odds on coming home after a tête-à-tête with a boar while on foot and armed only with a knife were too short to even call it sport, and has not mentioned it in his book. He would have been very impressed with Chiche Bilo. Perhaps the difference was in the skill of the hounds, but that would be hard to believe. There are surviving tapestries and drawings showing boar dogs that would make Hound of the Baskervilles look like a Chihuahua. A skilled boar dog has always been highly prized, and with good reason. An experienced hound was one that had lived long enough to develop a style in his tangles with boar without getting permanently ventilated. Other members of the pack would learn from him, thus decreasing the mortality rate of the entire pack. German paintings from the eighteenth century often show pack leaders wearing expensive chain-mail coats to protect them against the deadly tusks.

It is interesting to note that the quality of silence among boar dogs was as popular eight hundred years ago in England as it is today in Argentina. A letter survives at the Tower of London, written by King John in 1213 to Roger de Neville, mentioning that the king was sending, among other breeds, "fifteen varlets . . . and forty-four *de mota* (mute) dogs to hunt boars in the park at Bricstok. . . ." One speculates whether they were mute naturally or perhaps had been operated on in some way.

A boar hunt in Europe, by the 1500s, had become sort of a combination between the opening day of rabbit season in

Arbolito boar fighting knife with sterling silver mounts.

New Jersey and the Super Bowl. Huge beats took place for the pleasure of hundreds of sportsmen, driving great numbers of boar and other game before the huntsmen. As there were considerable pauses between the furious action, one Frenchman, Jacques de Fouilloux, suggested that between the more active phases of the hunt, a gentleman should have a young girl of the village at hand to take care of his more idle moments. You can see that hunting isn't what it used to be.

One of the only men of the modern era to hunt boar on foot with a knife for the sheer hell of it was Sir Samuel White Baker, an early explorer of the tributaries of the Nile River. In one of Baker's first books, *The Rifle and the Hound in Ceylon,* he describes chasing down Ceylonese boar on foot and killing them in the identical manner of Bilo. Baker, twenty-two years old at the time, favored a cut-down Highland Claymore, a double-edged piece of steel that was sharp as a razor, with an eighteen-inch blade. Weighing about three pounds, it was really a short sword. Describing the scene he would meet after a long run through jungle and ravine following his hounds and finally bringing the boar to bay in the thickest part of the forest, Baker said:

> The huntsman approaches the scene of the combat, breaking his way with difficulty through the tangled jungle until within about twenty yards of the bay. He now cheers the hounds on to attack, and if they are worthy of their name, they instantly rush into the boar regardless of wounds. The huntsman . . . immediately rushes to the assistance of the pack, knife in hand.
>
> A scene of real warfare meets his view—gaping

wounds upon his best hounds, the boar rushing through the jungle covered with dogs, and he himself becomes the immediate object of his fury when observed.

No time is to be lost. Keeping behind the boar if possible, he rushes to the bloody conflict, and drives the hunting knife between the shoulders in the endeavor to divide the spine. Should he happily affect this, the boar falls stone dead; but if not, he repeats the thrust, keeping a good lookout for the animal's tusks.

If the dogs were not of sufficient courage to rush in and seize the boar when *halload* [sic] on, no man could approach him in a thick jungle with only a hunting knife, as he would in all probability have his inside ripped out on the first charge. They are wonderfully active and ferocious, and of immense power, constantly weighing four cwt [400 pounds]. The end of every good seizor is being killed by a boar. The better the dog the more likely he is to be killed, as he will be the first to lead the attack, and in the thick jungle he has no chance of escaping from a wound.

Chiche confirmed to me what Baker had said. Without big, fearless dogs to hold the boar for him, a man wouldn't have a chance. A boar charges as straight as a spear, with his head low and shrieking like a banshee with a stubbed toe. He'll flatten a horse and unzip him with his razor tusks quicker than it takes to tell. Contrary to popular opinion, boar don't gore or slash with their tusks; they bite like a pair of shears. The lower tusks loop up and whet against the uppers, keeping them sharper than a carving set. When a boar is warming up to subdivide your carcass, the whetting sound is much like that made by your butcher just before he carves you a good steak.

A boar will almost always charge a man when fighting with dogs. If the dogs are weak from loss of blood or don't have a good grip on the boar, the pig may shuck them off like so many sparrows. Boar dogs are like dominoes—if one loses a grip, the others may be thrown off balance. Then, big shot, there's nothing between you and a quarter-ton of uncooked pork but a foot-and-a-half blade and your two shaking feet. I know, it happened to me.

There were needles of ice around the rim of the horse trough as we sucked up the last of our *maté* and mounted for the hunt. Two more *Dogos,* trotting behind the horses in their grim silence, joined the survivors of yesterday's fight. Chiche led us toward the river, about a mile downwind of the thicket where Day had been killed. Chiche and Angel had both whetted new knives and presented me with one as a gift. My sense of honor forced me to leave the shotgun in the corner behind the ranch house door. I later regretted it.

Puffs of cold dust were thrown from our horses' hoofs as we walked the mounts in line-abreast formation through the chaparral. In the distance, a pair of guanaco, desert cousins of the llama, stared and bolted away. To my left, a giant Patagonian hare hunched beneath a bush, frozen into hiding, then burst with a blur of speed into the surrounding thorny scrub.

A low whistle brought our eyes from the packed ground. It was Angel.

"Se fue por aquí, Patrón," he said, addressing Chiche and pointing to the set of tracks leading across our path. We dismounted as Bilo inspected the spoor and followed it, leading his horse. After fifty yards, a fresh pile of droppings lay on the trail. It was full of matted wool. Bilo gave me an odd smile, as if to say, "same one as yesterday."

Angel brought up the dogs on a multiple tether. Shaking with excitement, they were released and disappeared like silent wraiths on the spoor, with the little curs running behind. The lead dog was Tahpei, a big male given his Araucano name for bravery. He didn't look like the sort of dog you'd want to try to take a bone from.

Spurring forward, we followed at a canter, Chiche ahead and the big gaucho trailing me. I shifted the knife in my belt where the hilt dug into my ribs.

We covered three miles following the dogs, never hearing a sound from the curs. Four times the trail of the *Dogos* went off at a tangent with the pig's spoor until Angel shouted to stop for a moment. He jumped from his horse and stared at the ground. Grimacing, he pointed to the trail. Even I could see that the big boar had been joined by two others that were a little smaller and probably sows.

"*Pedro,* we've really got to ride now," Chiche said with a frown. "If those *Dogos* tangle with three pigs at once, we'll lose the whole pack. It's happened before. They're bred for fear-lessness and won't hesitate to go for a dozen boar." As if to answer him, a distant barking came to us from the river edge.

We covered the last mile as if possessed, and pulled up in the heavy cover near the riverbank. Fierce grunts and squeals mixed with the hysteria of the curs sounded like a steam calliope gone wild. Following Chiche and Angel with drawn knife, I bulled through the snags and thorns, wishing like hell I was going the other way.

I felt the wind whistling through my burning lungs as I ran with Bilo's wild Basque yell ringing in my ears. Suddenly, ahead I could see the movement of white dogs flicker through the small gaps in the bush. At twenty yards, a long slice on the side of Tahpei glistened a wet red as I saw him rush in like a mamba snake to grab the ear of a big sow. She shrieked and snapped her head, lifting the big dog off the ground with a lightning wrench, breaking his grip and tearing his powerful teeth through her ear skin. He landed on his back and re-gained his feet just before the pig hit him, her frothing, open mouth snapping shut like a bear trap just past his leg. A few yards to the right, the other three *Dogos* were trying to hold on to an enormous female, one dog on each ear and the third with his fangs sunk into the fat of her rump. She dragged them along the ground like a pro fullback in a Little League game, but none would break his vise-like grip.

There was a blur of Chiche coming in like a falcon from the sow's side, his left arm extended and the knife held low in his right. I saw him grip deeply into the pig's bristles, and drive the steel behind her shoulder, working the blade in the wound. The sow gave a terrible scream and began to thrash around with redoubled fury, lifting the heavy hounds holding her ears like two marshmallows. Chiche withdrew the knife and struck again, this time between the shoulder blades, sawing to find the spinal cord, holding on with one hand as the sow bounced him like a doll in her frenzy. Then, as if axed, she dropped without a quiver and lay still. He had found a joint between the vertebrae.

A hoarse shout ripped through the clearing. It was Angel yelling, *"Cuidado, Patrón! A la izquierda!"* Bilo leaped from the dead pig in time to see the other female bearing down on him, Tahpei being dragged behind with his teeth fastened deep in her flank. Three white streaks tore straight at her as Bilo shouted in Araucano, *"Kiah!"* Kill!

The *Dogos* rushed as one at the charging female. The center dog feinted at the animal's head, and, as she snapped at him, the other two leaped to her flank and grabbed her by the side of the throat. Slowed momentarily, she turned to slash at them and the middle *Dogo* joined Tahpei on the opposite flank. Bilo motioned Angel back and measured his charge. The split-second opening came and he was on her like a madman, stabbing and ripping. Her screeches turned to deep gurgling as thick blood gushed from her snout and open mouth, staining her clashing tusks crimson. With a last grunt she fell heavily on her side, kicking feebly in the grip of the dogs. A shudder ran up her spine and she was dead.

Blood-smeared and panting, Chiche got to his feet and called off the dogs mauling the carcass. They backed off and shook themselves, licking at wounds.

"A Dios gracias," puffed Chiche, *"que se fue el macho."* I looked at him questioningly. "I say, thank God that son-of-a-bitch male took off," he repeated in English. "He's a smart old bastard and left the sows to cover for him while he got away."

"Where do you think he went?" I asked.

Without answering, Chiche walked to the other side of the clearing and showed me the trail of the boar where it led down the riverbank and into the water. He pointed to a large island covered with thick undergrowth. "That's where he'll be, *Pedro,* and it'll be a rough place to worm him out."

Angel tied the horses to a bush while Bilo flipped off his *alpargatas* and I also removed my boots. Bilo said that even though it would be cold, we had better wade rather than bring the horses over. Cold? What a masterpiece of understatement. I felt like an icicle from the chest down as we struggled ashore with the dogs. Angel had to carry the curs, since there was no way they could be coaxed to enter the icy current, demonstrating considerably more sense than we did.

Walking slowly along the border of reeds where the shore met the river, Bilo found where the boar had come ashore and pushed his way through the heavy riverine growth. His path looked as though somebody had rolled an oil drum through the foliage. Even Angel's eyebrows went up. "Beeg wahn, no, *Pedro?*" Hell, yes, he was a "beeg wahn." My pigsticker began to look more like a paring knife. I was about to excuse myself to go back for my cigarettes when Bilo let the dogs loose. Bilo slapped my back and said, "*Pedro,* give me a hand with this one, eh? He'll be a real trophy." I was about to tell him that I wasn't really all that fond of fresh bacon when he turned and started after the *Dogos*.

The island wasn't as big as I thought it was, because within two minutes the little mutts began to sound off again. We heard the sound move about fifty yards, then steady and swell with the murderous grunts of the boar as he took on the dogs. Running full speed through the brush, I could hardly see Chiche and Angel until I burst into a clearing ringed by a heavy wall of nearly impenetrable brush. At several points in this wall, there were small tunnels bulled out by generations of wild boar. From one of them, surrounded by lunging *Dogos*, stuck the head of the biggest, meanest-looking, crook-nosed pig I have ever seen. His head was the size of a barrel, set with flaming red eyes above hooked tusks. The immensity of him made the 350-pound sows look like something out of "The Three Little Pigs."

Except for an occasional snort, the strange fight was silent. The boar had backed into the opening and knew his back and flanks were protected. Brave as they were, the *Dogos* also knew that it was suicide to attack head-on. He was huge, and he was smart, refusing to lose his advantage by attacking from his hole, no matter how the dogs baited him.

When he saw me, he changed his mind.

It was a dream where you couldn't run. As tall as my waist, hairier than a bear, and looking for murder, he burst from the tunnel straight for me. As he cleared the hole, the four *Dogos* were all over him, slashing for a hold in his flanks and backside. He paid absolutely no attention to them. I was fifteen yards away when he began his rush, but with the flood of adrenaline pumping into my brain, I had thought of and rejected three different ways to meet the charge before he covered half the distance. Not knowing what else to do, I ran straight at him, hoping my unexpected tactic might throw him off stride. As he was almost on me, I sidestepped to the right and he tore by, snapping his tusks.

Screaming with frustration, he wheeled around and lunged again, but two *Dogos* had grabbed his ears and fouled up his timing, leaving me somehow behind him. I made a leap for his tail and hung on to it with one hand, the other clutching for a grip in his hair. I hung on for all I was worth as he spun like a dog chasing his tail, banging one of the *Dogos* into my head each time he tried to reach me with his tusks. His snapping jaws were so close to my face they sounded like a bank vault closing.

Amid the tangle of dogs, pig, and me, I saw Chiche advancing. He screamed for me to hang on and lunged with his knife against the boar's unprotected shoulder as the pig swung to snap at me again. As if in slow motion, I saw the boar's left hind foot leave the ground and loop lazily to land perfectly in the center of my forehead. I saw stars for a moment, and then everything went black.

I don't know how long it was before I shook the cobwebs from my scrambled brain, probably only a few seconds. I was still holding the boar's tail with one hand as Chiche gently slapped my cheeks. Warm blood coursed down my face where the pig's hoof had split the skin of my forehead, dripping into the darkened earth already sodden with pig and dog blood.

I let go and rolled free, promptly falling on my head again. Chiche helped me up and steadied me. Angel lay on the ground, writhing as if in agony, tears welling from his eyes. I imagined him to be disemboweled. Finally I figured out that he was laughing too hard to stand up. Between peals of smothered mirth, he said something to me in Spanish. I asked Chiche what he wanted.

"He says you would make a very good *Dogo Argentino*, even though you were not supposed to catch the boar, but kill it." I began to realize I had never even drawn my knife!

Regaining as much composure as possible under the circumstances, I asked Chiche to advise the big, still giggling lummox that any damn fool could get a boar with a knife—we *norteamericanos* always used our bare hands. I was just a little rusty, that's all.

It took a couple of hours to load the three dead pigs onto the horses and walk them the five miles back to the *estancia*. On the granary scale in Chiche's barn, the big one tipped the balance at 596 pounds. I call him six hundred, because he must have left at least four pounds of blood in my clothes. That night, an *asado,* the traditional gaucho fiesta, was held in honor of the barehanded *gringo* boar-catcher. The whole town of Choelechoel turned out—all ten residents.

Chiche told the story of my prowess in fits and starts between the peals of laughter until it was time to carve the roasting boar. Before the first cut was made, the mayor called for attention. In Spanish, he explained that he had a token from his people in appreciation for demonstrating my new way of boar hunting, a trophy I had earned.

I carefully unwrapped the small box he presented to me. There, by the flickering firelight, I saw the ultimate trophy of my Argentine boar hunt—the freshly severed tail of my prey.

The next day we went back to the bird shooting I had traveled ten thousand miles to sample. It was great, but somehow anticlimactic. After all, how do you follow a pig act?

SOUTHERN
FRIED BUFFALO

SAGA — MARCH 1972

Asian red water buffalo.

Author's Introduction

In just one day's trek through the infamous Marajó Island jungles, I had been stung by fire ants, had my sump partially drained by dozens of leeches, nearly been electrocuted by an electric eel, and damn near hit by a fer-de-lance snake. A well-known hunting pal of mine suggested, without much regard for tact, that I ought to have been under observation to have hunted Marajó during the rains. But, since the red buffalo was protected in India and reservations were difficult in Vietnam, this was the only crap game in town. Australia was a bit far. Yet, of all the joys of Amazonia, perhaps the glass thorns turned out to be the worst.

About two years after the Marajó hunt, I happened to notice a lump in my left forearm. I squeezed it tentatively, and a clear inch of thorn, as brilliant and as sharp as Steuben crystal, slid out. It had been floating around my system all that time. Had it stopped in my heart or major arteries, I need not explain what the consequences would have been.

Dick Mason still lives in Brazil, in Mato Grosso state.

I must give you an interesting sidelight. Many readers of my work have asked me where that photo of me on the dust jacket of Death in the Long Grass *came from. It was taken of me, quite close to extremis, by Dick Mason during this trip. If a picture is worth a thousand words, that one is worth volumes.*

"I don't think I'd move right now, if I were you, old boy."

I looked up from my drink and across the glowing pile of Brazilian hardwood coals at Richard Mason. There was an odd look on his face. At my raised eyebrows he continued, "You see, that's a fer-de-lance just by your right leg, and any sudden movement will most likely make him strike."

The blood drained from my face like an upended wine bottle as I shifted my eyes to the ground next to the foot of my camp chair. The deadly snake lay inches from my bare, muddy leg, the distinctive yellow throat-patch gleaming dully in the muted flicker of the firelight. Fascinated, I watched the forked tongue flicker from beneath the hard sapphire eyes as he lay poised to strike. From the corner of my eye I saw a slow movement as Mason reached for the holstered revolver hanging from the support pole of the thatched shack. There was a series of oily clicks as his callused thumb eased the hammer back to cocked firing position, the six flat-nosed slugs rotating in their chambers.

"Damn!" Mason cursed under his breath. "Can't get him from here without taking part of your foot with him. I better not move or it just might set the bastard off. Bloody touchy, these night snakes, you know." I knew. "Listen, now," he said casually, "I'll try a body shot and figure that'll take his mind off you. Watch the gun. Soon as you see it go off, tip over in your chair to the left and throw your legs out of the way. The canvas bottom should keep him off until I can get one into his head." I nodded imperceptibly, not in much of a position to argue. Mason sounded as if he were chatting over the cricket scores in his favorite London pub.

The professional hunter's slightly bloodshot eyes glinted over the big leaf foresight of the silvery-worn pistol. The barrel held as steady as an anvil in his gorilla hand. Suddenly a spear of flame burst from the muzzle and I wrenched the chair over. The ground was still rising to meet me as the second shot blasted over the jungle encampment and blended with the

crash of the third. A yard away, the headless body of the
"Yellow Beard of Death" lay writhing on the ground.

Mason was already jacking out the smoking empties as I
picked myself off the dirt. He reached over and lifted the
squirming body of the tail, grunting at the unexpected weight
of the snake. Before he flipped it into the bush, I noted that
the first shot had gone through one of the heavy coils; another
had torn the lower neck nearly in two; and the third had
smashed the flat head into a pulpy smear. He walked to the
bottle of scotch and poured out a three-finger toss for me.
After one gulp, I handed it back for a refill.

"I think the people at *Saga* are trying to kill me," I told
him when my teeth had stopped chattering. "Don't you have
anything on this trialsized Guadalcanal that doesn't spend
most of its time trying to eat, bite, sting, stomp, gore, poison,
electrocute, or drown the tourists?"

Mason flashed his Daddy-won't-let-them-get-you grin.
"Marajó isn't a very hospitable place, I must admit," he said.

"Listen, Limey," I said, "if my insurance company ever
heard about this place, which fortunately is unlikely, they'd
kick my premiums a dozen cuts over an octogenarian with a
smoker's hack. Just one day in your little jungle playground
and I have been gnawed on by fire ants, halfdrowned, nearly
electrocuted, partially trampled, close-on snakebit, and by the
look of that Brazilian James Beard you call a cook, probably
poisoned." I paused to shudder down the rest of the scotch.
"Do you mean that people actually pay money to come down
here and play Rover Boy with you?"

"Booked for the rest of the season," he replied smugly.
"Of course, we don't get much return business." It figured. I
had been able to contact only one of Mason's previous clients
by telephone before leaving the States, a man fairly well known
in big-game hunting circles. When I asked him what hunting
conditions were like on Marajó Island in September, there was
a long silence in the receiver and then a short, nervous laugh.
"You're kidding?" he said hopefully. When I assured him that
I was not he simply said, "Well, I lost twenty-two pounds in
four days, and that was in the dry season, when things are

easy! If there's a tougher place in the world to hunt, I don't know about it. Still, if you want a red buffalo, it's the only crap game in town."

I began thinking very seriously about it. I had never said anything about wanting a red buffalo. *Saga* had. They had also wanted the exclusive story of Richard Mason, the young English guerrilla fighter who had cut a one-man swath through the Angolan MPLA terrorist movement when he was a white hunter there. He had almost single-handedly brought that local version of Mau Mau to a screeching halt by using their own terrorist tactics against them.

One glance at the map should have told me to return the ticket that arrived with my fate suitably inscribed in red carbon on the flight coupon. I was no stranger to South American jungles, having taken my share of jaguar, deer, tapir, and wild boar from British Honduras to Argentina, but I knew that the lowlands of the Equatorial Amazon were something else again. I would proceed from the jungles of New York to those of *Belém do Pará,* the ancient slaving capital of Brazil, directly on the Equator, at the mouth of the Amazon Delta. I would be met there by Mason. September, said the atlas, was the wet season in this charming corner of old Brazil. That's got to be the understatement of the year. Mason and I didn't walk out for dinner the first night in town, we waded. When the current was with you, you could do a fair breaststroke down the old, cobbled streets, and we pitched up like flotsam at a restaurant noted for its steak Diane. Reasoning that since I was to die wet and miserable, I might as well die slightly drunk, well fed, wet and miserable. I did the place proud. Over the famous Brazilian coffee—thick enough to float a bullet—I listened to Mason tell me about Marajó and buffalo. . . .

The Asian red buffalo is one of the most dangerous animals in the world to hunt. Period. Some confusion arises when hunters forget that there are two kinds of buffalo in Asia, and to put the domestic carabao or water buffalo, common as a beast of burden throughout the East, in the same league with the much larger wild red buff is like entering Joe Frazier in a Golden Gloves contest.

Originally from the remote areas of India and Bhutan, the buff has earned the respect and often the terror of some very famous and knowledgeable sportsmen. In stature, a big bull red buff weighs a long ton, just about the same as his African Cape cousin. He has the temperament of a constipated sumo wrestler and the tenacity of an IRS man. The Cape buffalo has a very efficient set of horns, to be sure, but the hat rack on a mature red buff is beyond belief. A total of better than one hundred inches is not unheard of, and a few will go better than 120.

They aren't called water buffalo for nothing, and this factor in hunting these behemoths has a lot to do with the odds that your first buffalo hunt may be your last. These unlovely killers are usually found in water over your nevermind, and unless you can wade a lot faster than I can, brother, you had better make your first shot count.

My good friend and hunting companion, Alvin Adams, told me of wounding a buffalo while on a hunt in the remote Kingdom of Bhutan. Hunting from elephant-back, Al followed up the bull, which charged his mount with such fury that the jumbo had to give ground and might have actually been knocked down had Al not been able to get in a quick spine shot that killed the buff. Alvin has hunted all over the world and killed the very rare black jaguar, but he feels that the Asian buffalo has no peer when it comes to pure mayhem.

Mason called for another cup of coffee as I asked him about the Marajó buffalo. From what I had heard of Marajó, nobody but an Englishman would live there on purpose.

"They were brought in at the end of the last century from India," he told me, "intended as beasts of burden for the rice fields in the northern part of the island." Mason guessed that they had been a few calves or half-grown animals, because as they grew up and stomped a half-dozen natives flat enough to travel airmail for less than a dollar, somebody figured out that just maybe these weren't the right kind of buffalo. How right they were. Somehow, they had been sent the red buffalo and not the carabao, which were introduced later. Meanwhile, the red buffalo had flattened their corrals and escaped into the interior, where they bred and became well established. For one thing, they had no natural enemies—the biggest, stupidest jaguar in the world would know better than to fool with one of these babies.

Mason told me that except for some areas in Australia, Marajó is the only place where they may still be hunted. Their extreme aggressiveness has caused them to be shot out and consequently protected throughout most of their natural range. This aggressiveness is probably the result of a very highly developed sense of territorial protection, which in many cases leads a lone buffalo to kill any cow, horse, or other buffalo that invades its domain.

In addition to the Asian buffalo, Marajó also supports a large population of jaguar, which live off the cattle herds that roam the island. Mason remarked that the Marajó jaguar was considered to be particularly dangerous owing to the fact that they live in close association with man because of his herds, and have largely lost respect for him.

The morning sky had brightened to the color of the white fur growing from my tongue as we piled aboard the little charter plane for the flight across the muddy Amazon Delta to the clouded green jungles of Marajó. An hour's flight in the single-engine aluminum parakeet brought us to Marajó International Airport—a choice of three different cow pastures on a ranch wrenched from the jungle. We circled it once, but Mason requested the pilot to take a run over his camp to alert his staff that we were on the way. As we peered down at the watery patches between the growth of low forest, a network of paths could be seen through the high grass and tangles. Mason intoned ominously that they were buffalo trails. After a few minutes, we swept low over a dark blob in a red mud wallow—a lone bull. I could see the long, mossy horns sweeping back from the massive head as the buff shook them at us. "My, my," said Mason, "touchy chap, isn't he?" The buffalo looked like a freighter moored in a small pond. "That, my valiant *compadre,* is the red buffalo . . . not the little black one that they let the dignitaries shoot, but the genuine article." One look at that animal and you knew right off that he wanted that airplane, bad. We flashed by and on to Mason's camp, half hidden beneath the jungle canopy. The wings rocked and three faces shone like wet ebony from the clearing and they gave us an acknowledging wave. The pilot reversed course and we were back at the pasture in a few minutes, bouncing to a mushy stop.

I stared at the two little characters who came walking over to the plane. They looked like twins, and neither one was over four feet six inches, but they were magnificently muscled and very handsome. Bright smiles gleamed as they greeted Mason with a lilting Portugese patois. I threw Dick an inquiring look as they each came over to me and kissed my hand.

Mason lit a cigar. "Cowboys like these two here earn the equivalent of about seven shillings, or, as you would say, one American dollar a month, plus enough *xarka*—dried beef—to keep them going. That kissing-the-hand gesture is a carryover from slavery, but nowadays it's just good manners to strangers. Shall we get started? It's a pretty good ride to my adobe *hacienda.*"

I climbed aboard one of the ponies and watched Mason fasten our gear onto a pack horse that had been led up with our mounts. He took off his boots and stuck his big toe into the tiny stirrup loop of twisted rope peculiar to the area. I followed his example. With one of the cowboys leading the pack animal, we started across several miles of open grazing land toward the west.

The first two miles were easy—open country spotted with cattle and the white, chicken-tame garça egrets, which stared as we rode by. Then we came to the edge of the forest. Mason stopped and loaded a round into the chamber of his .404 Cogswell and Harrison rifle, expertly lowering the hammer by holding the trigger back while softly closing the bolt handle. It would take only a small, silent motion to arm the big gun. "You never know," he told me. "Watch the branches carefully, particularly those near your face. Snakes often sleep in the shady limbs along trails during the day, and it's hard as hell to put a tourniquet on somebody's nose."

As we came to the first patch of swampy ground, Mason motioned me abreast. My pony had taken ten steps into the slimy morass when I felt him shudder convulsively and start to collapse under me. I leaped from the saddle, flat on my face in the filthy water, with one toe still hung up in the strange stirrup, positive I would be pinned under the horse in the muddy water. I thrashed my way free in time to see Mason leap from his mount and grab the head of my pony, now well under water. He was cursing steadily under his breath as he strained to pull the horse's head into the air, using a few phrases even I hadn't heard before. Basically, I gathered, he was referring to the doubtful parentage and somewhat bizarre sexual habits of the large electric eel that had flattened my horse with one jolt after the animal had disturbed the dangerous fish. In a few minutes the pony had regained consciousness and was ready to go again, apparently with no aftereffects from the massive shock. Mason told me that quite a few cattle are shocked and subsequently drown by stumbling into these eels, which possess enough juice to kill a man at close quarters. I must have been insulated by the saddle, as I felt nothing whatever.

A bit shaken, I followed Mason into the thickening murk of the deep jungle. He was chattering happily about the time last year he had been riding along this trail and came face to face with a particularly nasty buffalo. The brute had charged him in a narrow part of the trail, where it was impossible to reverse. The bull then smashed his horse into pulp, and Mason was barely able to grasp an overhanging branch and pull himself to safety, where he waited four hours for the buffalo to leave. Finally it took off and he was able to climb down for the long walk home. He chuckled. Mason has a great sense of humor.

Semi-open areas began to appear, the same we had seen from the plane earlier. The sun was now out, and the heat was bouncing in searing waves from the damp forest. I was damned tired and said so. Mason signaled a halt at the next piece of high ground, a grassy hummock jutting above the razor-grass-choked water. I slid gratefully from the saddle and plunked down on the matted foliage—but not for long. With a shriek, I leaped up slapping at my back and legs, afire with savage bites. Ripping off my bush jacket, I saw it crawling with tiny, scarlet fire ants, each biting ferociously. By the time I had beaten them to death, Mason was practically beside himself with laughter. When I had settled down a bit, he poured rubbing alcohol over the bitten areas, which took away most of the sting.

Ten hours after our start, we arrived at Mason's camp, shooed the scorpions out from under the antique French bathtub—where the hell *that* came from I wouldn't know— and started the camp boys filling it with heated, if somewhat muddy, water. We bent our jaws on some underdone *xarka* and settled down with a bottle of man's best friend and two plastic cups. After my second drink, our now headless friend had shown up. . . .

"At dawn, we'll push along and try to pick up the spoor of a good bull," Mason was saying. "You use that Holland & Holland .375 over there, plenty good for buff if you hit 'em right." I had nightmare visions of hitting one wrong. I probably shouldn't have asked what would happen.

"Hell," Mason snorted. "You can't very well miss! You'll be close enough to do him in with an ax handle. Only thing is, you'll be up to your adenoids in water, which is somewhat difficult to run in, should the necessity arise. After all, they *do* call them water buffalo. If you get caught by one that doesn't like you, the consequences are somewhat unpleasant, so just shoot him where he's biggest and keep shooting until I tell you to stop . . . or he stops you personally."

"Okay," I agreed, "but just remember that I owe a pile of alimony back home, and this is one way I don't want to get out of paying it."

I copied Mason as he stretched out in his hammock at practically a right angle. It was surprisingly comfortable, but at that point I could have slept on broken whiskey bottles. I hooked the mosquito netting around me and was asleep in a second.

Approximately five minutes later, I was being shaken by a rough hand as dawn broke over the trees. Mason handed me a cup of stiff coffee. "Better wear shorts," he suggested. "Long pants get too heavy when they're soaked with mud, and they don't keep off the leeches, anyway." We each ate a can of peaches and tried some more of the dried beef. It was no better this morning. As I was finishing, the bushes parted and a strange little man strode into camp. His name was Ramón Capybara.

"Ramón *what?*" I asked Mason. The capybara is the giant rodent of the Brazilian forests.

"That's right," he answered. "He's famous throughout the island as sort of a local version of Bomba the Jungle Boy. Claims his father was a capybara, but I've never heard his mother's comment on that! At any rate, he knows more about this western swamp area than anybody else." Ramón certainly was a weird-looking article, long hair and a loincloth completing the illusion, if it was one.

Fifteen minutes later we followed Ramón Capybara out of the camp toward the buffalo trails. Though it was still early in the day, the mercury stood at better than 110 degrees and the humidity was enough to permit small fishes to fly. After two slogging miles, the green cover gave way to Marajó's infamous thorn jungle. If there is any place quite like this anywhere on earth, I haven't heard about it. And don't want to. Every single bit of foliage was covered with thorns: straight and hooked, thick and short, long and brittle. They tore at our skins and clothing, gouging our flesh and piercing our shoes. Mason showed me some that he said were poisonous. I never doubted it for a second. In the middle of this tangle, we cut the trail of a big buffalo bull, his hoof prints the size of dinner plates, a peculiarity of the species that permits their immense bulk to cover marshy ground so well. We started tracking.

The spoor led out of the heavy trees and into the flooded grasslands with their knifelike razor grass that would really cut you as you brushed by it. A trail developed through the soaking undergrowth that was nearly impossible to negotiate owing to the deep, hidden footprints of buffalo, which were invisible under the two feet of muddy water. I stumbled several dozen times in the first mile, with sweat streaming off me from the intense heat and the effort of lifting my feet free of the sucking mud for each slurping step. Visibility was never better than six or seven yards, and we went along seeking the buffalo—who might well be seeking us—by ear. Blisters the size of pigeon eggs were growing on the tops of my shriveled toes and on my heels as the grinding wet canvas of my sneakers rubbed the skin off. After several miles of the hardest going I have ever experienced in twenty years of big-game hunting around the world, I had had it. In spades. Mason called a breather to remove the leeches.

At first I thought he was kidding, but one look at my thorn- and grass-cut legs revealed a grand total of twenty-three of the ugly, black bloodsuckers swollen fat with my juices. We each took a bite of the long black cigar Mason had brought along, and chewed the acrid tobacco into a paste. A good smearing of the tobacco juice applied to the leeches made each drop off, leaving a streaming hole in our skins. Mason had two more than I did, I noticed with satisfaction, but Ramón had only two. Apparently he tasted about as bad as he smelled.

Signs showed that the bull was still moving ahead of us at a good pace through the uncomfortably hot water. We sloshed onward, rifles at the ready, following the tracks, which were defined by still muddy swirls in the water. He had to be close. As I followed Mason, he suddenly came to a halt, frozen in the trail a few feet ahead. His hand was urgently pressed backwards in a stop signal. We stood motionless for some seconds, then he signaled me slowly forward. I could see the back end of a buffalo a few yards ahead in the trail. I looked at Mason, who motioned for silence as he looked the bull over. I could see nothing but a blob of black, muddy skin surrounding a ragged tail. Mason practically scared me to death by giving a hell of a shout, at which the buffalo took off down the trail like a submarine forcing its way over a sandbar.

"Not tonight, Josephine," he mumbled. He looked at my fear-drained face and said, "Hellish big bull, but only one horn. Must have broken it in a fight." He was sorry and said he didn't mean to panic me with the unexpected shout, but wanted to surprise the bull while he was at least facing away. We started the long, hot slog back to camp.

I have, in happier days, drunk good wines and even great wines, but I would not have traded a drop of the syrup from the can of peaches I drained back at camp for a barrel of the best. I would learn later that I had dropped fourteen pounds during my two days with Mason, and I suspect that half the weight was probably blood. My feet were tatters of broken blisters, leech bites, and embedded thorns. But it was almost worth it to see Mason a little winded. "Pass the painkiller, Bub," I called to him, "I'm going to amputate."

He flipped me the scotch bottle and I liberally applied a portion of the contents to my feet, and then took some internally. It didn't feel very smooth on the broken blisters, but the thorns had to come out since they were beginning to fester. I went to work with my Swiss Army knife, pausing occasionally for another pull at the anesthetic.

Mason and I had finished with our feet just as the sun began to slide down behind the marshes. It didn't make a whit of difference to the mosquitoes who were joined by legions of flying ants and other winged nuisances. For dinner, Mason presented me with a plate of paca, a sort of Texas-size rat that weighs about twenty pounds. It had been smoked, whole and ungutted, for about eight hours over a slow fire, then sliced and fried in bacon grease. Actually, it wasn't bad at all, much like lean pork—if you are partial to rats that taste like lean pork, that is.

Dick and I lied to each other for a couple of hours over the scotch before turning in. I called him over to my hammock to have a look at a strange varmint curled under my pillow, a long, metallic-blue centipede. Mason said it was a particularly dangerous type, showing the interest of a small boy in a new kind of frog. Really a charming chap.

I had been asleep for about three hours when I felt the gentle shaking. It was Dick, whispering softly.

"Hear him," he asked, "just on the other side of this strip of trees?" I strained my ears trying to filter out the hum of crickets and chirp of bats overhead. A bass growl rolled softly through the trees, making the back of my neck crawl. I didn't need Mason to tell me it was a jaguar, a big one.

"Let's go, he won't be there forever," he hissed at me. "I think he's made a kill—probably a steer from the sound of the crunch."

"Go?" I looked at his dim form. "Out there? At night? Good God, man, you've got to be putting me on!" I shook my head, listening to the cracking of bone between huge teeth and the tearing of flesh being ripped away. The idea of chasing a jaguar around through the snakes and spiders in the pitch black was somehow less than appealing.

Opening my mosquito netting, Mason shoved in my shoes. "Come on, you won't get a chance like this again." I was hoping just that as he slapped a shotgun in my hands and tossed four shells onto the hammock. "Load the rifled slug in the right barrel and the buckshot in the left," he instructed. "Carry the other two rounds between the fingers of your left hand—and don't drop them. They may come in handy." I had a picture of that. Mason half-opened the breech of his .404 and felt the cold brass of a big cartridge in the chamber. "Come on, come on," he kept whispering. I rolled out of the hammock.

"Right. Now he'll probably be too busy with that steer to pay much notice to us if we're quiet. Try to move only when you hear him feeding." I nodded in the gloom. Mason continued, "I'll go first with the light, and you stick right behind me." I told him he didn't have to worry about that one bit. We walked softly across the camp and entered the tangle of jungle.

Mason paused to whisper, "Slide your feet and feel that there's no twig or anything under them before you put your whole weight down on them." We picked our way through the looming trees like ghosts, guided by the low growls of the big cat as he ripped into his kill. The chrome end of the five-cell flashlight Mason carried gleamed ever so dully ahead of me, rising and lowering as he stepped in exaggerated pantomime over snags and rotting jungle debris. He stopped dead as the feeding sounds paused, then continued as the jaguar resumed his meal. I took care to step just where Mason did, hopeful that any snakes would first strike at him. After all, this whole thing was his idea.

Mason gradually slowed as the sounds came louder from the crypt-like blackness. He paused as I came up to him. "From the sound, he's about fifty yards ahead," Mason murmured with lips against my ear. "When I flip on this light, let him have it, both barrels, and reload as quickly as you can. Stay up with me, now right at my right elbow." We inched forward again.

My lungs felt full of hot gasoline, and the shotgun was slippery in my hands. I strained my eyes in the murk, but nothing except the crunching of the killer could be discerned. We must be almost on him. I knew Mason was trying to get as close as possible before turning on the light, but I thought he was overdoing it. I was supposed to shoot the bloody thing— not catch it!

I half-raised the shotgun and slid the safety off. At the tiny snick of metal there was a grunt and scurry of movement a few yards to our front. *"Now!"* shouted Mason and speared the light ahead—smack into a bear-trap set of gleaming teeth set in a blood-smeared muzzle surmounted by two flashing orange eyes. The big cat let out a screaming roar and flattened itself behind the mangled pile of meat that was the remains of its kill. I swung the shotgun up and caught the gleam of the brass bead foresight just under the jaw. A yard of flame stabbed from the muzzle as I fired both barrels almost simultaneously, oblivious of the heavy recoil. The big cat gave a huge leap to the side, twisting its muscular body in its dappled sheath of rosettes, and disappeared into the jungle growth.

"Goddammit," said Mason with surprising reverence. "Where did you hit him?"

"Chest and neck, both barrels . . . I think." I couldn't really tell, but that was where the sight had been. "He's got to be hard hit."

"Well, let's have a smoke and let him stiffen up." Mason lit one of his cheroots, then leaned over to put the match to my trembling cigarette. "This following up at night is one part of the job I don't like."

"You mean you're going in after him tonight?" I shook my head in disbelief. "In the dark?"

"Got to," Mason answered. "If he buggers off wounded, he may take to eating cowboys, and it wouldn't be the first time."

Handing me the .375, he reached over and took my shotgun and checked the loads. "Now listen. I'll walk forward with the light. You follow backward, facing our rear. Jags usually come from the front, but you never know."

He snubbed out the cigar and walked over to the edge of the cover. He glanced at me and I nodded back. We went in. The silver finger of the light probed the shadows, revealing nothing of the killer, but Mason stooped slowly over and rubbed a gout of blood between his fingers. He said nothing. Ten more steps and he stiffened into a crouch, the shotgun leveled from his hip, staring ahead. A soft gurgle came through the blackness. "That's your boy," he said out loud. "He's had it." The beam caught the cold gleam of an unmoving eye against the dark humus of the jungle floor, and passed on to reveal the jaguar, stretched out in death, his massive head between his forelegs. Holding the shotgun against the cat's neck, Mason slowly rolled him over with his foot, grunting with the effort. "He's a beaut," Mason whispered. Suddenly we were laughing, back-slapping and chattering like kids. The first barrel, the rifled slug, had taken out the top of the cat's lung and the buck-shot had penetrated well through its pattern on the rosettes. The way back to camp didn't seem nearly as spooky as we received the congratulations of the crew, on their way to skin the cat by torchlight. Fifteen minutes later, I was again asleep.

We were already a mile from camp by the time I was fully awake. Surprisingly, my feet weren't as bad as I thought they would be, probably due to the therapeutic qualities of Mr. Walker's finest. Ramón Capybara was sniffing hotly on another set of tracks that wouldn't have shamed a teenage mammoth. I followed behind.

After another several hundred miles in the muck, I was ready to believe our luck had held, when I heard a sound behind us. Mason and Ramón also swung around, having heard the same thing, and stopped dead in their tracks, looking past me with a certain apprehension. The trail where we stood was about eighteen inches wide, not leaving much room for passing traffic, human or bovine. Mason whispered that a buffalo was coming up the trail from our rear, probably looking for trouble if our scent hadn't put him off. He pulled me back farther along, giving a bit more visibility—up to about ten yards, now. We halted and raised our rifles, my heart pounding like a kettledrum as I waited for the buffalo to appear.

The sound of a heavy body moving through sucking mud came louder through the grass. I felt the blood draining as I waited, knowing that he would be on top of us before we could shoot. Sweat poured between my shoulder blades. I dared not move to slap the cloud of biting, whining mosquitoes as I stared at the screen of heavy bush where the buff would appear.

An indistinct black blur began to form through the grass, moving more silently now. It stopped. I could make out an immense horn gleaming with wetness, and then the shine of the dark muzzle. He swung the heavy head from side to side as he spotted us. A bawl of anger swept over us as he thrust out his nose and boiled the water to foam, his charge gathering speed. Mason howled to shoot. I put the front bead in the middle of the rushing mass and fired. The bullet slapped home with a meaty thud. The buffalo never faltered. I reloaded and saw the eyes looking at me as the huge black killer came through the grass, trampling saplings as if they were twigs. I fitted the bead right between the eyes and squeezed off, just as Mason fired, his muzzle blast deafening me as the shock wave slapped my face. Two black holes appeared in the skull—one over the right eye and one below it—as the bull lunged forward and fell in a soaking wave of spray at our feet. He never moved again. I let out a huge breath.

Even Mason whistled when he had a good look at the horns, long and savagely black, heavily corded with ridges showing smooth wear. His steel tape showed him to total 102 inches, one of Marajó's best. My first shot had taken off the

top of the heart and ranged down into the brisket, but it had
been like a bee sting to the buffalo. It had taken the brain
shots to stop him, and even then he had nearly hit us!

As we arrived back in the camp, we decided to take the
rest of the day to relax before the long ride back to the airstrip. Ramón rode out with two men and took the skull and
meat, needing three pack horses to accommodate the load.

Back at Belém do Pará, as I was about to board my jet for
New York, Mason asked me if, being a writer, I could give
him any ideas for promoting Marajó buffalo hunting back in
the States. I thought for a moment and suggested a contest
with a couple of trips as the prizes.

"How would that work?" he asked me.

"Well, I would say first prize should be two weeks, second prize a month."

MIDNIGHT
DATE WITH A
BLACK JAGUAR

SAGA — JUNE 1971

Head of male black jaguar.

Author's Introduction

The jaguar is a rare cat indeed. My personal estimate is that there have been twenty times as many leopards taken than jaguars. The black or melanistic phase of either cat still favors the leopard, if for no other reason than the sheer area it inhabits on three continents—Africa, Asia, and Europe—as well as considerable chunks of the Near and Middle East. The jaguar, which at one time ranged far into what would be the United States of America, could have been found as far east as Arkansas. By old reports, it was relatively common in Arizona and New Mexico.

Today, where jaguar hunting is legal, it can be done either the easy or the hard way. Dogs are very effective, as there is little a tigre or onça can do but tree, where it is fairly easy prey.

I have never espoused hunting at night, believing it to be generally unsporting. I must, however, bare my literary jugular and suggest that it is the most sporting way to hunt jaguar. This species does not generally come to bait as a leopard may, and hunting with dogs, although by no means easy, is a bit one-sided for the hunter. Calling jaguar with the roncadura (literally, "roarer") is a game not recommended to those who perceive a certain savagery even in bridge.

To be perfectly frank, even though I returned several times to the Xingu Basin, I never enjoyed it as much as I did Africa. The lush jungles are really quite sparse in huntable species, this dearth made up mightily by those creatures that hunt; I suggest the insects as the looming memory of any time in the Xingu. Yet it was an unforgettable and invaluable education and experience.

As a mad fisherman, I especially enjoyed the untouched

waters, which were even better than those of the Araguaia and Tapirapé rivers to the southeast, where we went bowfishing with Indians in the last volume. Oh, yes, I still have the pelt and headmount of my own black jaguar, killed only a month after Al Adams took the one described here. Mine was a bit simpler: no charge, just a second of stunned disbelief after answering the roncadura, *and a lucky shot. It might not have gone that way. . . .*

Nonetheless, in today's world, especially in the greater Amazon Basin, where huge earthmovers have done more than ten million hunters could have to ruin the habitat of the jaguar, the Xingu was an adventure that I shall never forget.

Today, I wonder if it is still there. "Progress" is very hard on last horizons.

James Donnelly halted his fork in midair; his face suddenly froze as the sound echoed through the darkness over our island camp. He glanced across the table at Mariano, the little Brazilian trapper. Their eyes met and held for an instant, then swung to the jungle and to the river that traced along its edge.

The deep, grating roar rolled down the valley again, over the now silent hills, through the giant trees and across the piranha- and crocodile-infested river. The nape of my neck prickled.

"Onça," said Mariano. "The jaguar is calling."

I looked at Al Adams. He looked at me. We both tried to swallow. Donnelly said nothing as he shoved his camp chair back and moved toward the battered rifle that was leaning against the tree near the dinner table. On the sand lay the *roncadura,* a hollow gourd sliced off at each end.

"It's a strange call, but I would say that chappie's looking for a little companionship," whispered James. "What say we just go on over there and oblige?" Our white hunter looked almost pleased at the prospect. Almost.

"Why, by all means," answered Al Adams. "Midnight matchmaking with lonely jaguars is one of my favorite pastimes. Any amount of fun." But he didn't look that anxious. "And just how do you plan on arranging this little moonlight tryst? In your planning, please bear in mind that I am too young to be eaten."

"We might as well use the same tactic that lady jaguars use to get gentlemen jaguars," said James. "We'll sweet-talk him." He scooped up the hollow gourd and placed the smaller opening to his mouth.

"*Oonnnghh, unnh, unnnh, unnh, unnh,*" James grunted. The answer floated back through the darkness—closer this time. My stomach felt like a nest of bats.

"What happens now?" Al asked as he slipped on his sneakers.

"Well, this can be a bit tricky at night," James said. "If we can get within range without spooking him, you'll have something like a second to fire when I flip on the light. In range, under these conditions, means around twenty-five feet or so. If you don't get him, he'll either run or charge. More likely, though, he'll come for us."

I was considering suggesting that Al and James go get that one while I waited here for another when James slapped a shotgun into my hands and nudged me to the sandy shore. By previous arrangement, Al would do the shooting and I would fire in case he didn't nail the jaguar, and the cat decided to charge. We had flipped a coin in New York, but now I was wishing the subject had never come up.

The dugout canoe glided to shore, where it ground the sand with a soft rasp. Mariano paddled while James took the front, with Al and me in the middle. We pushed off for the far shore.

"Swell, just swell," muttered Al. "If this thing turns over, there are going to be a lot of piranhas with heartburn. That's presuming, of course, that the crocs don't get us first. And if I do live to see shore, there's always Brazil's deluxe assortment of anacondas, bushmasters, fer-de-lances, scorpions, spiders, and—oh, yes—our lovesick jaguar."

"I don't think it's an Indian trap, though," said James without too much conviction. "Even though there's something strange about that call."

Soon the dark edge of the forest loomed ahead and we melted into its shadow. The canoe softly bumped the shore and James called a huddle to explain the assault plan. Nobody was joking now.

"We'll move into the bush about fifty yards and try to find some sort of a clearing," he whispered. "I'll give a couple more hoots on the *roncadura* and then clam up. The trick is to locate him before he spots us. We had better make the signals now, Al. I'll stand on your left and give you one tap in the ribs when I think he's approaching. Two nudges means get ready to shoot and three taps means I am going to shine the light at any moment. Got it?"

I could see Al's head nod in the gloom. He quietly jacked a soft-point into his .300 Magnum and snicked the bolt closed. There was a dull *tonk* as I dropped two green buckshot shells into the double barrel.

We moved off into the smothering darkness, rain from an earlier storm dripping from the leaves and down my neck, feeling like tarantulas as the drops trickled down my back.

Silently we picked our way through the bush to a gap in the jungle where a huge tree had fallen. James stopped and grunted through the gourd again, the answer blending with his echo from about two hundred yards away. I squatted next to Al behind the mossy trunk.

The minutes crawled by as we strained to hear the big cat's approach. Tree frogs screamed by the thousands, and the cicadas joined the jungle bedlam, fragmenting the night into slivers of jangling sound. A big croc swirled in the river behind us, and a tribe of Guariba monkeys howled from a distant ridge. I could actually feel the jaguar picking his way toward us.

There was a patter of drops from the leaves as the jaguar brushed a wet tangle. Then I heard the soft rustle of grass and the crack of twigs. A low growl crawled through the tangled bush to my front. Then silence. My mind was soon wandering back over the events that had brought me to the middle of a Brazilian jungle at midnight. . . .

It began over a New York lunch with my good friend, the internationally known sportsman Alvin Adams. With us was another friend, Charlie Cabell, president of Brazil Safaris and Tours in Rio de Janeiro. His outfit has the reputation of being one of the only reputable safari firms in that vast country, a country as well known for its red tape as its green forests.

Charlie was telling us about an incredible new area he had opened in the Xingu Basin. It had never even been penetrated, let alone hunted, and it promised some of the best jaguar hunting in South America. Al's ears perked up. He had taken most of the big cats—half a dozen tigers, a couple of lions, assorted African and Asian leopards, pumas, and even a magnificent snow leopard from the high Himalayas. He had hunted from Bhutan to Botswana, but he didn't have a jaguar—and he didn't want one let out of a cage and run up a tree in time for the arriving "sportsman" to pot it, as has happened with nauseating regularity in some Central American countries.

Two martinis later, we were booked into Xingu.

Three weeks later, my fantail still sore from the assorted vaccinations of a horrified family physician, our Pan Am jet rolled to a weary stop at Brasilia, the capital of this giant nation. It seemed more appropriate as the capital of the moon than of a country where, not more than a few hundred miles away, Indians were hunted with dogs less than ten years ago.

The next morning we met João Branco, our young bush pilot. As the Cessna 180 floated up from the runway, Al and I noticed something a bit unusual about the plane. There was no radio.

"How far do we have to go?" Al shouted over the roar of the engine.

"About 650 miles, *Senhor*," answered João.

"And what are we flying over?"

"That is jungle—the Green Hell."

"What if we have engine trouble and are forced down with no radio to call for help?"

"Is no problem, *Senhor*. The crash in the big trees would surely kill us, anyhow. Nobody could walk out of Xingu anyway. You don't worry. I never have engine trouble." Al shook his head and closed his eyes. João explained patiently that, since the last revolution, nobody, but nobody, was allowed to have a radio transmitter. We were pleased to see the little village of São Feliz appear under the right wing. We had made it to the jumping off point.

São Feliz was straight out of an early Bogart movie. The streets were busy with a collection of well-armed hairy characters. It was the only town of any description for hundreds of miles, and the tourist trade was mostly goatskin-capped prospectors and trappers getting a grubstake ready for another stint in the bush.

We spent the night in a "hotel," sleeping in hammocks strung from the mud walls. When we paid the seventy-five-cent bill in the morning, the proprietor apologized to us for the intermittent pistol fire during the night. "But, after all, *Senhores,* it was Saturday night." There were no bodies in the street as we walked to the airstrip, an unusual event for Sunday morning, we were led to believe.

James Donnelly, our white hunter, was waiting for us at the cleared patch of rain forest where the Cessna set down. I had pictured him, from Charlie Cabell's stories, as seven feet tall with a full beard, surrounded by a retinue of half-naked Indian maidens. He would be drinking an endless chain of beers, which he would open by biting off the tops of the bottles. He would certainly be festooned with knives, cartridges, and revolvers, if not grenades. Actually, I wasn't that far off the mark.

He *was* over six feet tall, did carry a revolver and bush knife, and did have a wild mustache. I immediately noticed, however, that there were no winsome aboriginal maidens in sight, and James did not drink when he was hunting. Still, he was not the sort of person you called "Jim." Ever.

A short canoe trip across the clear river and we were safely ensconced in our island camp.

The Central Xingu (pronounced Shin-goo) Basin is probably the most remote hunting ground left on earth today. Ten times as many people have been to the South Pole than have ever penetrated this vast, green carpet of jungle lying to the south of the Amazon along the fabled Serra do Roncador Mountains in central Brazil. Here is found the greatest variety of plant life in the world, 300,000 different species growing in the moist air and hot sunshine, forming an impenetrable maze hiding some of the most primitive and dangerous Indians left in the world, the Cayepo and Tchkurami tribesmen.

James Donnelly has been lucky with the Indians so far. But many others have not. A group of missionaries and their guides were clubbed to death about fifty miles from our camp last year, and nobody knows how many *garimpeiros* and *mariscadores,* backwoods prospectors and trappers, have entered Xingu, never to be seen again.

"Actually," James told me over a sundowner one evening, "a typical example of what can happen out here occurred just over there on the little river where we shot the capybara this afternoon. Six trappers came into the area looking for rock crystal and probably a few jaguar skins, despite government warnings. Somehow, they got their bearings mixed up and lost a lot of their stuff when their canoe turned over. Four months later, one of them turned up, more dead than alive, at a little mission on the Araguaya, about three hundred miles south of here. The sisters told me that he was raving about a river with golden sands—even had a good poke of gold on him. He also mentioned that his chums had all killed each other, quarreling over the strike. Each thought the others knew the way back but wouldn't tell, hoping the others would die and he would be left with the gold. Unfortunately, this fellow died before revealing any locations. Nasty bit o' country, this."

James Donnelly is no stranger to nasty country and close calls. In 1960 he bluffed his way out of a Congolese rebel military headquarters where he was being detained prior to certain execution. When his interrogator, a hefty colonel, got tired of beating him and stepped out to supervise a firing squad, another rebel, unaware of the colonel's orders, released James from the room in which he had been locked. James wisely at first refused to go, and the man threw him out with a warning not to hang around. That night he escaped into Uganda by swimming the crocodile-infested Semliki River in his underwear.

After a stint in North Africa as a writer and radio announcer, he made his way to Brazil, where he met his partner-to-be, the fabulous Count Andre Rakowitsch. The count, a Communist-hating White Russian, had come to Brazil after a stint in the German Army as a Panzer commander. Settling in the interior city of Goiânias, he got a job as a government surveyor working on the vast tracts of untouched land in Brazil's interior. His years in the bush as a surveyor, prospector, hunter, and adventurer brought Andre into contact with many of the most remote tribes; however, word of his fair treatment of the Indians spread through the bush to many tribes he had never heard of. Today, he is the only white man who holds the confidence of a half-dozen of the wildest and most dangerous of these tribes.

His first meeting with the fierce Cayepo came when he was suddenly surrounded on a sand bar in the lower Xingu. There were thirty warriors, a war party returning from an unsuccessful foray against a neighboring village. They eyed Andre's rifle, a prize worth a few of their lives. Thinking fast and taking a huge chance, he lowered the rifle and said simply, "Andre." The warriors burst into delighted chatter and insisted on taking him home for a week's feasting in his honor, so great were the things they had heard of him. During this stay, he made a personal deal with Pombu, the senior war chief, for hunting rights in their territory.

After meeting James Donnelly, Andre proposed a safari company to operate in the Cayepo section of the Xingu. James immediately accepted. A three-way deal with Charlie Cabell in Rio created an ideal team.

"Because of Andre's friendship, we haven't had any trouble with the Indians at all," James told me. "The only problem might be if some of the outlying tribesmen haven't gotten the word. You see, each year, usually in October, about eighty or a hundred warriors come down the river to pass the rains with their cousins, the Tchkurami, usually to pick brides. These courting parties are all young bucks, and as they send a foot party foraging on each bank while the main bunch goes by canoe, it's always possible we might be jumped before they realize who we are. This country has a long tradition of shoot first, socialize later. Ever since the first whites penetrated backwoods Brazil, they have always shot Indians on sight. Men, women, kids, it never seemed to matter much to them. In fact, as incredible as it seems, over ninety percent of all Brazil's Indians have been killed off either directly or indirectly by the whites. As you can imagine, the ones who are left are a little uptight about it. About the only ones left that are really wild are south of here in the Xingu National Park or in this area. There are only two whites in the park, and, above all, no missionaries."

Our first morning on the Xingu broke over the unnamed mountains to the east. A light breeze ruffled the thousand-yard-width of the clear river, the early sun reflecting off the rocks at the base of our island. I walked to the water's edge with James, his casting rod in his hand. The big gold spoon had hardly hit the water when he reared back with a shout, and a six-pound *tucunaré,* or peacock bass, slashed the surface to foam. Ten minutes later, his fillets were sizzling merrily in João's frying pan. Over a second cup of good Brazilian coffee, we made the day's plans.

"I think a reconnoiter of the area is in order," said James. "We'll try to spot some fresh tracks on the riverbanks and perhaps bang something for a bait."

"Can you bait jaguars like leopards or tigers?" Al asked.

"Well, yes and no," James answered. "They'll come to a bait sometimes, but here in Brazil we use baits more to locate a jaguar and keep him in the area so we can call him in or run him with dogs. But don't get any idea that there is much in common between jaguar and leopard. The biggest leopard I have ever seen was a hair over eight feet and weighed about

130 pounds. Two weeks ago my last client, Mr. Sliger, killed a jag that went over four hundred pounds. And Andre has a picture of one killed down in the Mato Grosso that was 470 pounds. That's even bigger than an African lion. The leopard tends to be shy usually, but the Brazilian jaguar—especially the Canguçu, the biggest subspecies—fears absolutely nothing. The Indians say the *onça,* as he is called here, eats quite a few folks on dark nights. Mariano here can tell you a few stories, like the night one walked up to him when he was in the bushes. It walked over like a big dog and put a forepaw on his boot so he wouldn't run away. It sniffed him, growled a bit, made a face, and then just walked off. Probably never saw a human before and wondered what new species of monkey this was. Or, as you may have noticed, Mariano doesn't smell very appetizing. He doesn't bathe much because of the piranhas. Another time, one kept him in his hammock for a couple of hours, sitting just under him and batting playfully at the hammock. Apparently it was fascinated by the swinging."

We spent the morning looking for fresh signs, but without any luck. At lunch, James suggested that I go downriver with Mariano about twenty miles and set up a fly camp on the shore. Maybe there was some sign in that area. We could probably kill a tapir or capybara. Al and James would join us with the cook, João, in the morning.

Ten minutes after my arrival at the fly camp, I knew it was aptly named. The air was alive with tiny black flies, each one packing the wallop of a small bee. After each searing bite a red dot of blood would congeal under the skin, making me itch like mad. These pint-sized cannibals seemed to relish bug dope like steak sauce, and the afternoon was a misery until a late breeze mercifully drove them back into the jungle. Mariano and I finally hung our hammocks and settled down to the lullaby of jungle noises.

About three in the morning, a dry, scraping sound awoke me. Easing my flashlight into position, I flipped it on. In a semicircle around our hammocks gleamed an even dozen blood-red eyes, unblinking and cold, despite their reflected fire. Jacarés, the vicious Brazilian crocodiles, had come to pay a call. Easing my .38 out of the mosquito netting, I canceled their dinner plans with a slug through the head of the nearest. As he flipped over, the others scurried for the river a few yards away. Mariano looked at me, shrugged, and went back to sleep. I didn't.

Al and James arrived in midmorning, and we immediately set out to try to shoot a bait. After a mile of silent paddling, Mariano spotted a capybara drinking at the water's edge. Seeing us, he turned and fled into the jungle. We pushed hard and loosed Gwendolyn, our one scarfaced jaguar dog, as we reached the shore. She flashed into the jungle and, after five minutes of barking, chased the big rodent back toward the river. As he broke cover, Al fired at fifty yards and placed his slug perfectly through the point of the shoulder. At full tilt, the big fellow turned a high flip and crashed dead on the mud.

Mariano took his machete and chopped through the carcass. We hung the front half near the ground from a gnarled tree near the beach. Mariano took the hindquarters across the river to a similar vantage point. Jaguars cover a very wide territory, James told us, but tend to travel along the riverbanks to intercept drinking animals.

After a short siesta—more a respite from the 115-degree midday sun than a rest—we decided on a bit of fishing for a change of pace. I wired a gleaming spoon to my spinning outfit and cast into a dark, slow eddy near a huge boulder. The lure was smashed instantly.

After a few minutes, I had beached a little monster. It had teeth like a bear trap, triangular and sharp. It was a black piranha, cousin of the smaller and more dangerous red variety, the real man-killers.

"We have another species here, too," said James. "It runs to about ten pounds and has choppers like a jaguar. It's called the *xipita*. There, you've got one on now!"

The light rod was nearly torn from my hands with the ferocity of the strike. He jumped, sounded, and slashed his way across half the river. Suddenly the line went limp. I reeled in and found that the heavy treble hooks had been twisted and crushed completely flat, as if a strong man had worked them over with pliers. The thick metal of the spoon was heavily scored by the teeth. It didn't take much imagination to guess what those razors could do to flesh. I could say nothing more than "Wow!"

"If you think that's something, put your rod away and I'll show you what the little ones can do," James called. "Bring your camera."

We started the motor and passed by the little fly camp to collect the croc carcass I had shot the previous evening. The jacaré had been skinned, and Mariano and James slung the bloody cadaver into the canoe. We moved slowly to the inlet of a small, unnamed river where James assured us there were sure to be plenty of red piranha.

After wiring two lengths of light cable to the croc, James smacked the water twice with his paddle. He swished the water into a froth as if some big animal were struggling. Then the carcass went over the side, held a foot under the surface by the lengths of cable. Thirty seconds later, there was a rosy flash as our first visitor tried a tentative nip. Then the little hellions really went to work.

Within one minute of submersion, half the carcass was gone. The water foamed and boiled like a cauldron of red poker chips as thousands of piranha seethed over the bait. The metallic clicking of the thousands of teeth sounded like a giant buzz saw as the flesh melted from the croc in a mad flurry of blood and spray. The meat was completely hidden by their bodies. And then they were gone, only the dull bones showing that they had ever been there. The whole process took less than three minutes.

I was stunned by their ferocity. As a boy I had seen the old movies on television showing Venezuelan *vaqueros* sacrificing a cow to the piranha to get the rest of the herd across safely. But this was unbelievable! A man who lost his balance there wouldn't live a minute. I was only too happy to leave the inlet for camp.

Later in the afternoon, Mariano returned to the camp from a scouting expedition of his own. He told us he had found a set of big pug marks that were no more than a day old.

He had followed them along the river for three miles, and they had never veered in their direction—straight toward our original island camp. It took half an hour to load the canoe, and the two dugouts were soon cleaving the current upstream, trying to beat the falling darkness and the ominous thunderheads that were looming over the furry, green mountains.

We had nearly made it back when the first rain came. In all my recollection I have never seen a more violent tropical storm, and I've seen it rain on five continents. The sky grew black, and the normally placid Xingu River was whipped with five-foot-high waves. The rain did not come down in sheets but in a continual horizontal lashing that stung our skins like buckshot. Mariano was barely able to turn the canoe before we reached shore. We spent a miserable hour huddled beneath trees, trying to duck the hundred-mile-per-hour winds. The air and sky had a greenish-yellow tinge; then it cleared exactly as if someone had raised the window shade in a dark room. Even the normally imperturbable James seemed impressed.

We pulled into the little island just after dark and tried to straighten up the shambles. Nothing important seemed broken. At least the gin had weathered the storm in good style, as Al and I were both quick to notice. We decided to test it for any possible contamination while João broiled up some delicious azulona, a beautiful blue partridge. It was halfway through coffee that the jaguar called from across the river. . . .

I could hear the jaguar breathing harshly just in front of me. My cramped legs screamed for relief, but I dared not even twitch. A squadron of mosquitoes assaulted my face and wrists as I strained to see some movement. But I only heard the heavy breathing. Suddenly, James's light lanced the night. Fifteen feet away speared by the beam, glowed two incredible orange orbs. They seemed detached, floating a few inches off the jungle floor. Gleaming white teeth flashed, and a screaming roar of rage ripped the night as I suddenly realized that it was a jaguar—*a black one!*

The black body tensed, the hind legs with their curved pale claws thrusting back into the wet earth as he began his charge. I watched him leave the ground in the curious slow motion of a man falling from a cliff to his death. The yellow eyes and ivory teeth floated closer to me. Curiously, I felt no fear. Suddenly he began to crumple in midair, somersaulting in a thrashing arc to the dark ground, roaring, biting, and throwing sticks and dirt with his slashing claws. He began to crawl toward us. He stiffened, then relaxed. A shadow came into the great golden eyes, and he was dead. I never heard the shot that killed him.

We stood motionless, as still as the dead jaguar, stunned by the realization that we had missed death by a split second. Al Adams let out a very long breath. His smoking cartridge case plunked to the dirt. James Donnelly shook his head in mute disbelief. I started my heart again.

Finally, James said, "I don't imagine you have any idea of what you've got here." He was still shaking his head. "That's about the top trophy any man can take anywhere in the world, the rarest of all cats. Snow leopards, clouded leopards, Siberian snow tigers, glacier bears, they're practically a dime a dozen compared to black jaguars. That one is, for your information, the third ever taken by a sportsman. Marco Polo sheep and bongos are like cottontail rabbits compared to the rarity of one of these."

We sat down for a shaky cigarette and examined the ebony beauty. He was in perfect fighting trim, two hundred pounds of rippling steel muscle sheathed in black velvet. His rosettes could be seen faintly beneath his dark hide. His teeth, incredibly long and pure white, gleamed from his gums like ivory tent pegs. I thought of how close I had come to a practical demonstration of their efficiency.

"You know," James commented back in camp over a café royal, "the black jaguar is considered much more dangerous than the spotted variety. The natives say that they are much more aggressive and behave differently from the others. I have a good friend south of here who control-hunts jaguar for cattle ranches. He's lost two complete packs of fine jaguar dogs to these black fellows. Each time he knew it was a black jaguar, but there was no way to call the dogs off the spoor. The jaguar would run and then ambush the lead dog, kill it, and then do the same thing a little farther on until he had wiped out the whole pack. A spotted jaguar will nearly always tree when pursued by dogs. I don't like to think what might have happened if Al hadn't made that fantastic shot on the fly."

"But how can that be, when black jaguars are born of normal parents?" asked Al. "It doesn't seem logical."

"Well, remember this, Al," said James. "We don't know very much at all about jaguars, let alone black ones. There are only something like twenty killed a year by sportsmen in all of South America. Sure, a lot are trapped and shot illegally, and the Indians get some, but the vast majority of the few on trophy room walls have been bought or shot on 'guaranteed' hunts. By the very nature of the impenetrable terrain that he lives in, he is virtually impossible to study. We know a little, like that the black jaguar, same as the black leopard, is a product of a recessive genetic trait. Same thing as blue eyes in people, but I don't think it's that simple. Personally, I believe that the black jaguars here, by breeding with other black jaguars, have developed into a separate species with some very different characteristics from jaguars on the whole. The Indians report seeing them mostly in pairs, which would bear out the idea of a separate group. Another thing, there is no question that the track is different—less space between the toes. Also, the call is more metallic and of a different pitch. They also call faster. Remember what I said when we heard this one?"

I had to admit that Donnelly had a couple of good points.

When dawn finally broke on our last day, we hung the big cat for some photos. James walked into his tent and brought out a surprise—two more black jaguar skins, even bigger than the one we had taken! He had bought them from the Indians some weeks ago, but hadn't shown them to us. He'd felt we might be disappointed if we took a spotted jaguar and then saw this pair of beauties. Mariano and I each held one as Al took what is certainly the only photo ever taken of three black jaguars in one picture.

Later that afternoon, João Branco banked the little Cessna down the valley and dropped smoothly onto the jungle strip.

We crossed the river slowly, drinking in the lonely vastness of the emerald jungle for the last time. Al had his trophy, the finest a man can dream of in a lifetime of hunting the far corners of the earth. But I had one I valued even more—my own skin.

THE HAPPY
SNOOKER

SALT WATER SPORTSMAN—
JUNE 1977

John Gorbatch with two huge snook.

Author's Introduction

You will be quite aware by now of my love of the snook, Centropomus undecimalis. *That the species attracts the complete attention of talented anglers as much as does trout or Atlantic salmon has been validated by Guy Carlton, and now by the veteran linesider John Gorbatch.*

If you've never watched the green flash of sinking, burnished sun over the horizon of the Gulf of Mexico and have never seen the murk writhe in to mate with the pre-moonrise blackness, you have missed a sensation of the sea that occurs in few places. Punctuated only by the schlop! schwok! *of feeding snook, stirring layers of photoelectric microplankton into submersed lightning flashes, there can be few feelings of such expectation, especially if you are tied to it by a slender tendril of monofilament nylon and a homemade plug.*

Smear on some repellent steak sauce and come along to the swift cuts and boiling eddies of Wiggins Pass. I think you'll have an interesting evening.

The figure of the man is dark against a pale ribbon of moon-washed sand where the beach meets the tide flowing from Wiggins Pass. Above the soft lap of night waves, there is only the imperceptible mesh of the reel's gears and the far-off *quaaarrrk* of an insomniac heron in the mangroves. The man pauses as the lure nears his feet, then lifts the rod tip, silhouetting the odd little plug against the sky, checking for possible weed. Satisfied that it is clean, he crushes a mosquito—unimpressed by the repellent label—then hooks a finger under the monofilament, watching the slick water for a swirl or the hollow, slapping pop of a feeding snook. A swish like a fencer's foil sounds as he casts again, the line whispering off the spool and through the guides with a dry hiss. The lure falls just at the edge of the current along the sandbar and, with sharp twitches, dances its dull, flashing path back through the black water, the line a laser track in summer phosphorescence.

The strike is not violent, more the sensation of snagging a heavy, rubbery log for the first two or three seconds, and the man rears back, driving in the steel with hard pulses that strip the drag. Then the fish realizes what has happened and begins a hard run, peeling off line in a single, spool-melting surge that ends in a white explosion of spray and the clatter of razor-edged gill plates against a wire leader. For a moment the huge snook balks, shaking its head, then streaks back across the mouth of the silent pass in a new run, the throb of its tail thumping up the line and through the man's arms as he applies all the pressure he dares, the rod pretzeled into a tight bow. He cannot see the fish, but he knows this is the one he's been looking for.

Ten minutes pass, and the man's forearm is nearly numb with the strain of tempering the runs, his heart almost stopping with each burst of jumps. But those irresistible dashes are growing shorter and he has been able to keep the light line free of ancient snags and cypress roots.

After twenty minutes he begins to take the offensive, gently pumping, working, easing the fish toward the shallows. *Easy . . . real easy,* he mutters to himself. Then, the oar-sized tail gesturing weakly, the snook is on its side at the sand's edge, the plug glimmering in the corner of its mouth. Gently, the man slips a thumb over the sandpaper teeth and slides the fish higher up onto the beach, not stopping until he is twenty yards from the water. It lies there, a striped platinum ingot in the dying moonlight. Panting with effort and excitement, the man hefts it, guessing the weight almost perfectly at thirty-three pounds. For John Gorbatch it is another best-of-season trophy, one more sprig in the laurel wreath of the best snook fisherman in an area that takes its "linesiding" seriously.

John Gorbatch has been called the Hank Aaron of snook fishing. Certainly, if the Red Baron, Von Richthofen, had been a fisherman, his scrapbook would have been no larger than that of this transplanted New Jerseyite who came to the southwest Florida area of Naples twenty-six years ago, determined to develop a technique for snook as effective as those he had managed with striped bass in the Atlantic surf. When I moved to Naples eight years ago, the first name I heard mentioned consistently with snook and snook fishing was his, and if anything, he has risen in regard since then to near-hero proportions. The local newspapers have recorded so many super-catches by John that the sports-page headlines now simply scream, *Gorbatch Does It Again!*

But how, I kept asking myself after a few years of serious snooking with no more than mediocre success, does that man always seem to catch the most *and* biggest snook in the country? What's he doing that I'm not, or vice versa? How does a fisherman working the same waters as thousands of fellow plug punishers consistently come in number one? The more than fifty cups, trophies, checks, and citations Gorbatch has earned prove pretty clearly that it isn't a matter of luck; anybody with that much luck would be living in Las Vegas. Then what was his secret? I determined to try to find out.

The first thing I learned was that Gorbatch's success wasn't a secret at all. When I fished with and interviewed him, he was more than happy to give me all the answers I asked for. One of the greatest points of curiosity was that, although most large snook are caught in the passes on live bait—pinfish and shrimp—Gorbatch uses only artificial lures, all of his own manufacture. John doesn't have a boat either, doing all his fishing from the beaches around passes. What were these mysterious baits and why were they so effective even without the advantage of a boat?

On the porch of his house, John obliged by showing me a

selection of his "clothespins," the lead-weighted, hand-carved mahogany plugs that he uses. They didn't look very impressive, roughly finished in silver or gold casually shaped like a minnow, but with very heavy stainless treble hooks firmly attached to tail and body, and no diving lip or other action-producing features. I noticed that although they were all the same size, they were of different weights, depending on the amount of lead core inserted into the drilled bodies. Asked what they had that commercial plugs did not, Gorbatch didn't hesitate with his answer:

"First off and most important, the hooks are better. I buy only the heavy, stainless imported kinds, which are too expensive for the plug manufacturers to use. These won't bend or straighten out like the commercial ones sometimes do under a lot of strain. After all, what's the point in spending all your time looking for monster snook that you couldn't hold on regular plugs anyway?" He picked up one of the clothespins and examined it. "Besides, a lot of fishermen don't have good lure-sense and don't understand how plugs work best. Conditions indicate lure choice, especially depth. If I find snook popping the surface, I use an unweighted plug. If they're feeding on the bottom on little crabs, I go to a heavier, weighted one. If I make my own, I get exactly what I want for any condition."

Gorbatch fishes the clothespin in a twitching, fluttering style that he varies in speed of retrieve. That it's effective can't be denied, no matter how homely the little dudes may look. Recently, he told me, he has been working on another idea that has proven quite effective in field tests. Liking a big white jig with a hair tail under some conditions, he found that the weight necessary for large size caused the jig to ride deeper than he wanted. Thinking back to his striped bass days on the Jersey shore, he recalled the block tin squid that had so often been a killer. Obtaining some metal by melting down the condensing coils of an old beer dispenser, he molded several jigs from this lighter metal, giving him the size he wanted, but half the weight of lead. In four sessions of casting, John has taken fourteen snook over eighteen pounds on the new jigs. He leaves the bright heads unpainted because he thinks the gleam of the raw metal is attractive to deeper-feeding snook that aren't actually on the bottom.

I quizzed him as to what he felt were the best conditions for snook fishing along the Gulf beaches, starting off by asking if night was preferable. He allowed that it wasn't necessarily so. He believes that, snook being quite shy by nature, it is the boat traffic in the passes that may make daylight fishing unproductive, rather than light conditions. On rainy or overcast days, fishing picks up because there is less traffic. As far as choice of tides is concerned, John prefers the two and a half hours before and after high tide.

Gorbatch is steadfast that the consistent catching of really big snook depends upon three factors: homework, rigid attention to detail, and persistence. The first of these refers to calculating external natural factors and relating your fishing to them. Tides, winds, and water temperatures are important to snooking. For example, he won't fish in a north or northwest wind, as it tends to dirty the water and cool it. In water temperatures less than 70 degrees Fahrenheit, John just doesn't bother. There are three main passes that he patrols and fishes, checking each one's conditions before stopping to fish. In the summer, the heart of the snook run, scattered inland thunderstorms may roil the water of one pass and not another, even though only a few miles separate them. Also, because of the distance, tides may be completely different at each one.

In matters of equipment and tackle maintainance, Gorbatch is a wild-eyed fanatic. For most of his fishing, he favors a medium-weight saltwater spinning rig with the reel's bail arm removed, feeling that this prevents tangles at night or possible broken springs. His experience has shown that twelve-pound test monofilament has enough authority under normal circumstances for even the largest snook, but in an area of mangrove snags he will switch spools in favor of eighteen-pound test where some horsing and praying are called for. His rods are fairly stiff-tipped, because John believes that power is necessary to drive home the big hooks into tough gristle. Because of the length of time required to wear down a big snook, he insists on an eighteen-inch length of No. 6 wire leader rather than a trace of heavier monofilament, which may be cut by the serrated knives of a snook's gill plates, or worn through by the rasping action of the rough teeth. A No. 7 swivel is the link between the leader and line.

Knowing through huge, lost fish the strains his tackle may have to weather when he hangs a lunker snook, John strips off ten feet of terminal line after every hour or so of casting and re-rigs, not wanting to take a chance that there could be the slightest nick or fray from barnacles or coral rock. Also, he insists on special, super-hard guide linings to add distance to his cast potential, as well as to reduce line wear in casting or retrieving.

It's John contention that more big snook are lost at the feet of the angler at the last moment than at any other time in the fight. He sees the problem as that of the angle of the hooks in the snook's mouth being changed as it is brought in and the distance between angler and fish decreases. The shorter the distance, the less elasticity of the line to absorb shock, and after a long fight, the hook may have keyholed through wear, permitting it to pull free.

Gorbatch advises that, as the fish comes in to be landed, the angler retreat up the beach with his rod tip low, then advance and beach him manually. He warns never to attempt to actually lift a big snook near the water, as it produces a thrash-

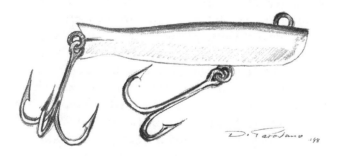

"Clothespin" snook lure.

ing reaction, but to slide it well up the beach on its side, with a thumb in the mouth. Leave the gills alone, or your fingers may look as if you've been hand-sorting samurai swords.

Drag tension is very important in fishing the big snook, which are capable of lightning surges that may shock-snap even heavy lines. John emphasizes that tension should not be measured directly from the reel, but that the plug should be hooked to a tree or piling while the fisherman backs off twenty or so yards and adjusts drag as he would when actually fighting a fish.

Color preference in lures is a favorite subject. He's a believer, through years of experimentation, in light, flashy finishes rather than dark ones, even for night fishing. John doesn't think snook see too well and therefore catch flash better than silhouette. For after-dark snooking, he prefers the clothespin in silver or red head with white body. The only color jig he uses is all white, day or night. For daylight casting, he normally uses various weights of the clothespin in gold, yellow, or yellow with black vertical stripes to suggest the sand perch, one of the staples of snook diets and one of the less frequently used. He doesn't go out lightly armed, either, and loses an average of a dozen jigs and several plugs per trip, which forced him through sheer economics to start molding his jigs in wholesale lots.

There are probably scads of fishermen who use the same types of equipment and tactics as John Gorbatch, yet without the constant results he manages. What's the difference? In a phrase, absolute persistence coupled with expertise. John is a devotee and fervent worshiper of the law of averages. When he decides conditions are right, he knows there are snook in the passes and just doesn't become discouraged. Neither mosquitoes, no-see-ums, thunderstorms, nor black nights deter him. He casts *constantly* with the irrefutable logic that you can only catch a snook if your lure is in the water doing its job. He probes every inch of water within reach, then works it again, aware that snook are usually moving and if there was nothing near his plug thirty seconds ago, there could be a critter fit to scare you under the next cast to the same spot. And it's logical to conclude that when he does sink those miniature grappling irons into the gums of a thirty-plus-pounder, he knows his equipment can handle it. His hooks won't straighten, his leader won't fray, and the experience of twenty-six years of monster snooking is with him. Of course, as John puts it, "Maybe it does require just a smidgin of luck. . . ."

THE DEADLY
NEW TUBE FLY

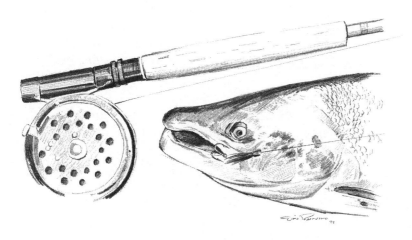

Cock salmon taken on tube fly in Iceland.

AUTHOR'S INTRODUCTION

Water has always meant a collection of magic places to me. The memories that pave my life have been so often quarried from the greenish Acid Waters off New Jersey, swarming with bluefish, the streaks of moon through a bed of water lilies on Lake Valhalla, in my native New Jersey, where a potbellied bass or three lay, the foam-bewhiskered amber of a Pennsylvania trout stream, or the impossible clarity of a Florida Keys tarpon flat. But then, just as with hunting, the joy of fishing is largely that of expectation. Yes, just like hunting, fishing is being in a lovely place that creates a state of mind not to be found in the fumes of combustion engines or the sweat-smeary ink of the morning's headlines.

It's pretty clear that God held fishermen in quite high esteem; or maybe it was just their patience. In any case, an awful lot of Disciples fished full time. I've never twitched a streamer fly in Galilee, but I suppose He would have approved. In any case, He's known for protecting orphans, drunkards, and assorted idiots. I'm sure I qualify somewhere. . . .

Horse racing has long been known as the Sport of Kings. Objection. I can only conclude that, with the exception of the northern European monarchs, kings in general have not tried to finance advanced romance with Salmo salar, *the Atlantic salmon. Any potentate could build a stable beyond peer before he could control the better salmon waters of both sides of the North Atlantic. Expensive? Don't even ask. It is classic supply-and-demand fare, and the latter so far outstrips the former as to be laughable.*

The Atlantic salmon is the most ridiculous fish to reach the interest of sporting masochists since the Deluge. To be properly outfitted according to reigning Anglo protocol on the best of British or Norwegian rivers, let alone the cream of the eastern Canadian streams, would run more than a couple of nice strings of polo ponies. Never mind the cost of leasing the water.

Fate, however, has sometimes twitched her beckoning, frostbitten finger and I have been able to fish some of these great waters. Still, I never had a better time at salmon fishing than in Iceland, where, as a guest of Chris and Sally Aall, old friends, I chanced to sample the Hitara River, north of Reykjavik, in August 1974. That I didn't write this piece until a year and a half later shows how long it took for my fingers to thaw out.

Herein, you will probably learn more of the tube fly than you really need to know. Well, I suppose that won't do, so I'll just ship you in to the volcanic black sands of the Hitara and see how your luck holds. . . .

Thε whole trip looked like a bust. Balanced on a small lava outcrop furred over with a light toupee of moss, I stood watching the glassy chute of glacial water slide down from the head of Steinastrangur Pool into the aquavit-clear depths, the dark silhouettes of Atlantic salmon suspended in its clarity like ants in amber. The fifty-knot wind that had screamed through icy teeth down the bleak, volcanic valleys for two days razored through my light windbreaker and stabbed my eardrums like frozen steel skewers. Iceland, I mentally mused, had not been misnamed.

Seven of us had been fishing the Hitara River, one of the best salmon waters on the Isle of Fire and Ice, for two straight days without so much as a swirl of cooperation. We had lashed

the surfaces of the best pools to near contusions with every fly
in the box, wet and dry, Wulffs, bucktails, marabous, nymphs,
and muddler minnows included. Nothing. At all. There were
plenty of fish in the pools, slowly turning from the molten silver of the sea to the pastel-dawn hues of spawning coloration,
but the drought of late August and the freak winds had spread
a case of communal lockjaw among the fish that nothing we
offered could cure. Exasperated and half-frozen, I watched a
gaff-jawed ten-pounder porpoise playfully in the slick water at
the base of the pool. I reached for a smoke. As I hunched over
to shield the flame from the whip of the wind, my lighter
slipped from numb fingers, clattered against the black lava,
and disappeared into the glacial run. Muttering a few comments I didn't learn in church, I reached back to a rear pocket
of my fishing vest and groped through the old lunch papers
and cigarette packs for the battered Marble's match container.
And found the envelope. Curious, I shook off the tobacco
crumbs and twigs and unfolded the air-mail letter, creased and
stained with insect dope and leader sink. The French stamps
rang a bell, but not until I opened it did I recall having received it from a crony in Paris, months ago. My mind on the
opening of the upland season, I had stuck it away in the
shabby old salmon vest and promptly forgotten its existence.
In one corner of the envelope lay a clump of odd, tangled hair
and plastic flies, and, stuck under the other fold, a thicket of
nasty little treble hooks gleamed out at me. Chris's note called
them "tube flies," and he professed a Rasputin-like power for
them over any salmon this side of the smokehouse.

I picked out one of the flies for a closer look, a small,
dark pattern. Unimpressive at best, it was simply a piece of
soft plastic tubing stuck male/female into a larger-diameter
piece and tied with a bucktail-hair wing completely around the
fly's head, like a grass skirt on a hula dancer. Obviously, since
the fly itself had no hook, the leader was supposed to be
passed through the fly's head and through the tube, and a treble hook knotted at the end. The fly body would be free to
travel up and down the leader, but water pressure or resistance
would keep it against the hooks while being fished. What the

Three styles of tube flies.

hell, I reckoned, I couldn't do any worse than I had been doing. I clipped off the No. 8 Blue Charm I had been fishing, pushed the tip of the long 3X tippet through the tube, and bent on one of the No. 10 treble hooks with an improved clinch knot. With the gale biting at my back, it was easy to swing the nine-foot rod and place the sinking-tip across and slightly down-current at the head of a deep, fast run through a lava fault on the pool's bottom. The line tensed in my numb fingers as the current swung it tight and across the clear, quiet water at the tail of Steinastrangur Pool. As the invisible fly reached the farthest point in its arc, I nearly fell off the slippery rock in surprise as a deep, silver flash gleamed up from the dark water. He hadn't taken, but a good fish had flashed the fly. Carefully, I cast again. At the same point of the sweep, the late Arctic sun reflected once more as the salmon swirled, yet the line still lay limp. My hands shaking from more than the cold, I reeled up the slack to rest the fish. I had his attention, but how to get him to take?

Remembering the old salmon axiom of a smaller fly for an undecided fish, I wormed out my fine-point scissors and clipped off the hooks. I shoved the smaller tube deeper into the larger so that the total length was reduced, and nipped away at the hair wing until it was half as long and full as it had been. Expectant as a bookie, I re-knotted the treble and repeated the cast.

The fly flipped perfectly into the water at the base of the run, line slicking through the guides of the long rod as I mended the cast. There was a big, metallic flash and a bulge of water. I dropped the rod tip sideways and tightened, the solid feeling of power throbbing into my arm as the trebles bit. The lower end of the pool self-destructed as eleven pounds of cock salmon hurled himself into a triple jump and bored away into a heavy run that banged the reel handle on my knuckles and made the drag scream for quarter. Fifteen minutes later, ignoring the icy water shocking into my right wader leg, lacerated by a lava outcrop sharper than a nest of punji stakes, I slid him like an anodized aluminum ingot across the volcanic ash of a tiny beach and mugged him with the lead-loaded priest. I lit a shaky cigarette and hunkered down in the wind to admire his bright, sickle-snouted beauty. The little black tube fly hung on the light leader just up from the corner of his jaw, where the tiny trebles were embedded in gristle. I felt as if I had just cured cancer, landed on the moon, won the Nobel Prize, all minor accomplishments compared to suckering a salmon when he's not of a mind to strike!

In the twenty minutes before daylight hemorrhaged somewhere over Greenland, I had beached another salmon, a pound better than the first, and finally, in a fit of overconfidence, broken off the fly in something that looked like a torpedo with teeth. Moses returning from the Mount with his homework had nothing on me swaggering back to the Grettistak Club with those two fish gilled on frozen fingers. I peeled off the ruptured waders, poured something very brown to keep the vapors at bay, and offered to answer any questions anybody might have concerning the finer points of salmon fishing. Dodging several thrown boots, I displayed the tube flies to my fishless friends, who had concluded among themselves that my two fish had been obvious suicides, probably depressed into taking the weird little fly by an aberrant moon phase or some such phenomenon. Ignoring their pooh-poohing, I poured another ounce of prevention and went to bed with a look of eagles.

By the end of the next day, had I been other than my usual, unselfish Prince of a Pal, I expect I could have traded those tube flies about even for $20 gold pieces. I caught and released five salmon that morning, the last a hyperactive hen fish of twelve pounds, in the home pool. Nobody else even got the threat of a strike. Smug as a Boston banker, I gave away four of the flies. That afternoon, all the men who tried them took salmon, while those fishing conventionally didn't have a take. Over that entire week, tube flies accounted for fifty-five salmon under the worst possible conditions of very low water, heavy winds, and "stale" fish. One salmon was finally killed on a standard-pattern wet fly, a No. 8 Silver Doctor. I didn't know what the tube fly had, but whatever it was, it had plenty!

In the fifteen months since first pulling that envelope out of my pocket at Steinastrangur Pool, I have spent a lot of time fishing the tube flies in different parts of the world, not only on salmon, but on other freshwater and saltwater species. Results have been impressive. Friends have fished them on Canadian Atlantic salmon in the Tabusintac, Restigouche, Miramichi, and Jupiter rivers, all with glowing results—so luminous, in fact, that a couple of them have sworn they will use nothing but tube flies in the future. I was high rod on the Owenmore River in Ireland's Connemara on dull yellow tube flies this year, having about twice the number of strikes of anybody else in the party. Since they were all better fishermen than I am, that makes the figures really significant. I haven't had a chance to do any trout fishing recently, but a pal tells me that tube flies are very effective on brown trout, rainbows, and

Arctic char as well as sea trout. That's a test I look forward to confirming shortly.

Techniques for using the tube flies on salmon vary little from tactics normally utilized in fishing ordinary wet flies. The cast should be across and downstream, in a searching pattern, little action or motion imparted to the swimming fly. Most strikes occur at the final swing of the fly's arc in the current, although it's by no means rare to have a strike at any point of the drift. Salmon really seem to hit the tube fly hard, rather than the more usual soft take common with other flies. About the only way I had no results with the tube fly on salmon was when experimenting with a Portland hitch or other "skittering" technique, but perhaps that was because conditions have been almost universally low where I have tried the fly.

Living in the great fly-fishing country of southwest Florida, I was very interested in finding out what reaction bonefish, tarpon, snook, and the like would have to the tube flies. On three trips to the Florida Keys, piscatorial pal Dean Witter, Jr., and I gave the tubes a real workout from Marathon to the Marquesas, off Key West, on both bonefish and tarpon, with the odd barracuda thrown in. Action was hot and heavy throughout. Bonefish took the tubes better than any type of fly I have ever tried, although on the grass and marl flats we had trouble with the tube fly's treble hook fouling the bottom. Dean jury-rigged a weedless guard from three strands of fine piano wire, and our problems were over. Casting ahead of a school of feeding and tailing bonefish, we would let the tube sink to the bottom and, when the bonefish were close enough to see it, scuttle it along with short twitches. They would run over like ladies at a girdle sale to grab it, usually giving a hookup if we didn't somehow spook them. Long, fine leaders were necessary in the crystal water, and we lost quite a few fish on cutoffs, but for pure action on the long rod, the tubes gave us more than I had ever had with bonefish before. We had several shots at permit, but for the usual reasons with the big sickle-tails, we were unable to present the fly properly. Maybe next time.

Tarpon, probably the greatest fly-rod fish of them all, are real suckers for the tubes. Tied in larger sizes for greater visibility, big school fish of 75 to 125 pounds will grab tubes like kids at a weenie roast. We worked the flats where the lunkers were cruising and feeding, the blue holes where they could be spotted loafing along on the tide running between the Gulf and the Atlantic and back, and the mangroves where twenty-five-pounders hang out all year long. All these tarpon preferred the tubes in red and white, yellow, all-white, and grizzly, and when a cast was properly executed and the fly stripped slowly in six-inch throbs in front of their faces, that mouth would open like a lid coming off a garbage can and it was stand by, brother! Last week I tried the tubes here on the Gulf Coast, and on a strong falling tide I took three nice snook on a yellow tube from under the mangroves, and a three-pound ladyfish as a dividend. In a deep channel hole where big tarpon frequently rest up for their nocturnal foraging, I tried letting the tube sink deep, then twitching it slowly off the bottom. I was rewarded with two fish: a fifty-pounder that I lost on the third jump, and an eighty-pounder that actually jumped into the boat with me. Apparently he liked the tube fly so much he wanted to see if there were any more where it had come from!

It's interesting to ponder just what makes the tube fly so effective. Of course, we'll never know, not being fish, but it seems to have that rare characteristic of "fishiness" about it, some inexplicable, ethereal quality that makes fish want to bite it, eat it, attack it. Like many great lures, it probably suggests food rather than imitating it, much the same as the very effective but highly unrealistically colored plastic worms so dear to the palates of big bass. Certainly, no bass ever made a living eating seven-inch long blue or orange worms in nature, but drop a plastic one in front of him and he'll usually grab it faster than pâté de foie gras.

Perhaps it's the circular shape of the tube flies—having no up or down—that presents a more attractive silhouette to fish. Or maybe the translucency of the plastic body refracts or reflects light in some very inviting way to suggest food. After all, most minnows are semitransparent, as are many forms of larval and crustacean life. Whatever the reason, the design in itself has several inherent advantages over standard one- or two-hook flies. Since the fly is usually run up the leader when fighting a fish, tubes are not as often torn and ruined by toothy species. Because the treble hook is separate from the body, it may be changed in size if more weight is desired for a deeper run or drift, switched when dull for a sharp one, or, in the case of tarpon, whose pig-iron-tough mouths make the setting of a treble hook difficult, replaced with a single hook for better penetrating qualities. The use of treble hooks not only permits smaller, less obvious hooks to be used on tubes with no sacrifice in holding power, but also gives a much better strike-to-hooked-fish ratio. Less weight also means a more normal and realistic drift in trout and salmon waters.

I wish I could tell you the name of the unsung genius who invented the tube fly, or when he did it, but other than indications that it's a European innovation, even the fly itself has been a close secret in most parts of the world. No wonder! Against conventional flies, even a dolt can look like a hero with it. At the moment, it can be a bit tricky to locate a batch, although most of the better British and European tackle stores will have some in stock. Word is spreading in this country about tubes, so you can bet it won't be long before they are generally available, but if you prefer to roll a few of your own, the formula is pretty simple. You'll need a needle, assorted hair, two lengths of tubing, one sized to fit inside the other, tying thread, lacquer, and a tying vise. Place the needle inside a one-inch length of the smaller tube, which should have a hole about the needle's diameter, just enough to admit the size leader you plan to use. The needle will support the flexible tube for the tying operation. Place the needle and tube in the vise as you would a normal hook for tying. Tie in a fairly sparse hair wing, 360 degrees around the head of the fly, in the same position as a bucktail or streamer; whip finish; lacquer the head, leaving the hole clear; remove the needle; and push on the larger-diameter tubing over the smaller to create the adjustable body length. You're in business. Except for a simple painted shank, it's probably the simplest fly of all—no hackle, tail, body material, horns, topping, tag, or butt—just tubing and hair. Trim the excess tubing to length, and the only remaining ingredient is water.

Anything the 20-Gauge Can Do, the 12 Can Do Better

SPORTS AFIELD —
NOVEMBER 1973

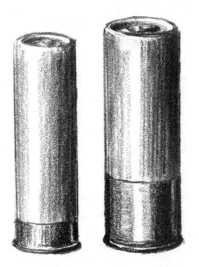

Twenty-gauge shotgun shell (left), twelve-gauge (right).

AUTHOR'S INTRODUCTION

So long as there are shotguns—or any firearms, for that matter—there will always be controversy as to which gauge is the most effective. Obviously, when properly applied to those particular shooting tasks for which they were designed, all bores perform well. Let there be no misunderstanding; I am extremely fond of the 20-gauge, but only within those areas of reasonable effectiveness. *The same goes for the 10-gauge. There are long shots in waterfowling where it would be a better choice, on the same basis that the 12 is superior to the 20, but I wouldn't want to hike one through the grouse mountains for ten hours or so. Perhaps I might usurp quite an antique concept and modify it to fit the idea: Unto each gauge there is a season. . . .*

I didn't have a chance to bring this up in this chapter, but I would firmly maintain that to start a beginning shooter—a boy, a girl, or a light-framed woman—with a .410-bore is self-defeating. Give it a bit of thought and you will realize that the .410, which is actually a caliber and not a gauge (gauge *meaning, by number, the quantity of pure lead balls that total a pound*), *may have low recoil, but it completely lacks the ability in any load to provide that satisfaction so necessary to a beginner at all but the closest ranges. Most feathered game is out of range of the capability of the .410, and miss after miss tends to severely erode the confidence crucial to the neophyte. What you are doing is actually handicapping the learner. Not enough power, not enough pellets to kill at usual ranges. To me, a man who kills his pheasants at long range with a .410 is certainly an expert, but he is also a game waster. He may do everything right, but it may also be beyond the ability of his gun.*

If recoil is a major factor and causes fright or flinching in a new shooter, use a bigger gauge, such as the 20 or even the 12, which has many kick-absorbing devices available today. At least when a new shooter does what he or she is supposed to do, the game will fall and provide the incentive to continue.

Look, I often shoot a 20 when conditions permit. There is nothing wrong with proper loads in a 20. It is simply a fact that it will not perform as well, given even slightly extended ranges, as will the 12. Sorry, but that's the way it is.

N ot very long ago, on a dull, cold January morning in the grouse covers of northern New Jersey, a love affair came to an end.

My brother, Tom, and I had been hunting hard for three hours, covering the lee slopes of Turkey Mountain where warm pools of wind-shielded sun had melted open patches of old snow, leaving dirty white islands in the shadows of birch windfalls and dark laurel thickets. Four—or was it five—times we had started at the distant whir of wild-flushing grouse, bursting from the tangles ahead, far out of range. After two months of gunning pressure, they were as shy as turkeys, refusing to hold for Tom's feather-footed little setter. Then, as we were about to give it up, the Englishman dropped into a solid point, his tail as rigid as protocol.

Carefully, Tom edged in from the right as I covered the left of a thick snarl of catbrier, sprawling ahead like an ancient barbed-wire emplacement. Glancing over to see that I was in position, he took a tentative step into the cover, his shotgun ready across his chest. One step was enough.

In twenty years of hard-core grouse addiction, I had never

had the chance before—and there it was. Two gray-brown buzz bombs erupted from the briers together, coming past me at an easy angle for my long-dreamed-of double. Reflex took over as I swept the twin tubes of the 20-gauge past the trailing bird, slapped the trigger, and saw feathers fly. Still swinging, I overhauled the leader, looking as big as a bustard as he lanced through the trees. At my second shot, he flinched and staggered, but kept airborne. Frustrated, I watched both birds clear the ridge and roll on wobbly, cupped wings out of sight down the mountain. Drifting spoors of feathers spun to the brown leaves with irritating slowness.

We searched with the dog for another three hours and finally quit, unable to find the hard-hit birds. Two fine grouse, ever more important in a dwindling supply of game and hunting land, had become food for foxes because I had asked the 20-gauge to do the job of a 12.

My affair with the 20-bore began with a graceful little Belgian import. Compared to most of the 12s of the day, she had lines racier than *Cap'n Billie's Whiz-Bang;* twenty-six-inch barrels that blended with a beautifully figured French walnut stock. She pointed where I looked, and got there faster than I could focus. I had bought her, I told myself, for the same reason I drank vodka martinis and fished a dry fly. It was simply a more sporting way to do things. Fifteen years have gone by now, and I still drift a Light Cahill and certainly still drink vodka. But I've had to swallow my illusions about the 20-gauge. She's just not enough gun for today's upland shooting.

A couple of years ago, when I was working for the travel division of one of the major arms companies, I had a unique opportunity to test the 20 against the 12 under varying conditions with a unique mixture of upland game. The company was just about to start marketing the 20-gauge version of their Japanese-made over/under 12-gauge, both very attractive pieces of hardware. As I was scheduled for a jaunt through Europe and North Africa to make arrangements for some gunning trips the company would offer, it seemed logical that I, and the other men on the trip, tote along a few of the new 20s for sort of an informal field test.

The trip started in the knee-knocking chill of Robin Sinclair's grouse moors in northern Scotland, near Caithness. Now Lord Thurso, Robin was quick to explain that the shooting in his area was of the type he described as "walk-up." He wasn't kidding. Using the 20-gauge field load of 2½ drams equivalent behind one ounce of No. 7½ shot, we slogged through the heather and gorse for a week, getting some very fine shooting over Robin's dogs. Each day I would alternate guns, switching to the 12 with 3¼ drams pushing 1¼ ounces of shot, carefully noting the results of each day's shoot in my notebook. After six days' sport, I tallied the results.

Taking care not to fire at birds much over forty yards, I had bagged exactly 26 percent more red grouse with the 12-gauge than the 20, with the same number of shells. Of the birds knocked down with the smaller gun, 31 percent were still alive when retrieved, against 11 percent with the 12. Except for gauge, both guns were as identical as they could be; the same model and both choked improved-cylinder and modified. The figures seemed significant, I thought, but a week's shooting on one species is hardly conclusive.

Next stop was the softly rolling Alentejo country of central Portugal, near the medieval town of Évora, where we hunted red-legged or Spanish partridge through the cork and olive groves. Much like chukars, hunting these birds on foot reminded me of nothing so much as ruffed grouse back home, except that the red-legs were smaller, faster, and if you can believe it, wilder. Fernando Fernandes, twice pigeon-shooting champion of a country that takes shooting very seriously, was virtually stiff with laughter at the idea of taking on *perdiz* with the 20-gauge. The box score for the group proved he was right; more than twice as many birds had been taken with the 12 than with the 20 under identical conditions. Incoming wood pigeons boosted the score for the 20, probably because they were taken over live decoys at about twenty yards when they came to stands of trees to roost. But, even at those ranges, the 12-gauge edged the 20 by about 8 percent.

A few hundred miles farther south, across Gibraltar, lie the great wetlands of northwestern Morocco, where I joined

PETER HATHAWAY CAPSTICK

158

the noted French shooter and gastronome, Bertrand des Clers, for ten days of magnificent sport with driven snipe, partridge, duck, and wild boar. Hordes of howling, screeching Arabs, burnooses hitched up around their shoulders, floundered through the flooded grasslands driving sheets of wintering Siberian snipe at us for six days. One of my shooting partners concluded after the next two beats that Moroccan snipe were "very small birds surrounded by vast quantities of air." It was a pretty accurate deduction in view of the performance of the little 20-gauge. Plucked, these jinking, twisting rockets weigh no more than a few delicious ounces, small enough to slip, time and again, through the poorer pattern of the 20-gauge load of No. 9s we were throwing. After shooting snipe three days with each gun, I had killed exactly 66 percent more with the 12.

That trip shook the foundations of my love affair with the 20, a relationship that got even rockier after a dozen trips through Argentina and Colombia, where I kept the test going on tinamou, martineta, paloma, and torcaz, which almost exactly equal our quail, pheasant, doves, and pigeons in body weight and habits.

Since 1969, as a professional white hunter in Zambia, Botswana, and Rhodesia, I have shot literally thousands of birds for food for myself and my clients—mostly guinea fowl, sand grouse, francolin, button quail and other species—with both the 12- and 20-gauges. The conclusion was inevitable: The 12-gauge, at normal upland ranges, will put more birds in your game bag under virtually any circumstances than will the 20-bore.

The killing of upland game with a shotgun of any gauge is reduced in its essence to one factor: how many pellets of proper diameter hit the target and where they hit it. Since the individual pellets in a shotgun charge cannot be aimed separately, the shooter must rely on the all-important ingredient of a uniform pattern of sufficient density to ensure that some pellets of the charge will reach a vital area and kill the bird. Obviously, a half-pound of chilled shot through the tail feathers of a rising pheasant won't do as much good as a couple of pellets in the head or neck. On the other hand, smaller birds such as woodcock, quail, doves and the like have less shot resistance, but also have smaller vitals to hit. Thus, an even, reasonably dense pattern is necessary for any upland bird hunted.

Equally apparent is the fact that any shotgun, of whatever gauge, is only as good as the charge it fires. For the sake of comparison, let's take as examples the two loads I have most often used to test the two gauges in the field—probably the most popular upland loads for either bore. The 20 shell is one ounce of shot over 2½ drams, and the 12-gauge, an equally standard shell of 3¼ drams, hustles 1¼ ounces of the same size shot through a modified choke. It doesn't take a Rhodes scholar to notice that you're throwing 25 percent more pellets with the 12 than with the 20, and throwing them harder.

Ah, you say, that's on paper. I don't shoot my birds with paper. Fine. Let's put you in a frosty Nebraska cornfield behind a dog that's acting as if he's been petrified. You catch a glimpse of a cock pheasant dodging through the stubble to flush, cackling in Chinese, just twenty-five yards away. By the time you get your heart restarted, flip off the safety, and slip the computer under your hat into gear to figure lead, let's say he's now about forty yards away. You pull the trigger on your 20-gauge, unleashing 350 No. 7½ pellets down the tube through a modified choke that prints an average of 60 percent of the charge into a thirty-inch circle at forty yards. If you've centered the pheasant right in the middle of the pattern, that leaves 60 percent of 350, or 210 pellets in the circle surrounding the bird at the forty yards. Is that enough to kill him? Impossible to say. It depends entirely on where he is hit, and how many shot actually smack him. I took a plucked, thawed pheasant from my freezer this morning and put him in the middle of a round 30-inch table on our terrace. It didn't take too much cogitation to decide that that bird was surrounded by a lot of table.

Let's try the same exercise with the 12-gauge. Right off, because of the extra quarter-ounce of shot, you have eighty-seven more pellets on your team than with the 20-gauge load. Over the forty yards, there will be 262 left inside that thirty-inch killing zone against the 210 for the lighter gun, which is exactly fifty-two more chances to put that bird in your game bag. I don't know what Jimmy the Greek would say, but those are the kind of odds I could get attached to.

Try it on quail with No. 8s, and the principle works even better, placing better than sixty extra shot in the target area over the 20-gauge. With 1¼ ounces of No. 9s, the advantage of the 12 is really tremendous, giving you about eighty-eight more pellets at forty yards in that circle.

Practically, because of the advantage of numbers of shot, the 12 will give you about the same pattern with an improved-cylinder choke, at a given distance, as a 20 with a modified. Or, you can look at it the other way—with the 12 you'll get the same density as with the tighter choke in the 20-gauge, but a killing area about 25 percent greater, because of the extended area of the density of the pattern. I don't know about you, but I don't always manage to fit the bird in the precise center of the pattern. The 12 gives me an additional room for error that can't help but put more game on the table, particularly in the case of birds not really well hit.

How about the differences in range between the 12 and the 20 for upland gunning? I don't know where you shoot, but the grouse, woodcock, doves, pheasant, and quail I hunt certainly haven't been getting any tamer in the last few years. Around a lot of the country, upland covers without split-levels on them are getting rarer than ruby mines or tax refunds. I can eat a cut-rate lunch and bowl a few frames just about where my first grouse fell in 1952, and if I was to try to retrieve my first pheasant, I'd probably get five years for jaywalking on an interstate highway.

Ten times as many hunters prowling a quarter of the acreage available twenty years ago are pretty good reasons why game is scarcer and harder to approach than ever before. What happens? Human nature raises its ugly head, teeth bared in frustration. People being what they are, they are inclined after long hours of hard tramping to try shots just a teensy bit farther than they should, in hopes of an odd pellet hitting head or neck. Unfortunately, they scratch down enough game to encourage them to keep trying it, leaving a high percentage of wounded birds to crawl off and be wasted.

At a time when every piece of game is more valuable than ever, I think we're actually wasting more birds than in previous years to undergunned and over-ranging shooters. I certainly don't advocate the use of punt guns in the upland covers; fifty years of increasingly better shotshells have proved that the 12 with field loads is sufficient for ranges normally encountered. But, at least in the interest of conservation, let's use enough gun for those ranges—which don't shade much over forty yards for the 12-gauge and less with the 20.

When the ammunition manufacturers developed the newer magnum shotshell loads, they didn't work on the principle that they should shoot farther, but that at any given range they would offer denser and better patterns and, therefore, more consistent game-getting potential. The concept wasn't to make the shot charge fly faster, but to add more pellets to the pattern at effective ranges. This is precisely the principle that makes the 12-gauge more effective than the 20-gauge with a lighter load.

Because a shot string tends to disperse as it flies through the air, the efficiency of a pattern is reduced as the distance from the muzzle is increased. Logically, if there are more pellets to start with in a charge of shot, everything else being equal, there will be more arriving at the target. Theoretically, this extends the range of a heavier load of shot over a lighter one through greater density of pattern at greater ranges. Unfortunately, this principle is only valid with the 12-gauge to a maximum of fifty yards, at more than which distance the 12 shouldn't be used on upland game. Of course, the distance with the 20 is considerably less. The shotgun pellet is a sphere, the worst velocity-retaining shape for any missile, and loses effectiveness past forty yards in a graph line like the Dow Jones averages for Black Tuesday.

Within practical ranges, however, there is a definite secondary advantage that the 12 holds over the 20. It's the fact that shot fired from a standard 12-bore field load flies faster and hits harder than a pellet of the same size shot from a 20. Let's use No. 6 shot for example this time.

At the muzzle, the standard 12-gauge load emerges at

nearly 100 fps faster than does the standard charge from a 20. This, in itself, is of relatively small practical value, although mathematically it does reduce the element of lead about 8 percent. What *does* influence the performance of the shot charge is the imparted greater muzzle energy of about one foot-pound per No. 6 pellet. This charge of sixes, as it begins its flight, has fifty-six more pellets in it than a comparable standard load of one ounce from a 20-gauge. Coupled with the additional energy of the rest of the pellets of the 12-bore, taken at 60 percent of the shot in a thirty-inch circle at forty yards, the potential energy total of the 12-gauge load is a fantastic 1,142 foot-pounds as against an even 800 for the 20. Certainly, no bird under the size of a Piper Cub can be hit with anything more than a small fraction of the total pellets. But each shot that does hit from the 12 will have the additional advantage of greater tissue shock, penetration, and bone-breaking potential due to its higher retained energy and velocity. This means more dead birds at any given practical range.

A great deal of the upland shooting I have done was conducted in areas of heavy cover where a considerable portion of the shot charge may be intercepted by intervening brush or trees. In this type of gunning, the 12-gauge, with more pellets and greater energy, has a much better chance of penetrating openings and breaking through light brush to score than does the 20-gauge.

When I first began to hunt seriously, I had trouble with close-lying birds such as woodcock, often shredding them just off the muzzle in a fit of overkeyed reflexes. I thought the 20 would prevent that problem, being a much lighter shell, but I was mistaken. Any shotgun charge, particularly with the new shot collars that reduce deformities and "fliers," is in all practicality a solid projectile until it has had ten or fifteen yards to start opening up.

I had a practical demonstration of the close-range destructive power of the shotgun in 1970 in Africa. Hunting francolin alone one afternoon, I bumped into a lioness with the broken strands of a poacher's wire snare deeply imbedded in her right foreleg. I was carrying a 20-gauge over/under stuffed with field-load No. 8 shot. About the time she had decided I could do with a little redecoration, I pasted her with the lower barrel at about four feet, full in the face. Her momentum knocked me down, but there was no need whatever for the second barrel.

Many of the hunters who complain about the "over-power" of the 12 at close ranges tote guns with tighter chokes than the Boston Strangler. If you're exploding birds past fifteen yards or so, I'll wager you are over-choked rather than over-gunned. If you do carry a full-choke gun in the uplands, remember your pattern with either the 20- or the 12-bore is only fifteen inches in diameter at twenty yards, and still but twenty-three inches at thirty yards. With that overconcentration of shot, you'll either miss your bird completely or blow him into peanut butter. In a situation of very close ranges, such as found with woodcock in very heavy cover, a good solution may be to make your first shell a brush load or "spreader" load, designed to open the pattern at closer ranges than with conventional shells. Try patterning a few with your gun and see how your particular barrel handles them. But, no matter how you look at it, upland gunning is a game for the improved-modified gun at most.

Most recently manufactured 20-gauges sport three-inch chambers to accommodate the new magnum shell of that size. Throwing 1¼ ounces of shot, this round is the basis of many shooters' contention that, because of the equal weight of shot, the 20 can do anything in upland gunning the 12 can do. *Theoretically,* with the three-inch shell it can. Actually, no way. It's not illogical to conclude that a charge of shot fired from a barrel of .615 diameter is going to behave differently from a load of the same size and weight from a barrel of .729, given equal relative choking. The 20 just doesn't handle the heavy load through the smaller barrel as well as does the 12. Take a sheet of wrapping paper out behind the barn and try it yourself. The density will be spotty and badly distributed. After all, what's the point of the three-inch magnum in the 20 anyway? If you want 12-gauge performance, then for heaven's sake shoot a 12!

About the last-ditch defense of the 20-gauge rests on the concept of its being lighter, and therefore faster on target. The 20 makes up in speed of handling what it gives away in range, cry the defenders of the faith. Thirty years ago, that might have been a hard point to argue. No more. With the development of space-age alloys, you can now take your pick from a tremendous selection of 12s that are within a very few ounces of the 20s—six pounds and change. My personal preference is to stay away from the ultralight irons for two reasons: First, excess recoil makes it tougher to get on target for your second shot and, second, the heavier guns seem to give me better follow-through when swinging on an angle shot.

Tell you what. If you still believe the 20 can do the job of a 12 in upland gunning, do me a favor. Take two boxes of shells for each gauge and head on down to your local trap club. Presuming you don't wander around in the field with your gun mounted, call for your birds from the sixteen-yard line in any style you normally use when expecting a flush. If you break as many birds with the 20 as you do with the 12, then please drop me a note. I'd certainly like to be your manager.

SHOTGUN PELLETS: IS BIGGER BETTER?

GUNS & AMMO ANNUAL—
1980

Canada goose.

AUTHOR'S INTRODUCTION

If I accumulated a good deal of questioning mail for my treatment of the Vlackfontein baboons, then this chapter brought even more of the letters I like to get. People all over the world, given the international nature of the Guns & Ammo Annual, *tried the concept I suggest here and they found that it worked, at least to their satisfaction.*

As I type this, this chapter is almost nine years old, but I had a chat only a few months ago with Gary Haselau, a seasoned professional hunter who, among other things, runs a large bird-shooting operation in southern Africa. One of his biggest offerings is shooting for Egyptian geese and those modern pterodactyls, the spur-winged goose.

At a professional hunters' convention last year in the Republic of Bophuthatswana, Gary told me that for the first couple of years he had started clients off with shot sizes No. 2 and 4, but was most disappointed at how many hard-hit birds were lost. Eventually he read this article and shifted to shot sizes No. 6 and 7½. He figured his bag of retrieved birds jumped up by about 35 percent. In a commercial operation, that is not small potatoes.

When I went looking for this particular article, it had simply vanished. One call to Gary at his home near Cape Town, and a copy was in the mail. He had kept it handy for reference purposes over the years. My thanks to you, Gary.

The way I see it, shooting is experience converted into learning. Well, here is something I have learned. Try it.

It was late on a golden, New Brunswick afternoon, the cooling September sun yet a hand's breadth above the last of the balding alders, the little bitch setter casting closely at the hand signals of Charlie, my guide. It would have been a great day even without what happened a few minutes later. Already we had found three grouse fumble-winged enough to blunder into the pattern of the delicate 20-bore, and Charlie's dark stained shoulder bag carried but one short of a woodcock limit. We had hunted easily since early morning, stopping for a lunch of willowspeared tube steaks with toasted buns and a short snooze, then, after combing some swales, had entered the last cover of the day, near a large, marshy flowage. It was then we heard it, that unique wilderness sound that stirs the stomach with its mixture of wild loneliness and excitement the same way a distant train whistle cuts into your thoughts late on a rainy night. It was the honk and gabble of Canada geese lifting off the flowage, five hundred yards away.

We listened for nearly a minute, savoring, almost tasting the sound when it suddenly struck us that it was growing louder! Through the tops of the snaggled low trees, dark shapes could be seen wheeling, forming, then straightening out into a great vee pointed directly at our piece of cover. Clearly, they meant to pass over us in easy range. I was very young in those days and might be forgiven the near coronary occlusion caused by the disappointment of standing smack in the path of my first flight of honkers, trembling hands clutching only a Browning Lightning Model 20-gauge, choked (for godsake) skeet one and two, each chamber loaded with seven-eighths of an ounce of No. 9 shot, an extra pair of shells customarily stuck between the fingers of my left hand. I had read enough about the legendary pellet resistance of the Great Birds (". . . the shot rattled off their wings like hail . . .") to know that my minimum armament should be a punt gun stuffed with a couple of pounds of old tire weights or, at the very least, a 10-gauge 3½-inch magnum belching a shot-put equivalent weight of BBs, even to have a chance of getting their direct attention. Nonetheless, I wasn't *about* to pass up a crack at one of these trophy birds, even if I was only packing a slingshot and a box of stale marshmallows.

"Shoot for the head and neck," whispered Charlie from his nearby crouch as the gaggle was about to break over our cover. "Pretend the head's a woodcock." I swung the twenty smoothly ahead of the nearest bird, concentrating on what I imagined I could see as his bright, brown eye, taking him early so I could stick him again a couple of times before he passed out of range. At my shot, only he could have been more surprised than I when, without a twitch, he just folded his wings and fell like a feathered bomber, actually forcing me to dodge him. Automatically, I touched off the top barrel at the next goose and he also spun to thump the soggy woodcock cover like he'd caught a direct hit from an 88-mm in the cockpit.

To date, nobody has ever remotely intimated that I am one of the world's better shotgunners, and, judging by recent activities, they aren't likely to fire up such a rumor. However, I had the ejectors working overtime that afternoon and two more shells chambered before the main flight was much more than just past overhead. Keeping my lead well out front at about forty yards, the same thing happened again as a second pair pitched downward, dead as virginity, tearing through the alders like pterodactyls to hit the ground. If I didn't wet my pants, it was close. I felt as if I'd just doubled on Siberian snow tigers with a fifty-five-inch-spread Cape buffalo thrown in. My wife, I believe, would describe the sensation in terms of having just come into some mind-boggling quantity of Green Stamps.

Okay, easy now. I know. Just lie back and breathe deeply. When you finally thought it was safe to switch back to *G&A* from *Better Homes and Gardens,* where at least you didn't have to put up with that triple-name screwball who kept telling you that solid bullets are better than soft points, that there is no such animal as hydrostatic shock, and that BB guns are really zowie good fun, now, just when you've been lulled into a cozy sense of false security, he's back! And crazier than ever! Great balls of chilled shot! He's saying that you should go goose hunting with skeet-bored 20-gauges throwing No. 9s! Now, now. Calm down. That's it, wipe the foam off your chin and put your feet back up, because we're going to try to take a nice, logical approach to one of the most interesting aspects of shotgunning, that little beauty being shot-size selection for the gamut of the feathered clans. (Unless, of course, you would rather discuss redheads, and I do not mean ducks. All mail answered in plain, brown envelopes.)

Aside from the time I spend in the hot sun, lashed by my wife with wet rawhide to the Coronamatic, custom-mixing metaphors and generally over-hyphenating for fun and profit, the vast majority of my business and private life has been spent somewhere between toting a Daisy Red Ryder carbine in New Jersey, to a double .470 Nitro in Zambia, Ethiopia, or Botswana, or a MAC-10 in Rhodesia. (While on the subject of my African career, I wish to state once and forever that what you have heard about me and that lady warthog has absolutely no basis in fact.)

However, despite that portion of my life spent professionally perforating elephants and other large, unsanitary fauna, my true love is shotgunning and I daresay that for every rifle cartridge primer I have popped, there is probably a full box of shotshells to match it. (That, for you students of the idiom, is a partially mixed metaphor with topspin.) I have had the great good fortune to have hunted birds of every size from the nyandu ostrich of Patagonia and his African cousin to hummingbirds (in the Amazon Basin) for museums, literally covering from Tierra del Fuego to Caithness, the northern tip of Scotland, and back down the European Continent; field testing for major arms manufacturers, from thrushes in Portugal, snipe in Morocco, and so on, all the way to South Africa. So far as I know, I've taken all of Europe's legal game birds including the auerhahn, and while I've not yet grand-slammed Africa's feathered friends, those left on the list are getting mighty lonely. The point of all this reflexive chest-beating is that I have had a pretty fair opportunity to observe on an extended firsthand basis the relative effect at reasonable ranges of different sizes of shot pellets on a wide variety of birds under an even wider variety of hunting conditions. One simply cannot do all this shooting without a few numerically rein- forced conclusions looming up against what one always pre- sumed was clearly and simply "foregone." As seems to be a continuing thesis with this, Yr. Obt. Svt., many of my practical observations just don't cut it with the standard, "generally ac- cepted" recommendations frequently proposed by various shotshell manufacturers as to what shot size to use for what species under what circumstances. The first light of pure heresy began to dawn after what I presumed was the "freak" quadruple with geese so many years ago in New Brunswick. Trouble is, it has been reinforcing itself with regularity ever since.

When I first started hunting with my father and brother at about age twelve, I was, as to be expected, impressed with the seemingly glaring fact that since bigger pellets hit harder and retain energy and velocity farther out than do smaller ones, clearly I should be shooting the hardest-hitting, biggest pellets I could get my hands on—within juvenile reason, of course, or I would have been shooting rifled slugs at rabbits. I have many times heard the standard dictum that on average, it takes five No. 4 pellets to kill a mallard duck at forty yards. As I grew older—and if not smarter, more curious—I started to wonder about this pellet-energy-equals-dead-duck routine. Didn't it in fact *really* matter where anatomically that mallard was hit rather than how many times obliquely in the fantail? Wouldn't a shot or two in the head or neck be worth darn near any amount of lead in non-crippling or meaty areas, I wondered? As the duck stamps rolled by each fall, it bothered me to see birds flinch in midair as they were body-hit, and big blacks and mallards hunch up to keep going out of reach if not sight. Except for birds killed at thirty yards or less, it came to me more and more clearly that really dead birds at fifty-five or so yards were all head or neck kills or collected by being crippled by broken wings. Sure, some had the bad luck to wander into a sizable chunk of the pattern of No. 4s and died instantly of body wounds, but not enough to convince me that the rela- tionship between shot size and decreasing pattern density as pellets got bigger and lesser in number was valid. I count a hit but uncollected bird against my limit, a tenet of sportsmanship Dad always drilled into me, so I determined to find out over the ensuing years, at least to my satisfaction, whether the answer was individual pellet penetration and energy or the mathematical odds of killing more birds by having more (but smaller) pellets in the kill zone, increasing the likelihood of a couple of instantly fatal strikes. I am now convinced that the latter will put more game in your bag.

I had better start apologizing to Elmer Keith, who I've got a niggling hunch isn't going to like this one bit. Elmer, as we all know so well, believes that if you're fixin' to put a hole in something, then, Pardner, make it a hole to remember! I very much agree with the Keithian Hypothesis as far as it concerns handguns and rifles, however, his hailing of No. 3 shot as The Answer in 10-gauge is out Elmer-Keithing Elmer Keith. Okay, Elmer, maybe No. 2s or even No. 4s. That's your opinion. *But No. 3s?* That's lily-gilding. (The reader will perceive that I am well out of rifle shot of Salmon, Idaho.)

Rather than simply sucker-punch you flat out with the latest heresy, let's just sneak up on what, after all the stables are cleansed, is the basic precept of shotgunning. Except for you, me, and a couple of other guys who are either dead or retired, most shooters just aren't good enough to hit a flying target with a single projectile frequently enough to rule out starvation, which is very negative to anybody's genetic advancement. By my research, the whole thing started off on September 31, several thousand years ago, when a shepherd by the name of Ralph, who found himself with a lot of time on his hands between Philistines, figured out that if he stuck two stones in the pouch of his sling he would have twice the chance of acquiring some Palestinian fried chicken on the wing than with one rock. Considering that this was before the hand-held calculator, it wasn't all that unimpressive a chunk of logic, either, Ralph finally got stuck at twenty, never having been especially swift at calculating cubits, spans, shekels, and the like. Besides, he ran out of fingers and toes. Yet he was smart enough to have his brother-in-law incorporate the Middle East

Multiple Projectile Sling Company (Pvt.) Ltd., which eventually proved that capitalism will yet out by diversifying itself into (under the Sherman Anti-Trust Act) what we now know as Winchester, Remington, Federal, and several other foreign subsidiaries including Browning and Beretta. Although these descendants of the M.E.M.P.S.C. (Pvt.) Ltd. have refined the basic product considerably, the principle of the concept hasn't changed one iota: the greater the amount of potentially lethal matter you can place at reasonable velocities in the immediate vicinity of your flying target, the better the odds are that he will collide with sufficient amounts of this matter to place him on the casualty list.

You will, by referring to the November 1976 issue of *Guns & Ammo*—enshrined, of course, in the timeless embrace of your *G&A* Binder of that year—note that we got mildly enmeshed in the ramifications of the multiple-hit theory whilst exploring the wonderful world of buckshot, to the irrefutable conclusion that No. 1–size buckshot is practically 75 percent more effective than the more traditional No. 00. That article was notable inasmuch as I received not one direct threat on my life. Maybe you only looked at the pictures?

We arrived at that conclusion based upon similar although not identical logic; that the very size of the larger No. 00 pellets and their fewer number per load, despite their slightly heavier individual weight, actually got in their own way. The load of No. 1 buck delivered far more pellets into the kill-zone of a deer at only a small fraction of individual pellet energy/efficiency loss. When the argument encompasses No. 2s or No. 4s versus No. 7½ or No. 9s, the premise of validity is more one of numerical superiority and kill-zone saturation, ensuring pellets striking immediately fatal organs if for no other reason than that there are so bloody many of them.

What I have been easing up to is that, despite what may be considered to be "traditional" shot sizes recommended for different birds, don't forget that the Acme Ammo Company had somebody in the Public Relations Department write them up and they may not necessarily be any more valid than the opinions of anybody else. The so-called "game-labeled" shotshells we see offered now are not under all conditions the best load for the bird described, at least not necessarily. This new packaging concept is a marketing ploy, which, if not only solving a lot of questions for inexperienced shooters, sure sells a lot of shotshells.

I have noticed that practically any "guide" I have seen published as to suggested shot sizes generally proclaims that something between No. 2s and No. 6s are the best medicine for ducks, and either BB, No. 2, No. 4 (what happened to Elmer's No. 3s?) or No. 5 for geese. This is rather like declaring that it will rain unless it doesn't. It is my experience that, with the possible exception of No. 6s for shooting big, passing ducks or geese, these sizes are much less effective than the smaller sizes, most of which aren't offered in high brass loads smaller than No. 7½ shot.

The shooter will, as a general rule, remembering that all shotgunning is centered around the laws of mathematical probability, have less cripples and fewer hit and lost birds with smaller pellets than with larger ones, provided the pellet employed is not so small as to be incapable of damage upon contact with a fatal organ. By this, I suggest that you could probably bounce four or five No. 11 pellets off a big honker's skull with no effect at fifty yards, but a single No. 7½ shot in the noggin or one or two in the neck would probably prove sufficient to kill. I mention the No. 7½ as I've had several go right through a canvas hunting coat, my shirts, skin, and enough meat to require considerable probing at just about this range. But, that's another story.

Point is, unlike the rose, a duck is not a duck is not a duck. A duck, or any other game bird for that matter, is composed of *parts* of a duck, some of which are vulnerable to even single pellet hits at sporting ranges, while other body areas can absorb the heaviest pellets without any appreciable immediate or even later effect. Ask any wildfowl field biologist what percentage of birds old enough to have made at least one migration are carrying pellets clearly visible through a fluoroscope, and he'll tell you the numbers are amazing. And, remember, he doesn't get many chances to inspect birds that didn't survive their wounds.

Shortly after Oliver Cromwell left the area, I was slogging

through a snipe marsh with Ed Zern, the great humorist, just outside Galway, Ireland, when off in the distance, I noticed a pair of ducks drop into a hidden culvert in the peat. I swapped the No. 9s in my 12-gauge over/under Beretta for a pair of high-brass No. 4s kept for such opportunities, and started after them. Easing up with the stealth of a stone-drunk mastodon, I was only able to get within forty yards before the birds, green-wing teal, jumped. I took a whack at each one in turn and was convinced I had probably under-held, as both continued on across the bog, hot on the process of making us eligible for long-distance rates. However, at about a half-mile, they banked into the piranha-toothed wind and headed back in our direction. We crouched down in hope we might get another crack at them when, at seventy yards, just as if somebody had pulled the plug, they *both* dropped dead at the exact same instant! Upon examination, I found that one was body-hit with three pellets, the other with four. They had travelled about a mile round-trip and it had taken all that time and distance for the effects to become, shall we say, permanent, and had they not come back our way they would have been food for foxes and we would have never known it. Had I kept the loads of No. 9s chambered, the much greater pattern density would almost surely have guaranteed a multiple head or neck hit, killing both instantly—and not just because they were small ducks.

Is that a pretty wild presumption? I don't think so, especially when one considers that there are only 135 No. 4 pellets per ounce whereas there are a spooky 585 nasty little lead spheres in an ounce of No. 9s. Therefore, on a weight/number basis, the odds of hitting a fatal spot are a genuine 4⅓ *times* better with the smaller shot than the larger! Okay, even if the No. 9 load was packing only an ounce and the No. 4 shell 1¼ ounces, the difference is still only about thirty-four more pellets, still leaving the smaller load an edge of an *extra* 416 pellets. You'd have to fire about three shots with the heavier load to put as many pellets in the air as one load of an ounce of No. 9s.

I will be the first to grant you that smaller pellets don't

have the individual impact at sixty yards that larger ones do, because of their lesser weight, and therefore lesser retained velocity and energy, but if you're shooting at ducks at sixty yards even with No. 2s, your *relative* pattern density will be so poor as to be flirting with unsportsmanlike conduct. Sure, you'll scratch down just enough to keep trying it, but it's for damned certain it won't help the waterfowl population much, let alone the tempers of the guys down in the next blind, and they may advise you of such sentiment. . . .

There's a little get-together every autumn in Amwell, New Jersey, which, so far as I know, is still a very good location to test your liver and digestive tract, modestly called the Duck Shooting Championship of America. Or maybe it's the World. I should remember because I came in second or third years ago, but at any rate, it's a very enjoyable and challenging shoot. One had twelve shells and six pairs of corn-fed flighted mallards, but the one thing I did carry away from such excuses to mingle with people who lie even better than I was the fact that I do not recall an exception where the winner did not use No. 8 or No. 9 shot on his birds, some of which were plenty bloody long shots. I promise you, especially if you were so unfortunate as to draw a local newspaper cameraman, usually a victim of St. Vitus' Dance, wearing a horse-blanket jacket and sitting in the open in front of your blind. Such gentlefolk do not tend to draw ducks to the decoys like flies to a dead horse. As best as I recall, the most frequent winner was the great Paul Whiteman, who swung a scattergun as well as he led a band. He wouldn't dream of using anything but No. 9s.

Same went for my old tarpon-fishing and duck-shooting pal, professional Everglades guide Ray Bradley. One of the better wingshots I have known. Ray favored a hand-loaded brute of a 12-gauge load of 1⅜ ounces of No. 9s in a three-inch Magnum Remington 1100, full choke. Brother, if he was remotely "on" a bird it went no place but straight down, even the toughest Florida mallard.

If you think back, you have probably seen the principle illustrated yourself. Have you ever, when without a retriever, had to surface-shoot a crippled duck with No. 4? I know I've sometimes had to waste three or four shells before lucking into a head/neck hit with the big pellets. The load of No. 4s looks like a mild hailstorm around the bird, but one of the half-dozen trap or skeet loads I carry when ducking just for such circumstances puts the crippled bird in the center of an explosion of water that looks like a Cape Horn squall. Thinking about it, I can recall only twice I have had to fire at a wounded bird with No. 8 or No. 9 without having it turn turtle on the first shot.

A pal here in Florida, one of the better local turkey hunters, uses only high-brass No. 7½ shot on his toms and claims to have been charged only once, although he lost his nerve on that occasion and was severely gobbled. When you consider that the head and neck of a bull turkey are as large in mass as a teal and probably twice that of a defeathered woodcock, you can see why he shoots only for these zones. He is very well known for never having done business with the Swifts Premium Butterball boys.

I'd purely love to get into upland game and the application of the smaller-pellet theory in this article, but that'll have to wait until they start paying me by the word. I will say, however, that an old, onetime market hunter who surely is now hunting around the bend, by the name of "Uncle" Hiler, insisted that there was nothing so potent in the upland tangles than—if you're ready for this—No. 12s, or, as they are also called, "dust." "Uncle," who spoke both grouse and woodcock fluently and had been known to drum on hollow logs during spring full moons, may have been taking the theory a bit too far, but it was mighty seldom during the season that there weren't a couple of grouse and woodcock limits aging on thongs hung from his rickety porch.

The table below represents purely my own choices, after much of an economy-sized life shooting a wide variety of game birds. Perhaps the best summation of the concept would be in application to one of the toughest and wiliest of all game birds, the African guinea fowl, of which I have hunted several varieties from Ethiopia to South Africa. Pheasant-like birds of steel constitution, I know of no other, pound for pound, capable of the

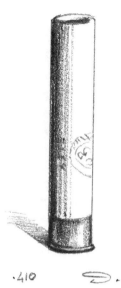

.410

.410 shotgun shell.

punishment his clan can take. Since they are practically the staff of life as a trade-off from buffalo or venison after six months in the bush, it's safe to say I've shot one hell of a lot of guinea fowl. When you carry a rifle in your hand all day, every day, you're bound to gain a reasonable proficiency, to the extent that when I didn't want to use the shotgun because of noise, I have hit flying guinea fowl as many as four times, all solid body hits, with a .22 long rifle and not had them fall. Yet, with anything between No. 7½ and No. 9 shot, a flushed bird within range is as good as dead from head and neck wounds.

TABLE OF SUGGESTED SHOT SIZES, PRESUMING 12-GAUGE DOUBLE BARREL OR REPEATING GUN

Species	First or Open Barrel	Second Barrel*
Ducks or geese over decoys	#8, 9	#7½, 8
Ducks or geese pass shooting	#7½	#6, 7½
Ruffed Grouse	#8, 9	#7½, 8
Doves	#9	#9
Woodcock	#9	#9

Species	First or Open Barrel	Second Barrel*
Pheasant	#8	#7½, 8
Turkey	#7½	#7½, 6
Crow	#9	#9, 8
Rail	#9	#9
Quail	#9	#9, 8
Chukar	#9, 8	#7½, 8
Rabbit or squirrel	#7½, 8	#7½, 6

*Same shot size should be used for third shot of single-barrel repeating gun.

TABLE OF SHOT SIZES FROM BB TO #12											
NUMBER	12	11	10	9	8	7½	6	5	4	2	BB
DIAMETER IN INCHES	.05	.06	.07	.08	.09	.095	.11	.12	.13	.15	.18
PELLETS PER OUNCE	2,385	1,380	870	585	410	350	225	170	135	90	50

AIRBOATING
FOR FLORIDA
QUACKERS

PETERSEN'S HUNTING—
AUGUST 1975

Hunting ducks from an airboat in the Florida Everglades.

AUTHOR'S INTRODUCTION

I guess practically every American state has something special to offer the sportsman, but few have the variety of exotic areas that Florida has. I had no idea when I wrote this article that it would be selected as Petersen's Hunting Trip of the Month. I guess it was a pretty good choice.

This was the first time I had gone a-ducking in Florida, and the change from chilblains to cattails certainly lent a different flavor to the proceedings. Of course, the great Everglades were spooky and enticing at the same time, but I had had no idea, even after six years' residence, that the shooting was anything like that which we experienced that great morning.

It is with deep regret that I must tell you that this was one of Ray Bradley's last trips. He was killed shortly thereafter in a highway mishap. I never went back to shoot teal where we had been; it just wouldn't have been the same without either the bellow of his laugh or the roar of the particular airboat. I have missed those days with Ray. Very much.

T he roar of the aircraft engine ruptured the predawn still like a squadron of Sopwith Camels on the Western Front. I gripped the back of Ray's seat, feeling the slickness of mist on the cool metal, a thin ground fog that gleamed and glittered like tiny snowflakes in the hard beam of his miner's lamp. With a touch of throttle, our craft began to move wraithlike down the corridor of blackness, the chest-cold cough of the motor growing into the deep purr of a pride of well-fed sabre-toothed tigers. Ahead, transfixed like mounted butterflies in the penetrating spike of light, thousands of mullet shattered the surface, showering diamonds against the velvet of the dark swamp. Four bright spots caught in the beam, glowing like red campfire embers, ten feet off the port bow. "'Gators," shouted Ray Bradley over the snarl of the engine. "That one on the left will go better than twelve, maybe thirteen feet!" I gripped the steel tubing of the seat a little tighter.

We thrummed on for another half hour, now out of the channel and on the vast saw-grass flats where the water lay over soft muck like a thin layer of lucite. We ducked under the big, black and yellow spiders cleaning their webs for another day of business and pointed together at the wakes of heavy-shouldered snook arrowing away from the boat.

Twice, raccoons stared incredulously as we passed, and a hunting otter slipped into a pool with a movement as smooth as twenty-five-year-old Scotch. I felt as if someone would soon ask me for my ticket. Disney never dreamed up anything as fascinating as the Everglades at 5:00 A.M.

The thinnest threat of false dawn was basting in its own juices somewhere over Miami when Ray's headlamp picked out the shaggy, waxy looming of mangroves ahead. A few short blasts of power pushed us over the spine of a dry mud flat and into the protected, lagoon-like expanse of water inside. It was a natural amphitheater, almost a perfect circle of heavy mangroves gripping the little pond in a high, Tiffany setting. I caught the flicker of movement in the light as fifty blue-winged teal bounced through the beam and away. Ray looked at me from under his hard hat and nodded. Dis was de place.

Bradley throttled back the airboat and swung it about as I unwrapped the short lengths of brown-dyed anchor cords and placed the decoys, a set of thirty mixed blacks and mallards, at the end of a channel between two clumps of mangrove bigger than duplexes. Before he flicked off the lamp, I opened a box of 8s for the Winchester Model 12 and screwed the Polychoke to the modified setting. I fed one of the red rounds into the chamber after checking the safety, then stuffed two more into the magazine. Ray struggled to outsmart the fastener on the coffee container, succeeded, and passed me a steaming mug. In the twenty minutes until shooting time, we drank the java and listened to the bellow of bull 'gators, the watery swirls of gar, and the croaks, squawks, rattles, screeches, and other verbal outcries of the thousands of herons, egrets, and assorted water birds of the great Everglades Swamp.

Dawn was through fooling around when Ray checked his watch and shucked three rounds into his Browning Auto. He had almost finished saying, "Let's open for business," when, with a hiss like a broadside of hot cannonballs, six teal materialized ten yards away, almost parting our hair as they power-climbed off the dark water and evaporated against the gloomy blobs of mangrove. There were no shots fired. Twice more, before it was light enough to pick out incomers against the background, scattered groups of bluewings scorched over and past us. With the mangroves blocking our view for more than fifty yards, they were on us and away before we had a chance to react, but after twenty minutes, the sky had brightened enough for us to spot a foursome barreling in from our left rear and swinging over the decoys. I heard Ray fire and saw the lead drake collapse, arching in a long slant to throw a plume of water on impact. I swung ahead of another drake and touched off, the rose of the muzzle-blast still visible in the half-light. Nothing. At all. Swinging the muzzle six city blocks ahead of his rapidly receding bill, I saw him stagger, then regain his balance, hurtling on. By the time the third shell was chambered, he was eighty yards out.

"Watch him, Pedro, watch him!" Ray whispered. "He's body-hit, but hard." As we followed the diminishing speck down the neck of water with bloodshot eyes, he suddenly folded and dropped from the early sky like a baked potato. I marked him down and we decided not to pick him up just then, while the action was hot. Seven more came in from behind us, but hung wide until a double broke off and came over to see about our open-house breakfast invitation. Ray dusted the first in a burst of feathers while I whipped the water with frothy strings of eights just past the fuselage of another until the third shot, when he was the apparent victim of coronary occlusion brought on by an excess of mirth at my marksmanship. I couldn't believe how much lead these birds required until Ray explained that, although we were sheltered by the mangrove circle, there was actually a fair breeze blowing up where they were flying and, brother, none of it was going to waste in terms of airspeed! I saw what Ray had been getting at when he had suggested I bring at least three boxes of shells, although over the telephone that night I thought he'd been into the vanilla extract.

As the sun cleared the furry edge of the horizon through the dishpan fingers of red mangrove, there was a lull. I lit a cigarette and watched the fighter groups of yellow-legs wheel, just for the pure hell of being alive. Ranks of white egrets flew in close-order precision just over us, and a pair of Louisiana herons tried to scream each other out of a particularly succulent minnow. Cobalt kingfishers reflected the early, low-angle sun and chittered their full-mouthed triumph back to their snaggled perches. I remembered the twenty years of northern duck shooting, the partial death by exposure that had always been part of a good duck morning, the ice water soaking through the new nick in your waders, crawling into the three layers of lumberjack socks, until your feet were colder than your wooden hands and ears. The screaming northeasters at the Jersey shore and the crunching tinkle of hoarfrost and skim ice on the little Connecticut ponds seemed a world away from this paradise.

I live in Naples, a smallish town with advancing symptoms of Condominiumitis, located right on the Gulf of Mexico about two hours from Miami, via either the newer Alligator Alley (U.S. Route 84) or the older Tamiami Trail, U.S. Route 41. Ray Bradley, born in Key West, was already a famous fishing guide before he moved years ago to the little village of Goodland, in the Ten Thousand Islands at the mouth of the Everglades. Bradley chose Goodland because, when winter water conditions slow down the tarpon and snook fishing, there is always great gunning only a few miles over the sawgrass to take its place. Ray got his first airboat more than a decade back and has been probing the deep 'Glades in subsequent models ever since, getting his clients back into the virgin waters where wintering ducks congregate thicker than mosquitoes at a nudist convention.

Airboats are really incredible contraptions, particularly to someone like me who never even learned to handle my Tinkertoys. Lots of roadside docks, mostly operated by Seminoles, offer ten- or fifteen-minute rides all along the Tamiami Trail between Miami and Naples, but fun as they are, there is no experience like getting out into the really thick stuff in a smaller hunting model such as Ray uses. The thrust of its twin-bladed-prop aircraft engine can push the flat-bottomed hull at incredible speeds even along dry ground, although I suspect that handling one with the confidence of a pro like Bradley is a lot trickier than it looks.

One would think that airboats were fairly simple affairs and would require rather little maintenance. Not so, says Bradley. Twice this season he's had decoys sucked under the prop guard and through the blades, necessitating the purchase of $414 worth of new blades. You can't buy a new prop a dozen or so miles out in one of the world's largest swamps, either.

Florida ducking depends to some degree upon the severity of the northern winter to push birds farther south. There is a fair population of birds all year long, but shooting is only at its best when there have been some cold snaps in the northern part of the flyway to stimulate migration, both of waterfowl and tourists. Teal always seem to be around, though, the point count of the species being low because of the immensity of the Everglades and the fact that few hunters have airboats. Ray Bradley, whom you can book by writing or calling him at Goodland Avenue, Goodland, FL 33933, also offers fine shooting for the bigger ducks: mallards, blacks, pintails, and many other of the puddle ducks of the Atlantic Flyway. The only problem I see is that you've usually shot yourself out of business before the sun clears the horizon, with the higher points charged against a daily limit of the larger ducks.

Without an airboat or swamp buggy, you had best forget about hunting the Everglades on your own. There's plenty to the old folk song that goes, "If the skeeters don't gitcha then the 'gators will." After only a few minutes with an experienced guide like Bradley, you'll appreciate just why they don't bother to chain convicts repairing the Tamiami Trail along the Everglades.

A nudge from Ray interrupted my reverie as a tremendous white-and-brown bald eagle stooped on a mullet-laden osprey, bluffing the hawk out of his breakfast, which the eagle snagged ten feet off the surface of the pond. I snuffed out my smoke and was about to say something to Ray when the flicker of wings caught my eye past his back. "Mark!" I hissed, and Ray froze into a lump of whatever camouflage is supposed to make you look like. From under the brim of my hat I followed them as they swung around, just thirty yards out, headed straight at us as if they wanted to share the coffee. "Now," I said, wheeling to fire.

Ray instantly called, "Hold it! Greenwings. Let's save our limit for the ten-pointers." The little greenies strafed the decoys and flitted over the mangrove barrier. I almost fell out of the airboat as Ray's favorite teal load of 9s pushed by four— you got it, four—drams equivalent of powder boomed unexpectedly right next to me. A single bluewing hen lay feet-up at the edge of the blocks, a bullseye of widening rings stretching away from her.

"Bingo!" I said with a tip of my cap. "Where did *she* come from?"

"Right down the middle, out front," he answered, thumbing a fresh shell into the Browning's pantry. "In fact, me bucko, here come four more. You take the left and I'll cover the right." I watched the bluewings growing bigger, until within a few seconds they were streaking flat out over the blocks. I held smack on the first one and he bounced as though he'd been belted with a jackhammer. Like grenade fragments, the rest of the flock burst upward, corkscrewing and dodging in all directions. A plump drake loomed over my muzzle, and I pulled above him as he climbed. He folded like a punctured accordion. My last barrel ventilated the backwash of another drake who zigged just as I zagged, the charge missing him by four feet. From the edge of my vision I saw Ray crumple a hen, another drake already falling to the water.

I asked Bradley what our total was, and after a minute of finger-counting and general cogitation, he pronounced it to be nine. "Best pick 'em up about now, 'fore a 'gator decides he needs 'em more than we do." He cranked up the airboat engine and we started for the long bird that had fallen at the end of the lagoon. The feeling of raw power as Ray fed throttle to the airboat was incredible. The tide had been falling and we were whipping through less than two inches of water at better than fifty-five miles per hour! Bradley had told me that his airboat could top ninety, but I reckoned I didn't want to be on hand when he proved it. With all nine dead birds in the boat, we taxied back to our shooting spot and got ready to collect the remaining eleven ducks on our limits. I still couldn't get over it. On the Florida point system, we were allowed a two-gun limit of twenty blue-winged teal, a bird that, because of his great speed, erratic flight pattern, and small size but excellent eating quality, I would rather shoot than a Canada goose. I love any kind of waterfowling, but when I can take a ten-bird limit of teal against two or three larger ducks, I'll take the teal anytime.

Although it was only a few days before Christmas, the temperature was in the low 80s by 9:30 A.M. I smeared some patent gunk on my arms and face to combat sunburn, no small joke with the glare off the water. We had sixteen birds, all bluewings except for a flashy shoveler drake I wanted for my collection. Eight or ten times, fast flights of mallards and blacks came over in easy range, but we held fire. Then, a few minutes later, we were caught flat-footed by a gang of at least thirty bluewings that skimmed the tops of the mangroves we had pulled the airboat against, swishing over the decoys with that sharp, hollow sound that only comes from a teal in a hurry. Perhaps their leader was nearsighted or just lonely, because, to our surprise, the whole flight swung around like an open fan at the far edge of the mangroves and hustled back over for another look. For four of them, it was their last indiscretion. Ray and I each killed an easy—if that term ever applies to teal—double, and that, sir, was that! We were back at the launching ramp on the Tamiami Trail before ten-thirty and Ray was saying, "You know, it's still early, and I know a couple of nice pockets of baby tarpon not far from here. Wasn't that your fly rod I saw in the back of your car?"

OLDIES ARE
GOODIES

GUNS & AMMO—MARCH 1978

Firing the obsolete but effective .44-40 Winchester.

AUTHOR'S INTRODUCTION

Despite his own great reputation, you have heard from me before of Colonel Charles Askins and my admiration for his gentlemanly friendship and skill at arms. Still, Charlie and I do hold differences of opinion as to guns and cartridges.

I suppose that I am really being unfair to republish this chapter without printing Charlie's initial ideas in full. But I do think I have reduced them fairly to the point where I am not taking unfair advantage with this rebuttal.

Charlie espoused the concept that a great many older standard or even somewhat obsolete cartridges should be cleared from the dealers' shelves and the money spent producing them at least partially spent to "improve" those worth saving. Being an incurable romantic, I immediately assaulted him in print in the same way we used to punch holes in our respective waterlines on safari, late at night and over something to keep off the chills.

Anyway, between the colonel and me, it has always been the best of fun. It was, in fact, he who talked me into writing my first book. It's hard to get mad at a guy for that!

As anybody who has been there will tell you, there is no part of the safari day so purely satisfying as just after dinner. Soft African voices are overlapped by a candy-box assortment of bush critters muttering in the lowering dark about the high cost of zebra steak, and the flush of the campfire blends marvelously with the glow of the sundowner half-finished in your fly-bitten fist. But, these are really just trimmings. The real feast is the talk.

Besides women and other species of dangerous game, the conversation usually turns to my favorite: the inevitable discussion of different cartridges and calibers and how bloody awful or magically wonderful they are. Now, if you were to pick somebody to deposit in that right-hand camp chair over there for a chat of such import, who could be possibly better qualified than a second-generation outdoor writer, a world-famous champion of practically every phase of the firearm arts and one hell of a nice guy, besides? You may, therefore, appreciate a small part of the pleasure I experienced for several weeks in Rhodesia in 1975 with no less an authority than Himself, Colonel Charles Askins, Senior Technical Editor of this magazine, who might just as easily, and with as much qualification, fill any of a half-dozen editorial slots of equal swat.

As the days drifted by, I began to learn several things about Charlie. The most obvious was that he was almost supernatural in his shooting, even better with a rifle, pistol, or shotgun than people said he was. The second thing I discovered was that he and I inhabited opposite sides of the ballistic spectrum, which made our long discussions even more fun. Now, one doesn't exactly argue with a man of the mental horsepower and literally world-wide experience of a Charlie Askins any more than you argue Relativity with an Einstein. However, after reading his fascinating article in the November 1977 issue of *Guns & Ammo* titled "Current Cartridges: Progress or Put-Off?" I couldn't but suspect that there might be a few half-mummified old conservatives like me out there who would like to expound the other side of the viewpoint.

In case you were trapped in a mine disaster or held by terrorists for the month of November and didn't read the article, let me try to offer the thread of Charlie's thesis: He believes that much of the "deadwood" should be cut from the offerings of the commercial ammo makers and that those older calibers that have proved to be effective game-getters be souped-up to higher velocities despite the industry pressure standards of the Sporting Arms and Ammunition Manufacturers Institute (SAAMI), who have presumably met in dark conclave to keep the .44-40 from attaining velocities over 5,000 fps. (SAAMI's position is that, for safety, commercial ammo must be responsibly loaded with pressures safe enough for older or weaker actions in which the round might be fired.)

Charlie further propounds that the funds theoretically saved from production of "obsolete" or ineffective cartridges could then be put into the improvement of existing "proven" cartridges or the development of new, even faster ones. Obviously this is an immense and admittedly slanted simplification of a three-thousand-word article and it's only fair that you go to your *Guns & Ammo* magazine binders—you know, the ones with the simulated leather and gold-embossed title on the cover and spine, right there on the shelf next to the Bible—and read Charlie's piece carefully.

Now, it seems to me that we're going to need somebody to moderate this discussion and keep Charlie from placing a big, blue-edged hole slightly north of my solar plexus, so pull up that canvas chair there, the one with the centipede curled in the seat, pour yourself something for the chill, and join us, *bwana.*

Perhaps you, like me, were interested in Charlie's observations of the .30-06 and .270 Winchester typifying the dreadful lack of ballistic improvement over the years in this country and therefore, by some captivating logic, the total lack of interest the arms manufacturers have in the American shooting man. His prime example is that the 150-grain, .30-06 bullet has only increased in muzzle velocity by 150 fps since Townsend Whelan used it in 1915; from 2,750 to 2,900 fps. (Actually, it has increased in factory standard loads to 2,970 fps, a matter of 220 fps. But never mind.) Even more insultingly, the .270 Winchester 130-grain bullet hasn't added one lousy inch-per-second since 1925 until the present, still crawling along at a disgraceful 3,140 fps muzzle velocity in factory loads. That's unpatriotic!

If you would please ask Charlie to keep his hands where I can see them, I wish to comment that this reasoning is based upon the premise that no matter how fast a bullet is going, if you can get it to go faster, it'll be a "better" bullet. Okay, fair enough. Classically, this is the greatest rift in the camps of ballisticians, professional or amateur. I squat proudly on the negative side of this hypothesis by reason of experience and observation. Much more germane, however, is the *fact* that even though the 150-grain, factory-loaded .30-06 round has not matured to a muzzle velocity of 6,000 fps or more by mere reason of its septuagenarian age, it is still one of the overwhelming favorites of American hunters and shooters and is damned likely to stay there. The reason that the .30-06 and the .270 haven't significantly increased in the foot-second department is the most obvious and simplest of all: they haven't had to. Both calibers are already more than adequate at their current loadings for virtually any task to which they might be reasonably put, and sales prove this to be so. Both are deadly, accurate, reliable, and flexible in a large variety of commercial bullet types. After all, if a cartridge is doing a superb job already, even though the loading may be ancient, why sacrifice the low recoil and fine field performance for a couple of hundred fps? I find the concept of the supposed "improvement" of the .30-06 or .270 Winchester rather like discovering the True Cross and then having it refinished.

An even more convincing argument against the Askinian Hypothesis is that of the .30-30 Winchester, which is about as ballistically stimulating as a dud firecracker. Yet it survives and even thrives because it does what it's supposed to do: kill deer, black bear, and other medium-sized game at reasonable, timber-country ranges. Death does not come in degrees. If a bullet does the job, why bother to crank it up higher than necessary with the resultant penalties of high pressures? If you don't go along with this, go buy a .338 Winchester Magnum, or—why fool around?—if you really want velocity and foot-pounds, Mr. Weatherby would be delighted to sell you one of his lovely .460s. (Please tell him *G&A* sent you.) Just leave the rest of us with our '94 Winchesters and our Remington '06s. I see you're a little low there, *bwana.* Pour yourself another. Me? Sure, I will, why not?

As far as the cartridge manufacturers in SAAMI are concerned, I, for one, thank God that they so well illustrate the principle of self-regulation of a mature and responsible industry. Can you imagine the results of a "velocity war" in which one would try to outdo the others by offering hotter loads of standard cartridges? Improving the .22 long rifle round is quite different from jacking up the .30-30. The SAAMI contention that factory loads must be safe enough for use in older or weaker actions is, to my devious way of thinking, one hell of a good insurance policy that you or I won't have to be separated from our older guns one day with an acetylene torch.

There may be another factor concerning the cartridge manufacturers that Charlie has overlooked: they are corporations and marketing organizations completely committed to that beautiful capitalist concept called profit. If they felt there was a valid need and a market for offering a cartridge based upon necking down a 40-mm Bofors case to accept a phonograph needle, you can bet the alimony installment they'd have it on the shelves by now. Cartridges, almost like life forms, seemingly are governed by the law of natural selection. If they are effective and fill a need, they survive and prosper. If they are better than they need to be, or are too close to another cartridge, they are relegated to anonymity and extinction. It's that simple. Yet, unlike many of America's major industries, the arms and ammo people have been admirable in their policies of keeping available cartridges for which they manufactured rifles or handguns but that are no longer in the spotlight. Charlie doesn't see it that way: As he says:

"Among those which are now relegated to the old-hack class are such bewhiskered numbers as the .22 HiPower, the .218 Bee, .25-35 Winchester, .25-20, .303 British, .303 Savage, .30 Remington Auto, .351 WSL, .348 Winchester, .38-40 and the .44-40. How much better it would be if the manufacturers simply dumped these old-timers and used the funds thus generated for the betterment of "today's' cartridges."

If you don't happen to like these arthritic hangovers,

blazes, man, don't buy them! Nobody is holding a gun to your head to use them. But, if you own a gun chambered for one of these Askins-damned rounds, it's very comforting to know that you will still be able to shoot it. Clearly, if not pristinely (.210 Zipper and others), the Winchesters and Remingtons feel they have a responsibility, having produced an arm chambered for one of their unsuccessful babies, to keep ammo available. Personally, I appreciate this. Sure, they make a profit on it, but many calibers are obviously kept in the line for goodwill and barely pay the logistics of their own production.

Charlie over there has made a very good case for the improvement of handgun cartridges in velocity and power, especially in the matters of the Super-Vel firm and the Auto Mag .357 and .44 pistols. I cannot, however, see these developments as in any way correlated to the case with extant rifle calibers such as the '06. My reasoning is that most of this work has been done in the areas of big-game hunting and, with Super-Vel, also law enforcement. The rub is that there *were* no really satisfactory revolver or pistol cartridges suitable in power and penetration for big game, and men like Lee Jurras were developing hardware that was new to the field rather than modifying a cartridge or cartridges that were already more than adequate for hunting, with the recent exception of the .44 Magnum, introduced in 1955. And, after all, the Auto Mag cartridges are no more than magnumizations in the same relationship to the original offerings as the .300 Winchesters and Weatherby Magnums are to the .30-06.

The modern critter crunchers, Weatherby and others, are clearly tailor-made for the high-velocity exponents and there is a great deal, indeed, to be said for them if your thinking embraces the shock theories of ultra-high speed and energy striking levels. We have discussed this before, and there are enough people looking for my scalp that I'm not eager to bring it up again. What matters is that I can't figure what Charlie is so excited about. If he would rather shoot the .300s than the '06, he should do so. But that doesn't mean we should give cement sneakers to any cartridge that doesn't whiffle a slug along at better than 3,000 fps or more.

If there is anybody more familiar with the 8-mm family of rifle fodder than Charlie Askins, I haven't had lunch with him yet. Ergo, I was surprised to see Charlie include the 8×57-mm Mauser cartridge as among those "neglected" by presumably being not loaded to full-case potential. By his own mention, more than a million 8×57s have been imported into this country, a substantial proportion of them Mauser Model 98s "liberated" as war trophies. In addition, many thousands of old Model 88 Commission rifles, also chambered for the 8×57-mm cartridge, were also imported into this country. Surely a great many are still in use, either in original condition or sporterized. Because of industry pressure safety standards, the 8×57 is loaded quite a bit below potential, and for a very, very good reason. The original bullet was of a .318-inch diameter, weighing 227 grains for military use. However, in 1905, the round was redesigned to a bullet diameter of .323-inch while the groove diameter of the Model 88 barrel remained at .320-inch. To fire full-power modern loads of .323-inch slugs (standard today) through a Model 88 barrel is, as the warning goes, hazardous to your health. Thanks to the chaps at SAAMI and their "old fogey" pressure standards, the reduced factory loads probably keep quite a few unwary shooters away from the proverbial pearly gates.

Possibly the most neck-pricking aspects of Charlie's comments and pleas for hotter—and therefore better—factory ammo is contained in his observations concerning the non-SAAMI bullet manufacturers including Hornady, Omark-CCI (Speer), Nosler, and Sierra, all of whom offer erudite and valuable reloading manuals containing data on a world of different calibers. Charlie made the statement, "Without exception every manual *suggests* [italics are mine] handloads which offer improved ballistics over factory standard loadings." Such is anything *but* the case.

To be fair, let's consult, with thanks for their permission, the Speer Reloading Manual Number Nine (October 1976, third printing) concerning the two cartridges of Charlie's own choice that he feels have shown much less progress ballistically than they should have: the .30-06 and the .270 Winchester.

Right out of the box, Speer, one of the major bullet

makers, proves that you don't have to be a member of SAAMI to offer your product responsibly to the American shooter. In fact, Speer goes well out of its way to emphasize that the principle of reloading is much more to obtain consistency and accuracy than to raise pressures and velocities. It most vehemently does *not* suggest maximum loads. I quote:

> The importance of accuracy is second only to that of safety; and although accuracy, along with safety, is a subject of central emphasis throughout this manual, one worthwhile acknowledgment seems in order. Accurate bullet flight is not necessarily related to high velocity.
>
> While it is true that the bullet moving at a high rate of speed will drop a lesser distance while traveling over a given range, the slightly greater drop of the slower, more accurate bullet does not impose the disadvantage many would suppose. The logic of this becomes apparent when one realizes that bullet drop is reasonably predictable: a factor which can easily be compensated for by a slight adjustment.

Speer continues this concept later, in its chapter describing use of the actual loading tables:

> Handloaders are cautioned to start with the lowest listed loads and gradually work up to maximum loads. Gun authorities recognize that a load might be perfectly safe in one rifle and dangerous in another. [Shades of SAAMI!] Thus, it is repeated: DO NOT USE MAXIMUM LISTED LOADS UNTIL LOWER CHARGES HAVE BEEN FIRED WITHOUT ANY INDICATION OF EXCESSIVE PRESSURES!

Obviously, these "maximum loads" must be red-hot, much higher in pressure and velocity than the equivalent factory loads, right?

Nope!

Let's examine Speer's data for seventy-two different load-ings of 180-grain bullets of different designs and their .30-06 muzzle velocities. That tight little club at SAAMI publishes factory MVs for the load as 2,700 fps. Yet, out of six dozen choices by Speer, only *three* of the highly cautioned "max-imum" loads exceeded factory ballistics, and at that, the fastest one is only a scant 130 fps hotter than the stuff in the green and yellow boxes. Of the non-maximum loads, only *two* equal the factory loading, and these by a piddling 10 fps and 29 fps respectively. Incredibly, the vast majority of Speer's loads are well *beneath* factory speeds, in many cases by several hundred foot-seconds!

So much for the '06; let's move on to the real eye-opener, the 130-grain .270 Winchester that Charlie chides so mightily. Don't fall off your camp stool or spill any of that booze. At the 3,140 fps at the muzzle for factory loads, with which Charlie agrees in his article, the store-bought .270 cartridge is *more than 82 fps faster* than the hottest "maximum" load published by the highly respected Speer. Progress, Charlie? How does one manage progress when one has already achieved perfec-tion? Further the defense sayeth not.

Come on, guys, let's have one more before we turn in. I've been wanting to ask Charlie a couple of questions about redheaded women. . . .

A LAPFUL OF
LEOPARD

OUTDOOR LIFE — MAY 1981

The late Carl E. Akeley with the leopard he killed bare-handed.

AUTHOR'S INTRODUCTION

Carl Ethan Akeley is considered the "Father of Modern Taxidermy," a title not lightly earned.

I first saw his work in New York's American Museum of Natural History in 1947, a small boy in hot flannel, dripping ice cream over his Buster Browns in the July heat. His bronzes of lion spearing, taken from his adventures with the Nandi of British East Africa, are still my favorite sculptures on earth.

Perhaps I always related to Akeley because he was an American who proved that my own dreams of going to Africa were not in vain. Akeley, at heart a sculptor, caught better than anyone else the action and reality of his still-unspoiled Africa. Yet he paid a very high admission fee for his exposure, killing a wounded leopard with his bare hands and being left for dead in the icy heights of equatorial mountains after being savaged by an elephant.

At last, in 1926, Carl Akeley paid his final dues for his lifestyle, dying of pneumonia on the high, chillingly wet slopes of the remote Virunga volcanoes of what was then the Belgian Congo, where he had collected specimens of the mountain gorilla for the museum.

Should you walk into the Museum of Natural History in New York City, you will see a magnificent diorama of the mountain gorilla, which actually is more than a memory to Akeley. It is an exact depiction of his grave, in the saddle between Mount Karasimbi and Mount Mikeno. The peaks in the background, behind the spot where his wife laid his tired and African-worn bones, are the volcanoes of Nyamlagira and Nyiragongo.

In creating his works for the museum, Akeley was the most generous of men, naming the display area after his *close friend Theodore Roosevelt. He also dedicated his only book,* In Brightest Africa *(1920), to the ex-president.*

The years have a way of saying thanks in kind: the Roosevelt Hall is now the Akeley Hall, and small boys like me from around the world still thank him.

The molten orb of dying sun hangs low over the snaggled, thorn-studded wasteland that is the Somaliland desert. The hard, copper light yields quickly to encroaching shadow as a bearded white man and a young black man pick their way along a blood-spattered drag mark. Despite the failing light, pioneer taxidermist Carl E. Akeley, who worked for the American Museum of Natural History, insists on continuing. He is determined to put a Springfield bullet into a big "hyena" that stole a prize warthog specimen and carried off the carcass of another hyena shot earlier. Although the hyena had been badly diseased and the skin was not taken, Akeley wants to shoot the thieving hyena for a replacement specimen and to stop the thefts.

Step by cautious step, he creeps along the sandy drag mark, the parched soil crunching softly beneath his boot soles. A slight motion off to his right through the tangled desert bush catches his eye. Without a thought, he swings up the rifle and fires.

He has made one of the biggest mistakes of his life.

The still twilight air is raped by the ripsaw snarl of a leopard that evaporates into the cover in a flicker of dappled gold and ebony. He realizes that the cat is the thief, not a hyena. Carl Akeley knows that following up a wounded leopard in thick scrub so dark that his rifle's sights are useless is not recommended to anyone interested in longevity. Not even certain the cat is actually hit, he decides to wait until morning to investigate, but it's too late. The father of modern taxidermy is in big trouble. The leopard, lying behind a bush twenty yards away, is in savage pain with a bullet-smashed hind foot and is not in the mood for a truce.

In America it would be called an arroyo or perhaps a gulch. In the KiSwahili of what they were spelling "Kenia" at the time, it would be dubbed a *donga,* but, in the Somali desert, it is known as a *tug.* It is a dry streambed cut deeply into the seamed, ancient earth by rare rains, and it is into this gully that Akeley turns and soon finds himself on a slightly raised island at a fork in the streambed. Taking a few steps, followed by his servant, he is unable to resist the temptation to advance to the point of the island to see if he can spot the cat. It looks as if the cat will soon kill the curious.

As Akeley spooks around the dry bush, peering into the dark pockets of shadow, he suddenly sees the leopard ghosting across the *tug* about twenty paces away. Again, the hunter snap-shoots. He jacks the bolt as fast as he can, aiming by feel over the useless sights. Twice, spurts of sand erupt from the streambed over the leopard. As Akeley lowers his aim and triggers a third round, the cat stops. It seems badly hit. The African behind the rifleman gives a shout of excited triumph, the beginning of a victory chant that is rudely interrupted by the vocal thunder of the streaking, charging cat.

Fear grips Carl Akeley's guts in a hard fist, the shock of real terror numbing him for an instant. Bravely, he beats off the fright and works the bolt of his rifle again. With what may be a world-record case of afterthought, he recalls that the magazine is now empty. A cartridge loaded with a solid bullet happens to be in his left hand. He realizes that if he can chamber it in time, he may be able to kill the leopard before it can close on him.

The cat charges in flashing bounds up one side of the island, and Akeley runs wildly down the other. At last, he clicks the round into place and spins around to face the snarls and grunts that are almost upon him. As the rifle comes up, so does the leopard. The cat smacks into the Springfield and knocks it flying. The fang-filled mouth hurtles straight at Akeley's throat.

Getting nailed by an annoyed or wounded leopard, judging by some of the dead and wounded men I have seen, must be rather like a long waltz with a freshly sharpened McCormick reaper. The terrific damage a leopard can inflict is due to his triple-threat—teeth, front claws, and rear claws. He has the added dividends of astonishing strength per pound, scary speed, unflinching courage, and perfect camouflage. There is also the matter of temperament. Leopards don't seem to like *bwanas* who put off-center holes in them. That the leopard has no trouble handling humans is well borne out by the simple fact that the second-highest-ranking feline man-eater of all time was an Indian leopard that killed and ate 425 men, women, and children. This cat, the Panar Leopard, may actually have been number one. Since many of the leopard's kills may have gone unrecorded, he probably outscored the Champawat Tigress, the accepted top killer. The difference between these two terrors was only eleven victims.

Most leopard charges begin at very close range, and the maulings that often leave a man as torn and tattered as a terrier pup's rag doll usually take only a few seconds. Tradition-minded leopards prefer to sink a faceful of teeth into the neck, head, or shoulder of the victim, providing a nice, solid anchor point for the rest of the job, which consists of recycling all points south with pruning-hook, gaff-sharp claws. In a whirling blurr of paws, old *chui* can slice through three layers of heavy clothing, the ribs, and an impressive part of the contents therein, taking about half the time it took you to read this sentence. Being squeamish myself, I won't go into the results of this technique below the navel. Of course, the hind claws are not idle while the front ones are at work. Leopards are well coordinated. To give a practical application of this speed and precision, there is a reliable report from Kenya in the 1920s of a single wounded leopard that mauled seven armed men and escaped untouched except for the original wound.

Carl E. Akeley was a sculptor, and he developed modern taxidermy techniques. Although he certainly was an intrepid character, he was not well equipped to collect his own specimens. It would have been flattering to call him a mediocre shot, and it fascinates me that a man so devoted to anatomical accuracy in the animals he mounted applied his knowledge so badly from the viewpoint of bullet placement on dangerous African game. One bull elephant he finally killed took an incredible 25 express bullets. That he was also rash around animals not noted for a sense of humor is typified by his problem with the leopard. This wasn't, however, the first time he had got in a jam. He had very nearly been killed a year earlier on this same expedition.

At nine thousand feet on the dense bamboo slopes of Mt. Kenya, he was warming his hands prior to starting on some fresh elephant sign. His double rifle was loaded and propped *against his stomach.* The spoor was fresh, all right, which became clear when he was overcome by the feeling that an elephant was right behind him. Whirling around, he tried to fire at the big tusker that towered over him, but he couldn't snick off the safety. The hawser-thick trunk lashed out with awful power and smashed Akeley in the face hard enough to tear his cheek almost completely off and crush his nose into bloody pudding. Dazed, he did not recall later whether he had fired or not. His next recollection was of a thick tusk thrusting for the center of his chest like an overweight javelin. By reflex, he actually grabbed it with his left hand, caught the other with his right, swung between them, and dropped to the ground between the bull's feet! The tusks stabbed deeply into the earth on either side of Akeley's chest and stopped only when they presumably hit a rock or buried root. Completely conscious, Akeley stared at the weird, gray-circled eye above him and felt the unbelievable pressure of the base of the trunk crushing him like a beetle. Blackness finally sucked him gently downward, and he passed out.

It was five hours before he came around. The elephant had probably become bored and left without stepping on the man, although the tusker stamped most of the low vegetation in the little clearing flat before making his exit. Through fuzzy vision, Akeley could make out a nearby fire through the cold mountain rain. His porters were warming themselves around it while he lay there, presumed dead, for good reason, in the icy chill. Neither Swahili Mohammedans nor Kikuyu tribesmen will touch a corpse, so the porters were merely guarding Akeley's body until word reached his wife back at camp. Unable to move or make a sound, Akeley lapsed back into unconsciousness for another four or five hours. He came to again shortly before dark and felt strong enough to give a gurgling shout, which spooked hell out of the bearers. Realizing that the boss wasn't *kufa* after all, they carried him to a makeshift shelter. Paralyzed, but feeling no pain, Akeley concluded that his spine was broken. Suffering from the cold, he got his men to pour a bottle of "cocktails" down his throat along with some beef broth and quinine, and soon felt warmer. Eventually, he managed to wiggle his toes, and that flooded him with relief because it proved that his back wasn't broken.

When Mrs. Akeley finally reached him, her consternation was understandable. Teeth showed through the rip in his cheek, his nose was smashed flat, and there was a crust of blood on his lips. Many broken ribs had been driven into his internal organs like spikes.

Thanks to a Scottish missionary doctor, so recently arrived in Africa that he didn't know elephant maulings were nearly always fatal, Akeley eventually recovered, but his internal injuries kept him in bed for more than three months. One might think he would have taken Africa's gentle hint, but he did not.

As the leopard, a flying streak of mottled murder, slams into Akeley, a tiny but most important error is made by the cat. Missing the throat, it lunges for the man's upper arm and clamps its fangs over the right bicep. This places the leopard off center just enough to prevent the claws from raking Akeley's stomach. The hunter, with the terrible strength provided by a massive surge of adrenaline, is able to catch the leopard's throat in a death-grip with his left hand while he tries to rip his right arm out of the biting mouth. It is a nightmare impasse. Each time he applies enough strangling pressure to loosen the grip of the jaws and move his arm, the leopard sinks the teeth home again in a succession of new wounds that moves down the arm as he pulls it away. Through the harsh, tearing growls of the cat, the sound of teeth crushing tense muscle and grating on bone is crisp in the desert twilight.

Akeley forces the cat farther and farther down his right arm, a new, mangling bite for every inch. In shock, he feels no pain. With the leopard chewing his wrist, the man is able to bend over, still avoiding the deadly claws, and fall down, pinning the leopard under him. His hand is now jammed in the leopard's mouth, and he wedges his elbows into the cat's armpits and forces the front legs apart. The claws just miss his chest but shred his shirt. Off balance, the leopard fights ferociously to twist under Akeley and bring its hind legs into play, but the soft sand of the *tug* bottom offers no grip. His strength draining fast from exhaustion and blood loss, Akeley thinks of the African and his knife, and shouts for him to come and help. The man, however, isn't having any, thanks very much.

With his right hand rammed so deeply down the cat's throat that the animal can't close its jaws, Akeley begins to sense that he may have a chance to survive if he can last long enough. Still keeping his throttling hold, he lunges up and brings his bent knees down on the leopard's chest as heavily as he can. To his surprise, he feels a rib break and repeats the savage, hammering blow with his full body weight. At once, the cat begins to weaken, still struggling, but badly hurt. At the end of his own strength, Akeley hangs on grimly, squeezing the spotted throat until the leopard is quiet. For many minutes, the man does not release his grip. Then he rolls off the body.

Akeley shouts to the African that it's all over, and the tribesman approaches, but has thrown away his knife in his fright. As he starts to look for it, the leopard begins to revive, scaring both men. Happily, the knife is found quickly and Akeley drives the blade home again and again.

Not yet realizing how badly mauled he is, Akeley examines the cat. That first, impetuous shot broke a hind foot, which may have caused the leopard to miss the throat in his leap. The second shot passed harmlessly through the loose skin at the back of the cat's neck. The hunter is able to walk and tries to carry the cat, but is far too weak.

Back at camp, Akeley is horrified to realize from its stomach contents that the leopard has eaten the diseased hyena, thereby greatly increasing the already near-certain probability of blood poisoning in Akeley. The hunter goes through the agony of having the innumerable fang holes syringed out with disinfectant. There are so many wounds that the solution pumped into one runs out another. Strangely, no complication arises from the bites, and Akeley survives to bring the world not only the great African Hall at the American Museum of Natural History but a collection of magnificent bronze sculptures of old Africa, which in my opinion, have never been matched. He wrote of his experiences in the excellent book *In Brightest Africa,* published in 1920.

To suggest that Akeley was lucky would be academic. Not only did the leopard miss its throat hold, thereby rendering itself unable to use its claws, but it was also a mighty small leopard. It turned out to be an eighty-pound female, about half the size of a large male. The odds against overpowering a big tom barehanded are about equal to those against my winning a Pulitzer Prize.

Akeley returned to Africa in 1920 to collect the mountain gorilla group now in the museum and, in 1926, while gathering data in the same area of Congo, died of an accumulation of illnesses. Appropriately, he is buried on the saddle between the high, wild peaks of Mt. Mikeno and Mt. Karasimbi. Which goes to show that if Africa doesn't get you in one way, it will in another.

ARTHUR NEUMANN'S OVERDOSE OF ELEPHANT

OUTDOOR LIFE—
MARCH 1981

The famous ivory hunter Arthur Neumann after having been tusked in the
chest by a cow elephant.

AUTHOR'S INTRODUCTION

Arthur Neumann is still considered by many historians of the ivory trade as the beau idéal *of professional elephant hunters. The only book he wrote,* Elephant Hunting in East Equatorial Africa, *is highly prized and rare Africana. It has pride of place in my hunting library. Although the book is generally believed to have been printed in 1898, the Africana bibliophile will tell you, as does J. G. Millais, who knew the great hunter well, that some copies bear the date 1897. In any case, this book is as rare as the ivory Arthur Neumann took under the most primitive and difficult of conditions in early east Africa.*

A British hunter, despite his surname, Neumann's prowess as an elephant hunter and the financial gain he achieved rank him among the geniuses of that bloodiest and possibly most dangerous of trades.

Neumann killed his first elephant in February 1894 in the vicinity of Mount Kenya, and was to spend several years pursuing elephant, often taking huge risks. His tribal African name was "Nyama Yangu," meaning "my meat." This was distilled by his black African staff to indicate that once Neumann decided on a tusker, it was as good as dead. Unfortunately, he ran across a big cow jumbo who had similar convictions. . . .

Neumann, according to J. G. Millais, the biographer of F. C. Selous, arrived back in England in October 1906, where he picked up a severe case of flu that left him weak and most depressed. The depression was, by all accounts, the result of his being rejected by a lady with whom he was hopelessly in love. After a visit to the West County, he returned to his "rooms" in London, where he shot himself on May 29, 1907. He was fifty-seven years old.

There was a most interesting and regrettably lengthy
apparent incident of parapsychological activity after
Neumann's death, in which he manifested his "spirit" to
someone he had known as a child all the way back in 1876.
Her name was Naomi Jackson, and such was the credence
afforded her "visitation" by "Uncle Arthur" that the British
Society of Psychical Research investigated the incident and
published an article in their journal in May 1908.

Whatever spirit it may have been that visited Naomi,
that of Arthur Neumann certainly lives on in the estimation
of anybody who has ever hunted elephant or who has ever
heard of him.

T he whine of mosquitoes is eerie and thin in the moist,
heavy air on the morning of January 11, 1896. In the snaggled
bush that borders the swamp along the northeast tip of Kenya
Colony's Lake Rudolph, professional ivory hunter Arthur Neumann and two black gunbearers, Juma and Squareface, are
walking fast to cut off a retreating herd of elephants, three of
which now lie in crumpled heaps, slowly seeping gore back in
the stands of dense *mswaki* scrub. It hasn't been a very good
morning; two of the *tembo* are light-tusked cows, the other a
young bull with teeth only twenty-five pounds per side. Still,
thinks Neumann, small ivory is better than none.

It has been nearly two weeks since his last kill, the past
ten nights of which have been stalked by nightmares of the
horrible death of Shebane on New Year's Day. He has only to
close his eyes to conjure up the image that will remain, dark
and awful, for the rest of his days, the last moment of agonized
life for his dead—and thoroughly disposed of—Swahili servant.

It had not been far from here, just to the north on the banks of the Nianam River where it flows into the vastness of great Lake Rudolph, the dark, murky current slow and casual as a swimming python. Twice that day, Neumann had himself taken a bath in the river, first at noon and then again near sundown, when he was accompanied by Shebane.

The hunter had washed and dried himself and was lacing up his boots, noticing that the Swahili had also gone into the water to bathe. Neumann finished tying his laces and was busy gathering up his things when the soft, quiet twilight was disemboweled by a sawtoothed shriek of pain and shock. Jerking around, he was stunned to see Shebane full in the jaws of a huge crocodile, lifted free of the water by his midriff "like a fish in the beak of a heron." Nothing for it. When the swirls ceased and the blossoms of blood had blended with the current, the river was again as if nothing had ever happened.

Shebane had been killed not thirty-five feet from where Neumann himself had been bathing mere moments before. Deeply depressed and likely not a little frightened by the deadly causality of Kismet, Neumann has had trouble these past days getting the sight out of his mind. Still, it was good to be back to the business of hunting, even if the ivory was nothing but toothpick stuff.

A narrow path runs along the edge of the swamp, no more than a thin swordstroke through the looming growth, as the men hurry along, anxious for another shot before the herd breaks off and heads into the heart of the swamp itself. Neumann is not thinking of Shebane now, but of the little .303 Lee-Metford service rifle in his sweating hands. Over the two and a half years he has been hunting elephant professionally, he has found that smaller herd animals such as these can be handled by the very light caliber successfully, saving his expensive express cartridges. After all, he is a professed "small-bore" man himself. Instead of the more standard 10-bore elephant guns (.775 caliber) considered minimum by other pros, he has been laughed at for preferring the "pipsqueak" .577 Black Powder Express with its 750-grain solid bullet. Such are the times.

But there is something wrong with the feeding mechanism of the .303; an annoying fault that a couple of times this morning has permitted the spent brass to be extracted and ejected, yet has not picked up a fresh round from the top of the magazine and chambered it. There is no time to switch rifles, though. In a few minutes the herd will be gone. Pulling ahead of Juma and Squareface, Arthur Neumann runs down the trail and smack into the biggest mistake he will ever live to make.

It's not the first time he has seen her, a three-ton cow with a half-grown calf at heel. She has already shown very definite signs of aggressiveness by a short charge earlier, but Neumann had spared her because of her small tusks and her calf, cutting the wind to avoid her rush. Two other elephants with her continue down the trail. Not her. With a silence that is in itself awesome, she immediately charges from close range, her trunk low, her speed churning up the few yards that separate her from the hated man. Arthur Neumann has no choice this time. No more Mister Nice Guy. Centering his sights on the spot that will pile her up in the frontal brain shot, he squeezes the trigger.

The hollow, muffled metallic click of the firing pin falling on the empty chamber is the loudest thing he has ever heard.

Arthur H. Neumann lived in South Africa for twenty-four years before taking up ivory hunting in British East Africa in 1893. From his classic book, *Hunting the Elephant in East Equatorial Africa* (London: Rowland Ward, 1898), the modern hunter can gain an unusually clear view of what it was like to be a member of what, on any basis, was one of the most elite companies of adventurers ever to penetrate a wilderness. Considering the hardships and dangers to which these men were exposed almost every day, and the number who died or were killed in the field, it seems reasonable to conclude that there were easier ways of making a living than elephant hunting. Still, a lucky, skillful man could make his fortune in a few years. If he lived, that is.

Neumann only hunted three years, taking two expeditions up the east shore of Lake Rudolph and back. Given what happened to him, his retirement after such a short career is not hard to understand. One wonders if the mere click of an ivory billiard ball or the tinkle of piano keys would not have been enough to cause him clammy palms in his later years, in which he achieved fame not only for his book but also for discovering a new species of hartebeest (which was named for him), as well as for his work in the field of butterfly collecting. At this moment, though, and for some time to come, it is most doubtful whether Arthur Neumann will *have* any later years.

He knows he is a dead man. With the chamber empty and the vicious cow almost on top of him, there is no choice but to run back down the slender corridor of thick bush that encloses the path as effectively as the walls of a brick alley. As he flees the pounding death behind, terror twisting his guts with cold fingers, he makes one last panicked effort to work the bolt, snapping the broken rifle back in the direction of the elephant without pausing to aim. Again, the ominous click. Dropping the rifle, he takes his last chance and hurls himself off the trail into the undergrowth, praying that the cow will pass him by. It is not Neumann's day. She hauls up in a cloud of debris and is on him instantly.

As Neumann tries to leap through the bush, the impact spins him around and he is lying on his back, supported by some springy brushwood, his feet pointing toward the path so he has a lovely, uncluttered view of the proceedings.

Kneeling over him, the enraged elephant lunges three times. Neumann's head is battered by the base of the trunk, large sheets of skin torn away by the rough contact, but his skull is somehow not crushed. Possibly the brush absorbs some of the shock. Then the tusks drive home, wrist-thick spikes as sharp as fresh-cut tent pegs that rip and punch completely through his right arm's bicep, piercing until the ivory hits the dirt below. The other tusk lances him in the chest, stabbing through the rib cage as the massive head pounds and grinds his chest, crushing and separating ribs. And then she is gone.

Does she think the blood-covered man is dead? She'd certainly have reason to. Perhaps she's worried about her calf. No matter. She abandons the tattered half-corpse and goes back down the trail.

Incredibly, Neumann is able to stand up and discover that he has no broken arms or legs. Later he finds that the cow has stepped on the buttstock of the Lee-Metford, leaving clear toenail scars in the wood, but the treacherous little gun is unharmed. Upon calling them, he sees his gunbearers come up, Squareface bursting into tears at the grisly sight of his master. Neumann is a bit miffed that neither of the men, who were armed, fired a shot, but forgives them in the light of past loyalty.

There is little value in following the day-to-day agonies of the mutilated Arthur Neumann over his long recovery. Completely out of reach of help, he should have died from blood loss, shock, internal injuries, and such on the spot. But he didn't.

Having himself carried back to camp, he spent the next days and weeks wondering just when death would come. As he waited, he nearly "went west" with terrible fever brought on by becoming chilled from water poured over his wounds to cool them and then being left lying in the wet when he would pass out.

Gradually the tusk hole in his arm began to close without infection, although he was unable to sleep or even sit comfortably for weeks because of the pain. Indescribable horrors oozed from his chest wound for more than a month, but the smashed ribs healed themselves naturally and the wound began to heal over. How the tusk missed the lung has never been explained.

On February 5, practically insane with pain, boredom, heat, and constant rain, he rose from his cot to kill a topi antelope, which he knocked over with his second shot. Unfortunately, the exertion brought on a complete relapse, and he spent another month suffering the hell of malaria and a world-record dose of galloping dysentery. Practically a skeleton, he at last nursed himself back to marginal health on native milk and eggs from a nearby village.

By June, Neumann and his safari had hunted back to El Bogoi, on the southern route back to Mombasa. His troubles were by no means over, although he had collected some exceptional ivory. Here, while stoking a campfire, he got a thorn in his right hand that became infected, quickly turning to blood poisoning.

Now, Neumann was a fairly low-key sort about his own problems, so when he writes that he was in such agony that he seriously considered amputating the hand himself, you can bet your lunch money that he was mighty uncomfortable. The hand got worse daily, until it was swollen all the way up his arm like a giant, psychedelically painted knackwurst. Having one of his men lance it deeply with a hunting knife must have been outstandingly unpleasant.

The operation did not help and probably complicated things further. Eventually the palm and the back of the hand burst and drained.

This whole process took another month, during which time he was confined to camp in awful straits. Even the draining of the hand and arm did little good besides relieving the painful pressure, as both were now half the normal size and completely useless. Eventually they healed, but were stiff for as long as Neumann lived. Incidentally, the only reference he makes to the problem once the hand burst is a casual mention of how really easy it was to learn to write with his left.

Neumann and the late, lamented Shebane were not the only ones to come to grief on the second Lake Rudolph expedition. At 1:15 on a dark morning not long before the end of the safari and safety, the gunbearer Squareface was killed and eaten by an enterprising man-eating lion, taken from inside a thorn enclosure close by where Neumann slept. As I said, it was a hell of a way to make a living.

BERRY BROOKS:
AMERICA'S
GREATEST BIG
GAME HUNTER

SAGA—APRIL 1974

The huge tusker that Berry Brooks passed up.

AUTHOR'S INTRODUCTION

I must say that at the time I wrote this piece, the title was no exaggeration.

I was sent by Saga *to Memphis, Tennessee, to interview Berry shortly after he became the first living American to be figuratively enshrined in the Hunting Hall of Fame, early in 1973. I stayed with him for four days at his fabulous home, not shyly called Epping Forest Manor, of British royalty fame, and found him to be a character fitting his reputation.*

A half hour cemented the credence of his expertise, not that it was ever in question, and I must say that I learned as much from Berry as I have on any three safaris.

Berry Boswell Brooks had been there and had done It—whatever It might have been. The record books proved that in any case.

Yet, given his accomplishments in the field of hunting, one might have swung the great brass knocker of his home, expecting a more chest-beating type. Not Brooks. Like his hospitality, he was understated, polite, knowledgeable, and most certainly in the top rank of quite a few sporting grandees I have interviewed. In a word, he was a gentleman worthy of being called a sportsman, in the word's truest sense.

More's the shame that Berry never wrote a book, but that detracts not a whit from his excellent films, which have raised hundreds of thousands of dollars for charity.

Berry Brooks was the epitome of the gentleman sportsman. Of course, he could afford his hunting pleasures, but what he spent in pursuing them he doubled in his charitable contributions to sustain the world sport of hunting. He died not long after our four days together. Perhaps it speaks well for the man and the hunter in that I hardly knew him, yet I miss him.

The first streaks of winter sunshine were angling through tall stands of papyrus as the Land Rover eased along the faint track of powdery *gussu* sand in Ngamiland, northwestern Botswana. In the left-hand passenger seat rode a powerful-looking man, his shock of pale hair blowing in the cold breeze as young Dave Sandenberg, on his first professional safari, wrestled the hunting car around soft spots on the edge of the great Okavango Swamp. As they cleared the tangled bush and swung onto the edge of an open *vlei,* the older man reached across the seat, grabbed Sandenberg's arm, and, without saying a word, pointed at something to their right.

Sandenberg looked across the flaxen grass to an odd lump that stuck slightly above the line of ragged vegetation. As he watched, a hundred yards away a small herd of zebra and wildebeest barked and whirled in flight. An immense lion, his heavy, dark mane rippling back to his flanks, stopped his stalk and slunk grumbling into the bush. The older man whistled softly.

"Lord, what a lion that is," he whispered reverently. He reached into the pocket of his bush jacket, extracted the two remaining rounds for the .300 Weatherby, and turned them thoughtfully in his weathered hand. "That's better than ten feet of lion if I ever saw one . . . come to think of it, I don't think I ever have."

"We'd better head on down to Liam's camp and borrow some ammunition before we take on that boy," Sandenberg answered. "I can pick up a tracker there, too. We'll need one to track and two to watch in this thick stuff, or he'll be in our laps before we know it. Bad bastards, these Botswana lions, you know."

The Land Rover bounced with new urgency down the fifteen miles of track to the camp of Liam Lynn, a well-known Kenya professional hunter who had come to work with Harry Selby during the East African rains. When the men arrived, Lynn and his client were back from an early hunt having tea under the spreading *n'gamo* fig that shaded the tent area. They didn't look very happy. Lynn's client brought over a .300 Magnum rifle shattered at the breech, the hardened steel twisted like a banana peel. The man was lucky to have escaped without serious injury.

"Just blew up on me," he said. "Damned if I know why."

Sandenberg and his hunter examined it, but couldn't figure out why it had happened. Since the man would now have to forget using that caliber, they borrowed a box of cartridges to supplement their own short supply. With tea hot in their stomachs and one of Lynn's Bushman trackers in the open back of the Rover, they returned to the spot where they had last seen the giant lion. The tracker's eyes opened into white platters as he cut the spoor. *"Tau entunanyana stelek, stelek,"* he kept muttering. One very large lump of lion.

A half hour passed as the men followed the Bushman through the tangled morass of snarled thorn and elephant-felled trees, the sweat from the surprising heat of midday oozing down their dusty temples. The big spoor became fresher and fresher until Sandenberg knelt to inspect a still-damp spot of the cat's sprayed urine.

Checking the safety on his .458 Magnum, he motioned the tracker back and whispered, "Must be lying up just ahead in the shade of that thick stuff. When you see him, he'll be close enough to poke with a stick, so knock him down and keep him down."

The client nodded and moved ahead of Sandenberg, the .300 low and ready. Silently, with every sense supercharged, they picked their way through fifty yards of gray thorn and grass, but the lion saw them first, when they were just twenty yards away.

With a terrifying roar, the big male sprang to his feet and instantly dropped back into a low crouch, his tail-tuft jerking as he dug his rear claws into the ground for his charge. The client put the sights on him, trying to find the shoulder for a crippling blow, and squeezed off a shot. Staring in disbelief, he saw the bullet rip a bloody furrow across the cat's back, eight inches high of his point of aim. With a deep grunt, the lion melted into a tawny blur streaking straight for the white-haired man.

Years of reflex flashed the man's hand down to the bolt handle to reload before the cat was on him, biting and slashing with razor-sharp claws. But the rifle's action was frozen solid. He smashed the steel as hard as he could, trying to free the chamber, hammering on the action with his bare fists, beating the heel of his hand into the color of spoiled liver. The action would not yield.

A blast of scorched air seared his face as Sandenberg snapped a shot at the lion, now only a few feet away. The 510-grain soft-point hit much too low, but knocked the lion off balance as it tore, mushrooming, through his guts. It broke the charge, and before the young hunter could fire again, the cat disappeared off to the side into the shadows. With Sandenberg covering the rear, the men walked several hundred yards into the open to let the wounded lion stiffen and lose blood from its injury.

Try as they might, there was no way to reload the client's rifle. Sandenberg remarked that it had made a tremendous noise at the shot, and that for some reason the cartridge had probably ruptured in the action. That accounted for the strange, high shot that creased the cat. Then he remembered the .460 Weatherby back in the Land Rover. A gift to Harry Selby from a client, it had been touted as the most powerful commercial rifle in the world. Sandenberg had asked if he and his client might try it out if they found a shootable elephant, and Selby had lent it to them. He lit a cigarette and sent the Bushman back for it.

Twenty minutes later, Sandenberg clicked three big rounds into the rifle and handed it to the hunter. They went back after the lion. Following the spoor, dirty with bile and visceral blood, it led them through the heaviest cover in the area for almost two hours of nerve-snapping tension. The tracker went first, crouched low to leave a clear field of fire for the hunters. They stepped through the brush as if walking a rotting tightrope over a snake pit, every sense quivering for the inevitable charge at close quarters.

Half-deafened by the blast of Sandenberg's turning shot, the client almost didn't hear the low growl behind him. The lion had doubled back on his trail to ambush the client from the rear. He spun around to see the lion a few feet away and streaking closer. He fired the .460 from the hip, shoving the muzzle at the cat in midair. The big bullet, with four tons of striking energy, caught the lion in the chest and, to the amazement of the hunter, smashed him completely backwards in a reverse somersault. The heap of dead lion was just three steps away.

Back at Sandenberg's camp, use of a pair of pliers clearly showed that the box of bogus ammunition had been double-charged by whatever idiot had hand-loaded them. Well, the client thought, a miss is as good as a mile. It wasn't his first close call, and he hoped it wouldn't be his last.

The man who thoughtfully sat flipping .300 Magnum cartridges into the Khwai River that afternoon was Berry B. Brooks of Memphis, Tennessee, winner of nearly every major award in the field of big-game hunting and conservation. The lion they were skinning would be among 160 other record-class trophies listed under his name in Rowland Ward's *Records of Big Game*. Twelve years after his first safari, he was the fourth man to win the prestigious Weatherby Trophy as International Sportsman of the Year in 1959. In 1963, *Sports Afield* chose him as one of the world's six greatest living hunters. He has won the Allwyn Cooper Trophy for the best head of Indian game, and the Nyalaland Trophy for the finest head to come out of Mozambique. However, his crowning achievement after years of hunting adventure on five continents came on the night of January 27, 1973, at the Grand Ballroom of Las Vegas's Riviera Hotel when four hundred of the greatest professional and amateur hunters in the world assembled to invest him as the first American in the newly formed Hunting Hall of Fame.

Theodore Roosevelt and Frederick C. Selous, the fine hunter and naturalist killed by German fire in 1917 in Tanganyika, were elected the two greatest International Hunters of the Past. Four living hunters were admitted to the Hall of Fame: His Royal Highness Prince Abdorreza Pahlavi, brother to the Shah of Iran, for Asia; M. Francois Edmond-Blanc of France, for Europe; and Warren Page, another famous American hunter currently president of the National Shooting Sports Foundation.

It is interesting that Berry Brooks would reach the height of his sporting career the same night as the man who had started a much younger Brooks in this direction sixty-five years earlier. In 1910, when Brooks was six years old, he met Teddy Roosevelt when the ex-President stopped by the Brooks plantation in Mississippi to borrow a pack of bear dogs from Berry's father. After a two-hour lunch listening to the great man spin yarns about his famous safari of the previous year, Berry decided that he would make it his business to hunt Africa also.

In 1914, as the drummer boy of the Confederate Veteran Company of Memphis, Brooks had a chance to see the Smithsonian Institute and the wildlife groups donated by Roosevelt when the company went to Washington. That did it. If Teddy Roosevelt could give an African Hall to Washington, then Berry Brooks could give one to the South. It took a little longer than the twelve-year-old expected—thirty-three years, to be exact—but in 1947 Brooks accomplished his goal.

Although he had already hunted extensively in Canada, the western United States, and Mexico, Brooks was really staggered by the game he found in the infant Kenya Colony just after the war. Nairobi wasn't much more than an elaborate whistle-stop on the Mombasa-Uganda line, where game often wandered into town. Zebra and wildebeest frequently had to be shot off the runways where, today, 747s land and take off like bees around a giant hive. Although lions are now found by looking for caravans of minibuses, Brooks never saw another party of sportsmen in more than three months' hunting during his 1947 trip.

Under the guidance of the legendary white hunter Donald Ker, Brooks and his wife and fourteen-year-old daughter wandered the length and breadth of the colony. They collected, among other choice items, an elephant with a pair of tusks for little Virginia, making her at the time the youngest female ever to shoot an elephant as well as having shot the best tusker for her sex.

After a few weeks of hunting in the bush, Brooks decided

to devote the rest of the trip to making a film. This footage was some of the finest ever taken of African wildlife. On his return to Memphis, the film was edited into his first full-length picture, *Passport to Safariland*. This film and others that he has made over the years have raised an estimated $500,000 for charity.

Before finishing his first safari, Brooks had agreed to donate a wing of the so-called Pink Palace mansion in Memphis for display of African game. It became the Museum of Natural History, and Brooks invested the place with thirty-eight species of game from Kenya, nearly all in the record class, including two whole shoulder mounts of bull elephants each worth $5,700. The taxidermy tab for his first safari alone was $75,000, and subsequent work raised this fee over the next few years to nearly $200,000. With such expenses, Brooks decided he'd better stick with the cotton business for a year or more. But in 1949 he could stand it no longer and booked Don Ker again for nine months of hunting in six countries.

Meeting Ker in Nairobi, they hunted down toward the Tana River, traditional home of some of Africa's finest elephants. During the preceding two years, Brooks had become fascinated with the idea of taking some really big ivory—something over 120 pounds per tusk. Even in those days, that was like trying to find a particular mosquito in a very large swamp. As the weeks rolled by, the two men walked hundreds of miles through the swelter, hoping for a glimpse of a fantastic old bull rumored by tribesmen to be in the area. *Hapana tembo*. No elephant. Plenty of smaller bulls, even some with hundred-pound tusks, but the lone monarch eluded them at every turn. Then, one morning, they found it—a spoor with prints bigger than garbage-can covers. Ker said it was less than six hours old.

The two men grabbed their rifles, called a gunbearer, and started on the track immediately. The morning was still cool in the highlands. They knew the bull would keep moving until the hotter hours, when it would stop to rest for a few hours in the shade. After traveling nearly ten miles, Ker realized that the gunbearer had forgotten the canvas water bag, but because the spoor was so fresh, Ker and Brooks decided to push on.

For five hours they picked their way through the waste country of *giri-giri* and wait-a-bit thorn, the temperature rising with every step as the trail led to lower ground. The February sun seared them unmercifully, baking the barrels of Brook's .470 Rigby until they were almost untouchable. Sweat dried into sheets of itching salt that chafed their necks and armpits raw, but they walked on. Then, as if by magic, there was the flick of a saillike ear from the shadows of a stand of *doum* palm and the shoulder of a gigantic bull elephant stood out from the dimness.

Brooks felt his pulse race as his eyes traced the length of the long swoop of dirty ivory, as thick as a telephone pole at the base and looping even farther than he had hoped. Slipping the safety catch from the Rigby, Brooks eased up for a brain shot. The ivory bead of the big double settled perfectly between the eye and the ear hole; up just a few inches and he began his squeeze. Slowly the bull swung around, and Brooks's disappointment was more bitter than the layer of dust in his dry mouth. The mighty left tusk was broken off two feet ahead of the lip, the bright glow of the fresh ivory gleaming in contrast to the stained mellowness of its mate. It was worthless as a museum trophy. Brooks and Ker turned around without a second glance, leaving the patriarch with his 130-pound single tooth to wander in Berry's dreams.

After three hours, Brooks knew he was in trouble. Neither he nor Ker had realized how far the elephant took them. With each step the American could feel his tongue swelling as it turned into a piece of dry leather in his mouth. He could not prevent the thick, white foam that formed at the back of his throat from blowing over his bush jacket, which made him look like a mad dog. Although Ker's body was more used to the dry conditions, he too was suffering, as was the Somali gunbearer, who was accustomed to the raw, northern deserts. Another hour passed. By now the men could do no more than walk fifteen minutes and rest five, a pattern that dwindled into walking five and resting fifteen as their bodies rebelled against the lack of water. Brooks was afraid he would pass out and the others would have to leave him, being too exhausted to carry him.

Brooks's tongue had swollen so much that he couldn't completely close his mouth. Foot by foot they fought onward until Ker decided to fire a signal shot. As the echoes of the blast blended into the hot silence, a tiny shout answered from far away. Chabani, the car boy, had begun to look for them and somehow missed the party and passed by in the bush. An agonizing hour later, he came up with the water and a shriveled orange that had been sitting on the dashboard tray of the car for several days. Brooks had a hell of a time chewing his half with his swollen tongue, but he wouldn't have traded it for platinum.

It was midway through this second safari that Brooks got another good look at the fate awaiting the careless or foolish hunter in the African bush. As Brooks told *Saga:*

"Don Ker and I had been out for three months and were hunting lion and buffalo in the Masai region. One morning a young *moran*—a warrior—came into camp to tell us there was another *m'zungu* or white man camped about ten miles away. Well, we were dying for someone to talk to and piled into the hunting car to go for a visit. When we arrived in the man's camp, the Swahili cook told us his *bwana* was off hunting with his *WaMericani* clients, but normally came back for breakfast about nine o'clock. As it was nearly that time, I took my binoculars and started to scan the plain for some sign of them and finally saw them coming from about a mile away. I told Don they were in sight and suggested we drive out to pick them up, but he opted for another cup of tea, not wanting to barge in on them.

"As they got closer, I had the feeling something was wrong and could see through the binoculars that they were carrying something on a litter. I got Don going, and we drove the Rover out to see what was going on. As we got up to them I could see that it was a man they were carrying and I had trouble recognizing Roy Lintey, an independent professional hunter I had met two years before in Nairobi. His whole face had been crushed and literally pushed up to the top of his head. He was still conscious, but in terrible pain and couldn't speak with his smashed jaw and cheekbones.

"I always carry a first-aid kit when I'm on safari and fortunately had several Syrettes of morphine in it. We gave him a couple and decided the best thing was to leave his clients in camp and try to get Lintey to the Game Department in Narok, some fifty miles away. Don got on the radio to the late Lynn Temple-Borham, who was in charge there and had him radio for a plane. On the way to Narok, I got the story from Lintey's gunbearer, who had witnessed the accident from a tree.

"The client had wounded a big buffalo bull through the guts and it ran into a five-acre tract of very heavy bush. True to his profession, Lintey told the client to wait on the other side of the tangle while he went in to root out the injured buff. Sending his trackers and gunbearers up trees to try to spot the bull, Lintey entered the cover alone with his .500/.465. He hadn't gone 50 feet when one of the men spotted the bull sneaking up on him and shouted a warning, whereupon the buffalo immediately charged. In the very thick bush, Lintey couldn't see the animal until it was almost on him, but courageously held his fire until sure of a killing shot. He made it, too, shooting the bull squarely between the eyes with the .500/.465, completely destroying the brain. But it was too late. Dead on its feet, the buffalo smashed into Lintey's stomach and then, almost as a reflex, wrenched his head up, catching Lintey full in the face with the boss of his horns.

"The official report stated that Lintey died on board the aircraft from Narok, but I believe he was mostly gone at the time we loaded him on. Things like that kind of get you to thinking."

By the time he had finished his 1949 safari, Brooks had hunted in Kenya, Uganda, the Sudan, Tanganyika, the Belgian Congo, and Northern Rhodesia, expanding the collection for the Memphis Museum. Although he finally did kill a fabulous elephant with tusks that weighed 114 and 109 pounds, it's typical of Brooks that he considers his finest moment hunting was with an elephant he did *not* kill.

A late afternoon in the Karamojong region of Uganda

found Ker and Berry stumbling across the track of a truly immense lone bull jumbo. After tracking for thirty minutes, they came upon the giant wandering alone through the low bush—an easy target even for a nearsighted man with a slingshot. Don Ker, who had been in at the kill of some of the finest ivory ever to come out of the continent, could do nothing but stare at the impossibly long tusks. They literally touched the ground when the behemoth lowered his head in walking! Famous for his conservatism, Ker estimated them at something better than 150 pounds per side, probably one of the biggest elephants shot in the past century. Brooks, who has seen a lot of big ivory, thought they came close to 170 pounds. They were even more fantastic because the tusks were well matched.

Without knowing why, Brooks broke his rifle and extracted the cartridges. Taking careful aim, he clicked the firing pins on the empty chambers and passed the rifle back for his camera. As the elephant wandered off, Berry took a series of photographs of the monster, which was at that time the largest ever photographed. Berry patted the unfilled elephant license in his breast pocket and turned away, a satisfied man.

That's the sort of thing that gets you into the Hunting Hall of Fame.

Throughout the nine months of his 1949 safari, Berry added almost sixty record-book trophies to the Berry B. Brooks African Hall in Memphis. Upon his return, however, he found that the growing cotton business began taking more and more of his time. For the next ten years he had to settle for completing the dream of the North American hunter—taking the Grand Slam in sheep: bighorn. Dall, stone, and desert species—one of the toughest orders in hunting. Elected to the Boone and Crockett Club for his achievements, he was also honored as an official measurer for the club, which keeps records of North American game.

As the years passed, Brooks had become more and more interested in Asian hunting. He was particularly interested in the rare and very dangerous species of giant wild oxen found in India and Indochina, the giant Indian buffalo, the towering gaur and his close, but even bigger, cousin, the seladang of

Southeast Asia. (The latter is considered by many to be the Holy Grail of lowland Asian hunting.) It is a great blue-black ghost of the bamboo that can stand *seven feet* at the shoulder—a will-o'-the-wisp killer so aggressive that not even tigers will stand up to a lone bull.

Brooks tried for years to obtain one of the five licenses issued annually for Indian buffalo, each time to find that the coveted permits had been grabbed by generals and maharajahs for their own sport. Determined not to go on shikar without a buffalo permit, Berry kept postponing his proposed hunt in India. It was his difficulty in obtaining these permits that directly led to the expedition that nearly cost him his life on four different occasions.

Early in 1961, a State Department friend of Berry's wrote him and said that he could arrange hunting permits for tiger, buffalo, and seladang in South Vietnam. Brooks immediately accepted and began correspondence with the recommended outfitter in Saigon, Etienne Oggeri.

Three months later, Brooks arrived in Saigon and was met at the plane by a tall, handsome man in bush clothes who introduced himself as Oggeri. Only that was it; the man didn't speak another word of English, a fact somehow not alluded to in the flowing prose of his letters to Berry. However, through the interpreter brought by Oggeri, arrangements were made to leave immediately for the Central Highlands hunting camp the outfitter had built near Da Lat.

Although they could not converse except in sign language (the interpreter had come down with fever and left), Brooks was impressed with the arrangements Oggeri had made for him. The camp, a pleasant location erected near some Moi aboriginal villages, sported a shower and attractive bamboo sleeping quarters as well as having fine food.

Deciding to try for tiger first, Brooks and Oggeri built several *miradors* or ground-level blinds, baited the clearing before them with sambar, a local staglike animal, and sat back to await developments. When, after several days nothing had taken the baits, Etienne proposed that he and Brooks ride into Da Lat for supplies. Brooks agreed and decided to bring along his shotgun to pot a few jungle fowl for the table. He would wait for Oggeri while he shopped, then ride back to camp with him.

While Berry had something to eat at a small sidewalk restaurant, Oggeri went off to pick up the supplies. The American was into his second cup of tea when he was astounded to see a sleek Mercedes pull up and a beautiful woman get out and walk up to him. "You must be Mr. Berry Brooks," she said in perfect English.

"And you must be the one who wrote me all those letters signed by Etienne," he laughed. She smiled, then her face turned serious.

"I am Madame Tran Le Chi, sister of Madame Nhu," she said simply. "I have come to warn Etienne." Brooks wondered if he'd been out in the sun too long without his hat. Madame Nhu was the wife of the political adviser to the government, Ngo Dinh Nhu, who was the brother of the President of South Vietnam.

"Etienne and I are in love and wish to get married," she continued. "I must not be seen with you. My sister is sending the army to arrest Etienne to prevent our marriage. He must go into hiding or he will be caught and deported—or shot."

Brooks felt as though he were in an episode of the Arabian Nights, as she quickly told her story. She had left her husband, a wealthy old Frenchman to whom her marriage had been arranged, and wanted to marry Etienne, her childhood sweetheart. Oggeri was the son of an Italian count who had come to South Vietnam twenty-five years before as an engineer, and had married a Vietnamese woman. Having lived in French Indochina at the time, Etienne held a French passport and was liable to deportation at the orders of Madame Nhu, who wanted to marry her sister off to another wealthy old man, this time a Chinese. As quickly as she had come, Madame Chi was whisked off in the Mercedes. Waiting for Etienne, Brooks wondered what to do next.

It took some violent gesturing to get Etienne back in the jeep, but finally he caught the gist of the warning, and began racing the car back to the safety of the jungle. Two days later a squad of armed soldiers walked into the camp, but Oggeri, forewarned by his friends, the Moi, simply strolled into the impenetrable forest until the little, pygmy-like Hill People sounded a laughing all-clear. Oggeri hunted several more days with Brooks, but the threat of soldiers combing the area for him forced him into hiding.

Berry took to hunting alone with a pair of Moi trackers, leaving at dawn and returning after long treks at dusk, exhausted and hungry from his constant search for the fresh track of a lone bull seladang. Finally, after three weeks, Berry cut the spoor of a huge bull. Even the Moi hunters seemed excited at the size of the great, splayed hoofprints deep in the forest humus. With the two little men working ahead like bird dogs, the American readied his .378 Weatherby and followed them on the spoor.

The hunters traveled two miles before coming to an immense stand of bamboo, pierced only by narrow, dark paths like the holes of giant worms. The decaying odor of the jungle thick in his nostrils, Brooks left the trackers and followed the spoor into one of the tunnels, stepping carefully to avoid making any noise. Sweat sheeted down his face despite the coolness of the area. Brooks knew what would happen if he met the seladang in one of the tunnels—visibility dim and no place to run—and decided not to think about it. Silently, he worked farther into the murk.

After fifty yards, Brooks could see a lighter area ahead where the tunnel ended, opening into an area the size of a small house. As he edged closer, he could see slight movement through the tough cane, movement that solidified before his straining eyes into a great, gunmetal-black animal that looked like a locomotive as it stared at him across fifteen yards. Brooks was staggered by the utter immensity of the seladang—*it stood a foot taller at the shoulder than he did!* He could clearly see the pale stockings on the powerful legs and the odd ridge of muscle that ran halfway down the giant's back. As he raised his rifle, the creamy horns with polished ebony tips lowered threateningly, and the monster rolled into a fast trot—straight at him. The crash of the Magnum was deafening in the closed area as Brooks sent a 300-grain slug just below the chin and into the center of the chest. The seladang lurched and staggered, but stayed on its feet. Brooks smashed him again and, like a toppling tree, the bull stumbled and crashed to the ground. He kicked for a few moments, gave a long, low bellow, and died. Alone, Berry Brooks had killed the rarest and most dangerous game on the Asian continent.

Shaking with excitement, Berry examined the great trophy. It would weigh better than three thousand pounds, considerably larger than the Indian gaur, which may reach 2,500 or more, in the case of a very big bull. Brooks took just the headskin and headed back to camp under the heavy load, deciding to return the following day with a work party for the skull.

Returning in the morning, Brooks, on a hunch, decided to leave his Moi party a few hundred yards from the bamboo thicket and check the carcass alone. He crept back through the tunnel and up to the edge of the clearing, with his rifle ready. Scanning every inch of the area, he finally decided that nothing had come to feed on the seladang carcass, and rose to his feet. Icy panic shocked through him as a paralyzing roar shook the clearing and a tremendous male tiger leaped from the far side of the carcass, where it had lain feeding, unseen. Cornered as it was, Brooks knew it would be sure to charge. At ten feet, he dropped it with a single shot from the Weatherby, the big slug tearing through the open mouth of the cat and breaking its neck.

A tiger and a seladang were pretty fair work for anybody. Satisfied, Berry returned to camp to oversee the skinning of the tiger and the boiling down of the seladang skull. He decided on a few days' rest before planning a possible trip down into the lowlands for giant buffalo.

Etienne Oggeri had to spend most of his time in hiding now, and was often gone for a whole week at a time. He did sneak back to check up on Berry, who had insisted that the shikar go on. However, since there was no one in camp who could speak English even when Oggeri was around, Berry was slowly going bush-happy because there was no one to talk to.

One day his prayer was answered in the form of a rather disheveled, unshaved angel who introduced himself as George. George was in sore need of a drink, and said so in a tone of Oxfordian English that amused Berry. Brooks had no whiskey, but offered him carte blanche to the camp's considerable wine stock if George would only stay and talk to him. Brooks had a deal.

George, who had no apparent surname, unfolded an interesting story. He explained that he was the son of French planters who had been executed by Indochinese sympathetic to Japan shortly after the outbreak of WW II. Chief conspirator had been the family's most trusted servant, who had personally cut off his father's head while George was studying at Oxford. Young George had taken the whole thing rather badly and had decided to become a drunk, an ambition in which he had realized true professional status. However, as long as Berry's wine held out, he'd be delighted to hang around and translate for him, since he spoke Moi like a native.

Two days later, George came to Berry and told him that a Moi had come into camp from a village nine miles away to ask Brooks to shoot a man-eating tiger that had killed one of the village women as she drew water the evening before. Brooks grabbed his rifle on the run.

Arriving at the village, Brooks discovered that the woman had been removed from the scene of the killing and placed in a hut in the center of the village. Knowing that the best chance to kill the tiger would be to wait for him to return and finish his meal, he begged the elders to permit him to use the corpse for bait. He reassured them that he'd see that the rest of the body wasn't eaten. But the chief and his two sons didn't agree, and insisted that the woman could not be moved. Brooks shrugged and decided to build a *mirador* anyway, in the hope that the tiger might show up, thinking the woman was still there.

Throughout the long afternoon and evening, Brooks sat immobile in the blind, his eyes glued to the vision slit. The shadows lengthened until a shroud of moonless dark settled over the forest, but Brooks stayed in the blind all night, hoping to shoot the tiger by flashlight beam. Nothing showed up, but he was certain the tiger was nearby, because of the ominous silence of the normally noisy jungle.

Late the following morning, thirsty, hungry, and exhausted, Brooks was forced to leave the *mirador* for some sleep and food. George had sent the jeep back in the morning with a native driver, being a bit too under the weather to drive after a night with the wine supplies. Brooks walked two hundred yards to the village, made his apologies to the Moi chief and his sons, took some photos, and got into the jeep. They had not been out of the village for thirty seconds when the whole place exploded into a furnace of towering flame. Blood drained from the face of the native driver as he rammed the accelerator to the floor, despite Berry's protests that they return at once to help. Neither promises nor threats of a 300-grain bullet in the head would make the driver stop and turn around.

Furious, Brooks returned to camp, where he had George question the driver about his actions. As he spoke, George began to look a little funny, too. Finally the Frenchman gave Berry the story: during the night, while Brooks was waiting for the tiger, a company of Viet Cong had surrounded the village. Brooks realized that was why the tiger had not returned, and why the jungle had been so quiet. George didn't know why, but they had decided to wait until Brooks left before burning the place and killing the chief and his family—the same man and his two sons whom Brooks had photographed a few seconds before leaving.

Brooks sat down heavily. Why had the Viet Cong permitted him to escape? A lone man with a valuable and much-needed rifle would have been no problem to kill in the darkness. Berry Brooks never could figure out a good reason why he had been allowed to live.

Two more incidents on this hunt led Brooks to believe that he might be pushing his luck. One afternoon he was sitting on the edge of his bed in camp, writing a letter to his wife. For no particular reason, he put down his pen and walked out onto the veranda of the little house. Just as he left the sleeping quarters, a huge dead tree crashed through the roof, crushed the bed, and knocked half the house flat.

A week later, the house having been rebuilt, he awoke from his normal hour-long nap a few minutes early and walked through a light rain over to the kitchen. When he was thirty feet away, a blue bolt of lightning struck the house squarely and smashed it into flaming bits.

For the third time, Berry Brooks had missed sure death by a matter of seconds.

Although not a superstitious man, Berry started to get the creeps. Since the lower river valleys where he had hoped to hunt buffalo were held by Viet Cong, Brooks began thinking perhaps he'd better put the cap on his Indochinese adventures before his family got a telegram of regret. Just a few days later, an incident occurred that convinced him it was time to pack up while he still could.

He and George had decided to drive over to a nearby Moi village for fresh eggs. Since the place was normally bustling by dawn, Brooks and the Frenchman were surprised to find the village empty. Pulling into the square, Brooks saw something lying in the dust. He didn't have to get closer to know what it was—the chief of police.

The Viet Cong, on a political raid, had hit the place about four o'clock that morning, decapitated the chief, and then cut both hands off three men who protested. Brooks tried to dress the stumps of the two mutilated Moi, who had not yet bled to death, but it didn't look very hopeful. Shocked and depressed, he and George returned to camp.

The following morning, two cooks from the camp showed Berry where a squad of VC had approached the place, then set up camp about a mile out. Clearly they had been scouting the camp. Berry threw his guns and trophies into the jeep and headed for Saigon.

It's almost anticlimactic that Brooks was dragged off his airplane and jailed, all his belongings impounded without explanation by four South Vietnamese officers the following day. Somehow, he managed to be released from the police station to spend the night in the deserted Caravelle Hotel. There he met a mystical Swiss whom he was able to bribe to get him passage out of the country. While Berry waited in his hotel room, bullets ricocheted off the concrete and the building shook to VC sabotage explosions. The police station where he had been held was bombed and many people were killed. This raid presumably destroyed his trophies and his ten thousand feet of film. At midnight the following night, Brooks was smuggled by the Swiss onto an airplane that deposited him, the only passenger on the flight, in Bangkok.

Four years later, he got back much of the film, damaged by water, and, surprisingly, all his guns and trophies that had not been destroyed by the blast. That same year he also got a telephone call in English from the elusive Etienne Oggeri, who had escaped across the border to Laos, ending up in the United States, where he was teaching jungle warfare to the Green Berets at Fort Bragg. With him was his wife, the beautiful Tran Le Chi Oggeri, who had slipped away from imprisonment at her sister's hands and made her way to New York.

In the years that followed his Vietnamese shikar, Brooks hunted the lower Sahara regions of Chad and the Central African Republic with Clause Vasselet. This time he was after rare desert game including scimitar-horned oryx, aoudad, Dama gazelle, addax, and Lord Derby or giant eland in the old Oubangi-Chari region of French Equatorial Africa. He safaried in Mozambique, where he won the Nyalaland Trophy for a super bull nyala.

In 1967, the giant Indian buffalo license finally came through, and Brooks spent three months bagging a 111-incher that cinched the Allwyn Cooper Trophy for him. He took a fine gaur and tiger, and finally capped off the hunt by killing a sloth bear that had ambushed and killed three women in Madhya Pradesh.

Today, back in Memphis, Tennessee, Brooks putters around the museum like a bird-dog puppy a week before the season. *Saga* asked him his plans.

"Well, I'll tell you. I've been looking around for a *really* exciting place to hunt. . . ."

THE BLACK DEATH

THE AMERICAN HUNTER—
AUGUST 1979

A bull buffalo looking for trouble.

I suppose it all comes down to Cape buffalo not having a very good sense of humor. Mixed with his cast-steel constitution, this makes for a rather unpleasant combination when the odds swing over to his side in the thick bush.

We've already spent some time outlining the generally uncooperative attitudes of Inyati, *and this paper portrait merely enhances the truth of his blood-and-thunder reputation. But he is also composed of nice, red meat, about the most prized single item on the mind of any central African tribesman.*

I don't think anybody knows how many hunters or simply ordinary people who are unwittingly in harm's way come to a literally sticky end with the buffalo. This is by no means rare; if anything, it is a typical result of rudeness to Syncerus caffer. *Perhaps I should have called this piece, "Requiem to Fantastic."*

As corpses go, it was a real humdinger, the kind even a big-city coroner wouldn't forget in a hurry. It hung fifteen feet in the air above me, draped like a torn mannequin over the spiked branch of yellow acacia. My thumb instinctively slipped onto the safety of the Evans .470 Nitro Express double rifle. Literally dead center, smack through the solar plexus, was a hole large enough to accommodate a fair-sized pumpkin if you shooed off the hundreds of iridescent green flies and white maggots swarming over the torn mess. Two days of hanging in the searing sun and spring humidity hadn't been especially beneficial to the general odor of the immediate area.

I started Invisible, my Number Two man, scraping away a shallow grave. Silent, my ancient, gnome-like Awiza gunbearer cut a sapling and pushed the dead man from his grisly perch to land with a foul thump beneath the` tree. The ground was mostly rockless, sandy clay, so we covered the grave with staked-down mounds of the meanest thorn bushes we could find to keep the hyenas and jackals from invading the poor man's privacy.

The spoor told the whole tale as simply and clearly as a Dick-and-Jane book. A mangled, smooth-bore muzzle-loader lay fifty yards away, the fired percussion cap still pinched in place between the hammer and nipple. The wire-bound stock and barrel looked ready to be stamped into scrap. We retraced the big, splayed hoofprints easily to a shadowy stand of thick mopane, where the two old Cape buffalo bulls had stood, dozing away the afternoon heat. The splintered end of a sap-oozing twig showed where the bullet had clipped it before it went on to slam into meat—too far back, by the look of the dried blood. Probably guts or stomach. The wounded bull had immediately charged, while the second had run off a few yards and stood, confused. The hunter, a Senga tribesman whose name we later learned was Fantastic, had dropped the gun and run for the shelter of the big tree. He was still ten feet short when the bull smashed into him, shoving what was probably the right horn completely through the man's chest, back to front. The unbelievable power of the charge's impact had, by the look of the wound's diameter, pushed the horn clear up to the base. Then the toss had thrown him free, straight up to where he happened to land across the branch, probably already dead of a crushed spine.

Then the buff had stopped, probably perplexed that the man was no longer in sight. For what must have been several minutes, he charged here and there before he smelled or saw the blood leaking down and spotted the body. From a point some four feet above the trampled ground, the bark had been bludgeoned and torn from the tree where the bull charged it, repeatedly trying to knock the man free. But the cruel thorns held the dead man, and the bull gave up, returning to the dropped gun, which he proceeded to pulverize until he wandered off with his pal to nurse the terrible pain in his guts.

It was now my job to track him down, root him out of the thick stuff, and stamp him "canceled." As Game and Elephant Control Officer of the district, it was my responsibility to kill him before he bumped into some poor beggar and put on his act again. Having been in on the demise of something around one thousand Cape buffalo, or *M'bogo,* as he's called in KiSwahili, or *Inyati* in Fanagalo, the central and southern African equivalent catchall language, I knew enough not to be very keen on the idea.

At first light the next morning, we broke camp and immediately made for the Lundazi River on foot. As is my custom, I carried the .470 myself at any time visibility was less than one hundred yards. Silent tracked ahead, looking for spoor, while I covered him by watching the sides and far front. Invisible, just behind me, carried the water bag and my extra cartridges and iron ration provisions for at least one night in case we had to sleep on the trail.

We cut spoor after about an hour of hunting, that of a pair of bulls for sure, leading from the water's edge and then back at a lazy angle into the heavy bush. I very much wish somebody would come up with a more appropriate term that I could plagiarize. "Heavy bush" simply does not fairly describe the vegetable morass of almost solid growth that lines the Lundazi to a depth of three hundred yards from its banks. It's rather like calling Rocky Marciano a sissy. Visibility is not measured in yards, but often in fractions of feet.

My tracker has found a lovely pile of near-steaming pasture-patty, not even glazed over. You stick your finger into it and discover it's not fifteen minutes old. It also contains, you note with no little interest, large, dark clots of blood mixed in with the fecal material. Guess who.

We follow the spoor for another forty yards until a very convenient, thigh-thick sapling appears. As you cover the bush ahead, Silent, who is well named, sneaks silently up the trunk until he is twenty feet above the tops of the surrounding ground cover. An errant swirl of wind doesn't do much for your confidence as you steal a glance up at him. He's staring hard at something, obviously indistinct, about fifty yards off. It seems like two weeks before he points with his chin and holds out two fingers; then a single finger up and another down. One bull is standing, the other lying down. Pointing a line of direction, he looks expectantly down at you. Go get 'em, boy. Oh, me, oh, my. Silent, who is not stupid, will stay in the tree where you can see him, giving signals if the buffalo move. Like straight at you.

Following his pointed azimuth, you snick the safety off the Evans and begin creeping forward, picking each step in slow motion, walking on the outside edges of your sockless desert boots. After ten yards, you look back at Silent, who simply nods. Still there. Ahead, there is nothing but the shadowy tangles of branches, leaves, and grass woven more densely than an Oriental rug. Every few yards you lie flat, trying to pick out the silhouette of a leg or the movement of a flicked tail or ear. Nope. You'd think that a couple of critters that push a ton or so would at least crack a twig or swish a leaf; maybe even break wind or something. Not bloody likely. You pause for a moment to persuade your heart to stop pounding so loud you couldn't hear an express train if it was coming right at you. Fear and raw nerves make you sweat, and your legs feel like spaghetti. You're not scared, you're terrified motherless.

Then an astonishingly familiar bovine odor smacks you in the face. And you realize you can hear the flies! You freeze into an idiotic statue, one foot off the ground. When you can smell them and even hear the flies, you have a fair hunch they're not awfully far away. Your sweat-stinging eyes probe every inch of alternating light and shadow ahead and to the sides as you try to lower your leg without losing your balance. That would be cute! A step. Another. Where are they? You want to shoot them, not take them prisoner!

Then it's there, its very size making it nearly invisible in the dappled play of sun. But what is it? Well, you reason, if it smells like a Cape buffalo, makes tracks and droppings like one, draws flies and has a big slab of grayish-black hide with sparse bristles near enough to count, then it is fairly reasonable to assume it *is* a Cape buffalo. Or, at the very least, *part* of a Cape buffalo. But which part and which one? You don't want to cash in the unwounded one unless you have to. Long, very long, seconds creak and crawl by as you strain to figure out what you are looking at and whether it's the end that bites. Maybe just another few steps closer. At six yards—African yards are much shorter than the ones used to measure American football fields—your brain slips into panic overdrive. From between two leaves, a single, baleful eye is staring right at the center of your stomach. That's all, boys. You don't get paid *that* much. At eighteen feet, you couldn't give a howl in hell which bull it is. Hopefully, he doesn't yet realize what he's looking at either, so now's your chance. With the sneakiest possible movement, you level the Evans. The ivory bead mates with the vee of the single express rear leaf; hold slightly over the eye and squeeze off.

The muzzle blast smothers any sound of bullet strike, and for an incredible millisecond there is silence. It is, however, a mini-millisecond because now the air is alive with shouts from Silent, very unsociable grunts from a couple of feet away, and the noise of the radical rearrangement of some local flora. The second bull, whichever one he is, has unquestionably had his attention gotten and is charging, bearing down invisibly through the heavy bush with an irresistible power that is hair-raisingly awesome. You jump a few yards to your left as he breaks cover, exactly where you were standing, attacking the sound of the hated gun. He is clearly not very happy with you.

The reflex that has kept you alive through all these uninsurable years in a never exactly dull business has the .470 doing its little act all by itself. As he swings toward you—head high, changing direction—a charming, white-edged hole appears between his eyes, right at the base of his big, black, wet nose. He's hardly hit the ground, blood pouring from his ears, before the Evans is broken and new rounds chambered. Another solid throws a puff of dust from the back of his neck. Sure he's down for the count, you spin and level the rifle back at the place where that spooky eye was, holding it in its marvelous balance by the pistol grip, index finger on the second trigger, while you fish out another cigar-sized cartridge from your pocket with your left hand and reload the fired chamber.

You need not have bothered. The first bull is lying where he dropped, the solid slug neatly through his left eye as he looked at you. He's as dead as your innocence and the tax shelter combined, but, even though .470 Kynochs are worth their weight in sterling silver, you stick to the rule that's kept you ambulatory and swat him in the nape of the neck anyway.

The urge for a cigarette and a long, absolutely obscene scotch are overwhelming as you sit down ten yards away. You manage the cigarette on the third try, just as Silent and Invisible come up wholesaling the usual *"eeeeehhhs"* and *"aaaaahhhhs"* of the excited bush African.

When we had the bulls rolled over, and the fat, red ticks were beginning to drop off the crotch area, sensing death, we were able to determine that it was the second bull that had been wounded. Silent dug out a wicked chunk of iron reinforcing rod that had passed through five coils of intestine and lodged against the far skin's inside. The people in this part of the world have great imagination when it comes to ammunition. A couple of feet forward, and it would have been a fine lung shot and the late, lamented Fantastic would have been the village hero.

By the time we had taken the interior fillets and tails for table fare, as well as the ears to turn in to the government, the circle of human vultures had moved in. They had likely been following us from the village all day, waiting for the sound of my shots. When we finished the walk back to the Rover, I took a healthy belt of scotch, grilled some of the fillets, and spent the rest of the day driving back to base camp. I certainly hadn't enjoyed the business of following up somebody else's wounded buffalo, I reflected as the hunting car rocked and scraped along the light bush track, but it sure as hell beat the *real* fight for survival, back in civilization.

RETURN OF THE MAN-EATERS

PETERSEN'S HUNTING—
OCTOBER 1983

A massive crocodile basking on a sand bar.

AUTHOR'S INTRODUCTION

Man-eaters, as we all know, have been limited to lurking in the foxed pages of very old books, usually in half-calf and gilt. After all, this is nearly the last decade of the twentieth century! Imagine such trash as people being eaten by crocodiles within a few hundred miles of Egoli, the Zulu name for Johannesburg, South Africa, the City of Gold!

It always strikes me as strange that great peoples such as the Americans never seem to pause and realize that there are far more humans being attacked, killed, and eaten by their own grizzly bears today than in the time of Lewis and Clark. True, there are probably not as many grizzlies, but their concentration in parks, supplied with a constant source of bipedal prey such as hikers and backpackers (who now are advised to wear bells on their pack harnesses to forewarn grizzlies), creates a much greater saturation percentage of man-eater to prey than was the case two hundred years ago.

Actually, a grizzly bear is rather a Cub Scout compared to such accomplished people-processors as lions, leopards, and, especially, crocodiles. Considering just the last species, there are still about ten people a day eaten by them throughout Africa, Asia, and Australia. Oh yes, the American alligator does his bit too.

As I write this, in July 1989, I have increased my files of croc man-eating by dozens of incidents. Dozens? Hell, scores. Before giving the most slender details to support the contention that the crocodile is as dangerous now, if not more so, than it was centuries ago, let me explain that space will not permit more than the briefest accounts of recent attacks and killings. Also, kindly bear in mind that these are highly selected from many times their number, such attacks not always proving fatal. Newspaper reporters have some difficulty in interviewing people inside crocodiles' stomachs. Bad acoustics, I suspect. And let us never forget that many croc attacks go unreported simply because they usually occur in wild regions where communications are primitive. I remember several occasions during my years in the African bush in which one or another village dweller simply disappeared near a river. The people just accepted that crocs had once again struck.

- *December 7, 1983: A three-year-old girl was taken and never seen again while her mother was washing clothes in the Great Usutu River in South Africa's lowveld. The child screamed at being caught by a leg and the mother tried to chase off the croc. The waters closed over the croc and its victim. This was the latest of three years of killings by crocodiles in the Usutu.*
- *January 1, 1984: As reported by the Zambian Information Service in Lusaka, crocs had killed twenty-five children from one primary school alone over the past five years. Although a pump had been installed for drinking water some distance from the river, it was ignored. The local chief was severely beaten for not controlling the crocodiles.*
- *March 27, 1984: Residents living along the banks of the Great Usutu River at Siphofaneni, Swaziland, say a large man-eating crocodile has eaten one of them each year for the past eleven years. It has also eaten hundreds of heads of livestock. Mr. Lufto Gamedze, a community leader, has been quoted as saying that the croc was owned by a witch, since repeated attempts to kill it have failed.*
- *May 12, 1984: A crocodile killed and ate a Britisher, Nigel Cox, in the author's old base, the Luangwa River of Zambia. It was likely a group attack, as a black game guard was also killed and his body never recovered. Cox refused to heed warnings about the Luangwa crocs. He believed they were not dangerous. The proof was in the pudding. It turned out to be him.*

- *August 28, 1984: At Hoedspruit, South Africa, a six-year-old boy was killed and taken by a croc. The pond, bounding the Blyde River, was being drained to find the boy and his killer. No further report.*
- *December 20, 1984: Muzikayifani Ndlovu was expected to lose his leg after a croc attack in the Umfolozi River of Zululand. He suffers greatly from nightmares after ripping himself loose from a croc of unknown size.*
- *February 20, 1985: A crocodile actually took an Australian woman from a tree where she had fled, about 230 kilometers southeast of Darwin. She was attacked in the bush some distance from water, and crawled for four hours after breaking free. She was found by a ranger.*
- *May 6, 1986: Three people were savaged by crocs in the Zambezi River near Mana Pools, Zimbabwe. Mr. Hugh Lloyd lost an arm saving his son, Jeremy, while a British tourist was severely bitten in his attempts to help Jeremy.*
- *January 7, 1987: A Kavango soldier vanished in the croc-infested Kavango River in northern Namibia, where he had been swimming.*
- *October 11, 1987: The postmaster of the Caprivi Strip settlement of Katima Mulilo, an Afrikaner by name of Kobus Slabbert, was grabbed by a crocodile in the Zambezi River while in the very act of warning women and children to clear the water. He and his party were enjoying a barbecue on the bank of the river, some of the guests splashing in the river, when Slabbert went to warn them of the danger of crocs. He was grabbed by the ankle, and despite his immense strength and bulk of 286 pounds, was whisked away. Portions of his body were discovered two days later. Slabbert twice surfaced in the jaws of the croc and was advised to stick his fingers into the killer's eyes. Apparently he did not have time.*

Before Americans feel too smug, let's remember the tragedy in Englewood, Florida, in June 1988, when an alligator seized four-year-old Erin Glover and dragged her to

*her death. The alligator had lunged at the little girl as she
and playmates were walking near a lake.*

*Quite certainly, "Return of the Man-Eaters" is not the
appropriate title of this chapter. They have not returned;
they have never left.*

The last dawn of Sweetness Vilakazi's short life edged the
sere, brown horizon of KwaZulu with typical and terrible heat.
As the shimmering globe of sun flooded over the drought-tortured crops and into her beehive-shaped grass *kaia,* Sweetness
rolled from her simple bed, balanced on stacked bricks to raise
it above the reach of the dreaded *tokoloshe*—the Zulu equivalent of a free-lance leprechaun—and checked to be certain
none of the hairy water spirits lurked beneath, ready to render
her unworthy of a husband. Satisfied that she was alone, she
shrugged into a faded calico shift and stepped outside.

Already, many of the married women had left for the
fields, hoes on shoulders, before the first threat of the January
summer day began to hammer down, and were now sweating
in the parched, khaki-colored mealie patches that should have
been as green as the wing of the *isithathabantwana,* the praying
mantis—the-green-one-who-takes-children. It would be a very
bad year, Sweetness thought, scuffing the powdery dirt with
coated toes. This should be the time of the rains, yet her
KwaZulu homeland was still burned and naked. What, then,
would happen when the dry winter came in April? Ah, well,
decided Sweetness Vilakazi, thoughts were for men. . . .

As she had done since the time her mother had trained
her to balance a tiny vegetable tin on her head as a child, she
swung up the envied plastic jerry can and started on the worn
path to the Hluhluwe River, which muttered the muffled

speech of dark water beneath high banks, some 200 yards away. *"Sakubona,* Sweetnessi," called a woman as she passed, and Sweetness smiled easily on her way to death, which lay, unseen, only twenty long, barefoot paces ahead, waiting and hungry a few feet from the well-worn notch in the red clay bank where women drew murky water for their families. "Hua!" thought Sweetness Vilakazi, "but that hussy Beauty Mkunzi was foolish to let that crocodile take her water can." And, she remembered, just the next day Bongiwe Mkwandi had been caught by the hand by a big *iNgwenya* but had pulled free, although the crocodile had badly hurt her. She was still in the *hospitali* at Empangeni, Sweetness recalled, and cast her eyes quickly about in hopes of seeing Bongiwe's strapping husband, who might well be getting lonely by now. What foolish women, decided Sweetness, to let themselves nearly be caught by *iNgwenya*. Humming a snatch of "The Wedding Song," she felt the cool caress of the river water sluice over her toes as the slow, brown liquid flowed into the neck of the jerry can.

Of course, she never saw it, the camouflaged log just beneath the torpid surface. An explosion of muddy water and ivory teeth erupted before her, savage fangs and irresistible power crushing the bone of her arm that gripped the water vessel and clamping her flesh as solidly as a lion trap. Her scream of protest and agonized surprise had just welled in her constricted throat when, with a wrench and a twist, she was under the surface, the panic of her filling lungs unfelt because of the agony of her splintered arm. In seconds, the calm, brown waters of the Hluhluwe had closed, only the flirt of swirling, slow current marking the place where Sweetness Vilakazi had ceased to exist.

Sweetness Vilakazi was never seen after that day in early January 1983. Nor have the corpses of nine other human crocodile victims killed in the Nkundizi area of Hlabisa been recovered in the roughly four months since they began to die.

Why were they not more careful, knowing the danger only too well? I doubt that it could ever be explained to a non-African; perhaps it is just the way of things with the hunter and the hunted.

I can never seem to stop a small shake of my head every time I pick up a newspaper or magazine and see the Nile crocodile enshrined with the Cudjoe Key beach mouse, the California condor, the Hawaiian monk seal, or the rusty numbat under the enveloping wings of the word *endangered*. It may seem a touch strange, but I would suggest, as have some enlightened wildlife experts, that in some very extensive areas of Africa, the odds of getting eaten by a crocodile are about as good—or bad—right now as you read this as they were a hundred or more years ago.

I suppose that, these days, when the lightning development of mind-boggling technology is so astounding as to numb us, it's hard to keep in mind that some things *never* change. For sure, one of them is the croc. The other, as typified by the killing and eating of Sweetness Vilakazi, is the fact that man is a quite natural prey for old *iNgwenya*, which has been snacking on lithe, dusky maidens for as long as they have been hanging around the banks of lakes and rivers. This is, of course, much less than the 170 million years that the crocodile has been open for business, but it seems that it has filled in its idle moments admirably since humans came on the scene.

It's worth an instructive look at the particular situation in which Sweetness Vilakazi had all her life memberships canceled, because the circumstances are, at least in my experience, classic croc fare that still seem beyond belief to the average American.

The Nkundizi area of Hlabisa, a section of the Zulu homeland of KwaZulu, sounds exotic enough, but in fact lies only about two hundred miles from the ultrasophistication of Johannesburg, the City of Gold. Call it a round trip between New York and Philly. Well, the Hluhluwe (Shlush-*shloo*-weh) River has plenty of crocs, make no mistake, but it's not especially noted for its saurian population. The interesting thing is that of the nine humans recently eaten in company with 114 cattle, nine goats, and three dogs, not a single one of the late tribesmen was reported to the authority responsible, the KwaZulu Nature Conservation Department.

The *induna*s, or headmen, had for generations taken the croc danger as just a normal ingredient of bush living or, as they put it, a "natural disaster." Actually, they were informed only in the 1950s that they would be prosecuted for such unenlightened, anticonservationist activities as trying to kill the crocodiles that were regularly eating their people. Although it could have been little consolation to widow Pauline Dlamini, whose fifteen-year-old son and breadwinner was eaten by a croc in January of 1983 while gathering aquatic wild plants, protests against the wave of human slaughter were finally lodged with the local magistrate. No, no, and no again ruled the various parks boards and conservation departments. They would try to remove a *particular* man-eater, but, as was the case with the Hluhluwe crocs, there was no way to determine which crocs were guilty. A general thinning of the crocs was declared liable to "disturb the ecology." The Zulus would just have to take more care or find someplace else to get their water.

I suppose one could make a point that the Zulus living along the Hluhluwe have it pretty easy compared with the Zambian natives resident in the Kapinda region of Zambia's border with Zaire on Lake Mweru Wantipa. According to the Zambia *Daily Mail* (which, one presumes, would hardly go out of its way to advertise such a primeval state of affairs in a country as enlightened as Zambia), an average of thirty people a *month* are killed and eaten by crocs. That's one a day, as of July 15, 1982! The Kapinda villagers report that a shortage of fish, the mainstay of the local diet for both people and crocodiles, has led to the crocs becoming so fierce and aggressive that they are hunting humans as far as 550 yards from the water's edge. At an average of thirty per month, it would seem that the tactic works pretty well!

Certainly, it shouldn't be presumed that Zambian crocs have some sort of racist preference; it's just that the obvious population proportions in rural Africa dictate that blacks are thousands of times more likely to turn up on the menu than whites. A terrifying exception to the rule was Andrew Theunissen, a senior police official who came about as close to being crocodile fodder as you can get while he was swimming in the massive Lake Kariba, part of the border between Zambia and Zimbabwe (formerly Rhodesia).

According to the report in the *National Enquirer,* which Theunissen wrote in June of 1982, he was in the croc-infested water in the first place because of his own pet theory, which proclaimed that crocs won't attack a man where fish are plentiful. Well, Andy, back to the old drawing board. . . .

Theunissen, who was checking out the equipment on a police boat near the town of Binga, was suffering from a headache and decided that a dip would be just the ticket. It was nothing compared with the headache he was about to get. Floating quietly about two hundred feet from where he had dived off a dock, he was paralyzed with terror when an eight-foot crocodile grabbed him by the head, an armory of teeth shearing his scalp and grating on Andrew's skull with "an unbelievable crunching, grinding noise." He reached up and tried to grip the jaws with his hands, noticing how dark it was inside the croc's mouth, all air shut off from his bursting lungs. Theunissen struggled for all he was worth, feeling the savage teeth peg deeply into his hands and fingers. Suddenly, he was free!

In a growing cloud of watery blood, the policeman tried to fend off the reptile with his hands and feet, barely avoiding the terrible slashing of fangs as the croc snapped repeatedly at him. Upright in the water and belly-to-belly with the animal, Theunissen fought until he was able to kick and push himself off. He thrashed out in desperation and finally felt the greasy mud of the bank under his fingers, pulling himself clear in a last burst of terrified energy. Fortunately, his fellow officers saw him and got him to a hospital. Despite a major collection of stitches, Theunissen was really very lucky that the extent of his injuries was a severed nerve in his lacerated scalp, which left one side of his face permanently numb, and several severed finger tendons.

Just as in the case of Sweetness Vilakazi, though, and probably thousands of others, the pattern was completed the next day; another policeman in a different part of the lake was attacked by a crocodile. He didn't have Theunissen's luck, however. The "endangered" croc killed and ate him.

It seems to me that those folks who don't tend to think of croc hunting as among the more diverting of Africa's hunting

pleasures haven't tried it. A big croc, accompanied as it normally is when sunning by tick birds and plover sentinels, is
tougher to get within range of than a paranoid bull turkey, and
is certainly one of the greater stalking challenges in the world
of hunting. Add to that a fatal target zone of only a few square
inches that can only be hit from side angles or above, and you
have a classic game animal for the precision rifleman. Still, the
real problem and challenge of croc hunting is *after* the shot,
trying to retrieve the carcass. The perfect placement of a brain
shot normally causes a few seconds of tremendous tail flurry,
which often carries the body into the water to be lost to the
jaws of its pals. If you're lucky and the croc was pointed the
right way when you shot it, though, you now have the interesting project of dragging it back to land.

This was the proposition facing a pal of mine in southeast
Africa whose safari client had shot a big croc on a river sandbar a few seasons back. For count-on-it sure, his African safari
staff weren't *about* to go get it and drag the water-supported
carcass back. The client allowed that he hadn't paid his bill
yet, and that left my friend, John. Walking down to the bank,
he fired a few rounds from his .458 into the water to spook off
any close acquaintances of the deceased dragon and started
wading up to the base of his chest, the rifle held above. About
twenty yards short of the dead croc, he felt something grab his
left leg with terrifying power, and the next instant he was
flipped off his feet, the water closing over his head. Breaking
the surface, in the sloshing billows of dirty liquid now rapidly
staining with big red blossoms, he saw that a big croc had the
calf and shin of his leg meshed tightly between its teeth and
was spinning to tear off the living meat and bone. He got a
lungful of water as he was knocked down again, trying to contain his panic but gagging and screaming in terror. Somehow,
he realized that he still had his .458, a Brno bolt-action stoked
with 500-grain solid bullets. Despite the fact that the rifle was
full of water, he reckoned he was as good as dead anyway, and
fought to flip off the safety catch. Feeling it under his thumb,
he jerked the trigger while the gun was still beneath the surface. There was a violent *whump!,* the exploding barrel badly

lacerating his hand as the action was blown apart. As he dropped the gun, he felt the croc release him. Floundering toward land, half dead with shock and pain, he was relieved to see the client run in to help him ashore. That the French hunter happened to be a physician probably saved John's life, since the man was able to stop the bleeding long enough to make the six-hour drive to a clinic.

Africa doesn't have a monopoly on crocodile attacks (a man who wounded an American crocodile in Biscayne Bay in Florida in the 1800s was killed by it when he tried to—of all things—kick it), and a recent report by United Press International from Kuala Lumpur, Malaysia, is certainly interesting. Although not the Nile crocodile of Africa, the equally deadly "mugger" or marsh crocodile (or possibly a salt-water croc, a species that killed most of a Japanese force of one thousand men stranded between Ramree Island and the Burma mainland in World War II), was reported at twenty-six feet and having a track record of at least eleven successful human kills as well as having bitten several more people who weren't inclined to stay to dinner. Over a three-year period, according to the UPI report, this particular beastie had terrorized long stretches of the Lupar River in Sarawak, formerly a prime prospecting ground for commercial hide hunters.

As of October 31, 1982, the super saurian was still giving the Lupar constabulary the slip, although the brute had been reported seen at noon several times; alas, no sharpshooter had been able to perforate its skull with a bullet. There is hope, however. Six veteran Malay witch doctors and two scientists of indeterminate qualification have joined the dragnet. It's not clear what the witch doctors are doing, but the scientists have been wandering the riverbank with their Sonys or Hitachis, playing the recorded chirpings of newly hatched crocodiles in hopes of either stirring maternal instinct in the (almost surely) female man-eater or tempting her to infanticidal cannibalism, which would be far more likely. So far, no go. Wonder what the score is up to by now?

Before leaving the different species of crocodiles to their continued depredations, bear in mind that we have only discussed *two* African locations. Even the relatively urban Zulus don't think much of reporting chopped damsels to the authorities, so you can guess what may actually go on in the *real* boondocks. Just a bit of finger counting can only leave one with the conclusion that the thousands of people killed in such remote areas as Mozambique, Angola, Ethiopia, or Congo-Brazzaville—all crocodile strongholds—must aggregate huge numbers.

For our sins, we in the southern United States are gifted with the alligator. And, for my money, the 'gator is the classic case of "preservation" gone stark, raving bananas.

When I was a kid, alligators spent most of their time seemingly queued up at the back door of Johnson, Smith and Co., the world's biggest novelty house, which sold bushels of the babies by mail order along with exploding cigars, chameleons, and highly realistic fake dog droppings. Placed on the federal endangered species list in 1967, the alligator had a record of attacking man outside of Gary Cooper Everglades movies that was pretty unimpressive. Ah, but that was before they got federally subsidized.

Today, conservative official estimates figure 'gator populations in just three Gulf counties at about ninety thousand! A fifteen-footer got itself arrested casually wandering down a street of $200,000 houses in Missouri City, Texas, just last June. Charming. Zany. Colorful, right? Not if you are one of the growing number of people who have been or will be mutilated or killed by alligators.

It wasn't funny to Sharon Elaine Holmes, who never got past the tender age of sixteen. You see, she was the first documented case of fatal alligator attack in the United States. She was dragged to her death—with her father trying to pull her out of the 'gator's jaws by her hair—drowned, and partially eaten in a state park near Sarasota, Florida, in 1973, back when 'gators were still considered endangered. That was seven years after the species became strictly protected, and four years before it was downgraded to "threatened" status. At the time, game biologists and state officials declared the terrible tragedy a "freak incident." Turns out it wasn't. In fact, it was just a preview. . . .

Since the death and dismemberment of Sharon Holmes, alligator attacks have been increasing with spooky frequency, from zero between the time of the first Spanish settlers through Sharon's death in 1973. Just last August, two University of Florida students were fortunate to rescue an even-more-fortunate classmate from the jaws of a ten-footer near Gainesville. Chris Palumbo, a twenty-year-old engineering student, was spotted in a local lake disputing possession of his left arm with a 'gator, which was trying with some success to eat it. The alligator took off when the two rescuers got close with a boat, but Chris's arm was reported severed in two places.

Mr. Dennis David, who is coordinator of the Nuisance Alligator Program for the Florida Game and Freshwater Fish Commission, advised UPI in June of 1982 that alligator bites are rare, averaging about three per year, with the last official death by 'gator in 1979. Presumably he is speaking of the Florida population only, which is composed of 500,000 to one million 'gators, depending upon whom you choose to believe. (That still seems like one heck of a lot of 'gators to be called "threatened," at least by me!) My notes show some thirteen 'gator attacks that featured major bites around the United States in 1981 alone. And these are just the ones that made the newspapers. In less than five months of 1982, for example, there had been 2,336 officially lodged complaints against nuisance, problem, or dangerous alligators (or all three) in thirteen Florida counties alone! Consider that the statistics included the cold months of January and February, when 'gators tend to be sluggish, and there is some indication of how big the problem is getting.

There is little doubt that the alligator is suffering from the same "familiarity syndrome" that affects such otherwise people-wary species as African lions and grizzly bears. That familiarity breeds contempt through close association and loss of predator respect of man in artificial circumstances, such as those of parks and reserves, is easily borne out by the alarming increase of attack rates by alligators. Those animals, once naturally frightened of man, may have now grown blasé by over-protection and increased association to the point that they are now deadly dangerous. I doubt that it will be the case, but perhaps a clipping I found in August of last year is a foreboding indicator of the future:

ALLIGATOR FOUND IN NEW YORK RESERVOIR

New York (SAPA-AP): After years of debunking stories of alligators living in New York sewer systems, municipal officials were astounded to find a small alligator in the reservoir.

"I couldn't believe it," said Mr. Andrew McCarthy of the Department of Environmental Protection.

Officials began hunting last week when residents near the reservoir began calling to say that they had seen an alligator.

On Monday two department employees spotted the alligator on a rock. It jumped into the water and swam away before they could get to it.

Later that night, accompanied by an expert from the zoo and a Mrs. Myra Watanabe, a university professor who has captured alligators in China, among other places, they succeeded in bagging it.

The alligator was taken to the Bronx Zoo, where experts examined it, pronounced it healthy, and placed it in a cage.

I suppose it won't be long before it's "Hey! Canada! Look out behind you!"

BILTONG

THE AMERICAN HUNTER—
SEPTEMBER 1979

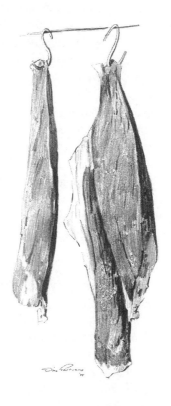

Sticks of biltong drying in the shady, cool air.

Author's Introduction

The Africa of Golden Joys described by Shakespeare just might be chromatically misleading. Of course, the rich drench of grass and sunset are pure balm to the soul, but I regret to report that they are not edible.

I'm not about to research who suggested in an early advertisement than an unremembered number of people could not be wrong, but it was fairly good advice. The same applies to biltong.

I never encountered biltong until I was given a stick about two feet long and as thick as my forearm by Johnny Roxborough, who was carving hunting trails for the old Luangwa Safaris company back in about 1969. He had a "ration license" for something around six buffalo to feed himself and his work force, and had made a most plenteous heap of this African beluga sufficient to share with me. From the first molar-twisting gnaw, I was a devotee.

Of course, being dried and not cooked, it sounds repulsive. Ah, but dear friend, look into the manufacture of satin sometime. Have you ever smelled caviar still in the process of conversion from fish eggs into foreign exchange? If not, then indulge me, who cannot stomach a deviled egg, yet who believes that biltong is the finest treatment of game meat. . . .

Unfamiliar as I am with the protein alchemy of pickling, I suppose biltong is sort of a dry-pickled meat. No, it is not cooked in the sense of its being exposed to heat, but then neither are smoked salmon, dried chipped beef, or the so-popular "snack sticks" offered at many delicatessen counters.

Most Americans assert that biltong is a form of jerky

gone wrong. Even Bob Ruark, in his Horn of the Hunter, *described it quite erroneously as being thinly cut and openly spread on bushes to dry. He was wrong, as the classic biltong of central and southern Africa is much different. The difference is due to the long dry season that east Africa does not enjoy. I see no point in developing the theme, as that's what this chapter is all about.*

I have had safari clients who refused to try it for reasons of their own, proclaiming that they did not think it would be good. So much for epicurean snobbishness. They were the poorer. In fact, I can say that I never had anybody try biltong who did not like it, vegetarians excepted.

Thus, if you take a deer or moose or elk, please humor me and try what I suggest. Make a bit of biltong. In southern Africa, it is the most common and pleasurable method of preparing game meat. It lasts nearly forever without refrigeration, and kids prefer it far, far above Popsicles. Nobody ever accused biltong of building anything but strong teeth!

I have not mentioned some herbs and flavors that may be incorporated. Many local folk like coriander, thyme, and perhaps a whisper of sugar or sage in the "wet" stage. Whatever, I think of it best as a preserved sort of African chili. Do it yourself!

Since the first day when man awoke beside the carcass of a kill too large to eat at one ravenous gorging and noticed that smaller scraps of his meal had begun to shrink and dry, dehydrated meat has been a staple food of innumerable generations of mankind. It is still one of the most popular and delicious preparations of game meat.

For the American hunter, few adventures offer the exotic flavor of an African safari. And mixed with the memories of heavy-maned lions and scimitar-horned sable are also the savory recollections of classic safari foods. For many veterans, the most delicious reminiscence is of that most traditional of all bushveld snacks, biltong.

When Yanks first see biltong, they tend to dismiss it as an African form of jerky. It is really quite different from the thinly cut, sun-dried meat of the U.S.A., and, in the opinion of many who have tried both, considerably more tasty. Biltong is an Afrikaans word from the Dutch-based language of the Boers. It refers to the rump cut often used in biltong making. As a sportsman's food, either a main course or emergency ration, it is not only practical because of small bulk and light weight, high protein value, and stability, but it is great tasting as well. Eight ounces of biltong contain as much nutrition as a four- or five-pound steak and needs no refrigeration or preservative other than to be kept dry. In a tight spot, even a foil-wrapped pair of dried sticks can keep a man alive for days. I proved that it will last literally for years under normal, dry conditions when I recently found three sticks in a cartridge bag I hadn't used since cropping elephant in Zambia in 1969! It was still tasty, even if a bit dry for my preference.

Biltong is usually produced in the southern African winter, which is the dry season. It may be made from the meat of a wide variety of antelopes—eland, kudu, impala and Cape buffalo being favorites. Most African game has extremely lean meat, the only fat being around the heart and kidneys, making it perfect for biltong. Animals with marbled flesh, such as hippo, are not suitable for biltong-making. When the muscle tissue is fully cured, the fat veins remain the same, giving one the impression of eating a candle. Even in Africa, commercial biltong is generally made from beef and is as commonly sold at rugby matches as is popcorn in our movie theaters. Because of the multinational passion for the stuff, it commands very high prices despite its light weight. Sportsmen probably use 90 percent of the meat from their carcasses for making biltong for their own and friends' use.

I ran into something of a problem a few years ago when I returned to my Southwest Florida home during the safari off-season to find that neither Cape buffalo nor kudu was on the resident license. I eat biltong the way Churchill smoked Coronas, and it didn't take long to figure out that my meager supply of Everglades venison wouldn't be enough to last me out the winter. I also noticed that the inherent humidity of the Gulf Coast made biltong production a chancy and frequently impossible operation. I began to experiment. You can imagine my delight when I found that the lowered temperature and reduced humidity of an air conditioned room created a perfect artificial climate for making biltong.

Although the sales of commercially made, artificially formed and flavored beef jerky are steadily increasing, biltong is still almost unknown in the United States. Among my friends, however, it's starting to catch on. If you've got a chunk of lean elk, deer, or moose venison in the freezer that you haven't been able to coerce your wife into cooking, why not convert it into biltong?

Biltong is nothing more than strips of lean meat, seasoned with plain salt and black pepper, which is shade-dried in a space low enough in humidity to permit it to dehydrate either naturally in wind or artificially in air conditioning. During the drying process, the meat will lose about 85 to 90 percent of its weight. There is no odor. The salt stops bacterial action and draws the moisture of the meat to the surface, where it evaporates in the dry air. The pepper is added not only for taste but because it keeps flies and insects completely away. Here's a checklist of the things you need to turn out a batch of your own:

- Lean meat, at least 8–10 pounds before trimming
- Non-iodized salt or finely crushed rock salt
- Coarse- or medium-ground black pepper
- Large bowl or basin
- Sharp knife and sharpener
- Box of paper clips, medium to large

- Heavy cord
- Cutting board

The choice of meat, especially when beef is used, is quite important. I often use baby beef, which is less fatty than many of the more expensive, grain-fattened cattle. It's also a lot cheaper. I paid $1.29 per pound for this lot of twelve pounds total weight. The tenderness of a cut of meat is more a detriment than a bonus for biltong, which, when dried properly, is stiff and hard. Any medium or large game such as deer, elk, or moose may be used. Almost any part does fine, whether neck, rump, legs or the spinal erector backstraps. In trimming leg meat, though, separate the muscles and remove the sinews that run through them. Smaller game such as rabbit or squirrel is not appropriate, nor is bear or pig because of possible parasites and strongly flavored meat. American bison is some of the best biltong meat I've worked with.

It is essential in preparing the meat to remove as much fat as possible. Fat is layered between muscles against a sheet of gristle that should be cut away after partially separating the muscles with your fingers to start the cut. I prefer a skinning knife with a sharpening stick for touching up the edge to separate the whole meat chuck into two or three muscles along their line of natural cleavage. In the case of beef, expect to lose something over one-fourth of the gross weight through trimming before the prepared meat is ready to slice for curing.

For convenience in hanging the strips and to provide maximum surface area as well as saving space, the best way to slice the strips is in an opening coil, something like a continuous apple peeling. Remember that shrinkage will be extreme, and try to keep thickness about one inch. Width doesn't matter nearly so much, as strips may later be split for storage or carrying.

Place the strips about five pounds at a time into a large bowl and cover thoroughly with non-iodized salt. After turning out a batch or two, you will have an idea how much salt you prefer. Don't pile it on. Coat it so that some salt reaches every portion of the surface evenly. With a kneading motion of the hands, mix the strips completely to be sure the salt is spread well. Add a liberal sprinkling of black pepper—medium or coarse—until the meat is well speckled after more mixing. If the meat seems a bit dry, sprinkle on a small amount of water from your fingers until it is slick enough to dissolve the surface salt without really wetting the batch down. Place the bowl in the refrigerator and let it stand overnight.

The following day, prepare the drying cords by taking a loop knot every few inches, far enough apart so that the hanging strips will not touch each other when suspended. If you are curing the meat outside, string the cord between branches of a shady tree, where the biltong will receive the most breeze, out of reach of pets or animals. Bend one paper clip into an S shape for each strip of meat, and hang the biltong with one point deeply in the meat and the other through a loop. If the humidity of your location is higher than about 75 percent, you will have better results curing your biltong inside. Place it in the direct flow of an air conditioner or duct, and, if possible, further aid evaporation by directing a small fan over the meat. If you have a dehumidifier, use it, although it's not really necessary.

The question of how long biltong should be cured depends upon several considerations including humidity, thickness of the strips, and your personal taste and texture preferences. Addicts like me tend to like it best still wet in the middle, and somewhat flexible though dry on the surface. Those who haven't tried it before will likely enjoy it dryer. I cure a batch for six days in air conditioning at 70 degrees Fahrenheit.

Experiment with three or four smaller batches of two or three sticks each, varying thickness and seasoning as well as hanging time. When you have found the ideal texture and seasoning for your taste, you may stop the drying process by freezing the strips in tinfoil. This isn't necessary unless you plan to keep it for a long time and prefer it wet.

Biltong should not be wolfed down but savored, and may

be eaten in stick form by gnawing if you have healthy teeth. As a snack, it is delicious sliced thinly. Should you develop the passion I have for the stuff and want to be able to keep a reasonable supply hidden from your pals, it is best only eaten in an attic closet during the dark of the moon.

VIDEOS IN THE LONG GRASS

THE AMERICAN HUNTER—
DECEMBER 1986

Dennis Gerber, left, and the author with a buffalo killed on an award-winning video.

AUTHOR'S INTRODUCTION

Hey, Mom, look! No hands! I'm a video star! Well,
there was nobody more astonished than I was to hear from
Ken Wilson, president of Sportsmen on Film of California
(near enough to Hollywood to count) with the financial
suggestion that we do a series of hunting videos together.

I didn't think I would enjoy the process, but it turned
into a bucket of fun. The first three videos won the 1986
Television Movie Awards for the Best Nature/Wildlife
Production, and I was to learn that a later production
entitled "Capstick: Hunting the White Rhino," had won the
1987 Television Gold Medal Award for Conservation and
Wildlife.

Of course, announcing the triumph on "The Larry King
Show" of August 18, 1987, didn't hurt sales. The videos
have flourished.

I have never forgotten how men like Dennis Gerber
and Rick Morgan actually ran up to ten miles a day with
forty-four-pound video cameras on their shoulders, filming
all the way. Out of breath, they shot tapes that were as
steady as if filmed from a cement-set tripod. When I found
out that Gerber had six Emmies to his credit, it became
pretty easy to figure out why.

Trust me, all credit is to the film crew, as we were
hunting in very dense bush at times and the visibility hardly
permitted vision, let alone broadcast-quality filming. They
were brilliant. And courageous.

I suppose it just goes to show how perfidious the lenses
are to make me look fairly knowledgeable and everybody in
sight at least slightly heroic. Still, it has always been my
contention that the most dangerous thing a professional

*hunter or, even worse, a professional writer can do is to start
believing his own press. You have to throw one hell of a lot
of press reviews to stop a buffalo, a lion, or an elephant. . . .*

I t wasn't dangerous.

It was deadly.

The three lions—two real monsters, big even for the
Chobe region of northern Botswana—were less than thirty
yards away. On the ground, the cover certainly wasn't the
same as it had appeared from the air. What had looked like a
golf course from a couple of thousand feet was actually a snarl
of scrub mopane, terminalia, and conbretum, the impossible,
chest-high scrub that makes lions invisible until you step on
them. This always leads to highly interesting events. . . .

Gordon Cundill, Esq., our scoutmaster, motioned that he
could hear the lions breathing in a patch of really thick stuff
just ahead, and urged our minor army into battle. Gordon
loves to battle with lions, the two of us having sustained a
charge from the biggest male I have ever seen or taken, nine
feet five inches between the pegs, the previous June. I shot it
eight times, all in the right places save one (a hair over the
spine), while Gordon had three hangfires and a complete dud
through old ammo for his .500 Nitro Express double rifle. This
inspired some language I do not believe I shall include in this
piece.

I don't think there has ever been another time when I had
hoped with more fervor *not* to find a lion I had been hunting,
but that was certainly the case with these three, so dangerous
were the bush conditions. Botswana lions, I can assure you
with clear eye and the experience of conducting many safaris

in that region, have the poorest sense of humor of any of the breed I have ever encountered. I recall it passing through my mind that I really need not have been there in the first place but for my shot at becoming a video star. Hollywood! The Big Time! Me and Cary Grant. Dolly Parton, Stewart Granger. Wow! My name in lights!

It all started with a letter that arrived two months late from Ken Wilson, a six-foot-five producer who had already made some videos in Tanzania and who had decided to put together a series of major productions because of the success of his company's earlier shooting and hunting tapes. He had already been in touch with Gordon Cundill, at the time the managing director of Hunters Africa, one of the oldest and largest safari firms in Africa, with more than twenty camps in Botswana and Zambia alone. The weird thing was that I had worked with Gordon on several safaris the year before in producing my book *Peter Capstick's Africa: A Return to the Long Grass.* I accepted the assignment and suddenly found myself within body-odor distance of three lions and three feet of visibility to work with.

When I previously mentioned a minor army, perhaps I understated the group. With the number of people we had, D-Day would have gone much more easily.

First, there was Gordon Cundill, whom I have partially described. There was Ken Wilson, who does much of the shooting in the tapes and who is a fine hunter and shot. He is managing partner of Sportsmen on Film of Tarzana, California, the producer and director of the series. The cameramen were Dennis Gerber, who, if you don't mind, is absolutely tops in his field with six Emmy awards, and Rick Morgan, a six-and-a-half-foot video man of outstanding ability. The sound and some of the filming were done by Chip Payne, who exhibited great skill and ingenuity in the bush. I am most indebted to these men for their work, often meaning fourteen hours a day.

The safari staff was backed up by a rare American, Jeff Rann, a top pro who was born in Afghanistan. Another of the pros of high repute was Ron Blackbeard, who is a descendant of the 1820 settlers to South Africa but whose family has been associated with Botswana, formerly Bechuanaland, for generations. We also had Robert Ramajaga on the team, so far as I know the only black professional hunter in Botswana, and a grand man, a brilliant tracker and shot who has true knowledge of the bush.

Obviously, the first order of business for the video series was the lions. Lions take time. They sometimes take a lot more than that in the chest-to-head-high scrub of April. Happily, the video film crew had never been in on an African hunt for dangerous game, and they hadn't the first clue of the peril they were in, wandering through the horror of pre-winter bush. If you wanted to bet that I was nervous as hell, you'd win.

Lion hunting in heavy cover is a very tricky proposition under ideal circumstances (which don't really exist), but to have a battalion tagging along is a waste of time. Despite our Hollywood crowd, which looked like opening night at the premiere of *Lawrence of Arabia,* we still got to within thirty or so yards of those lions until one, the smallest, thundered off. You just can't believe how much noise they can make on hard ground. Sounds like a bloody herd of buffalo.

Gordon and I had a conference of war. Agreeing that there were plenty of lions around, we decided to split up, Ken Wilson and Rick Morgan going with Jeff Rann, while I decided to take off on my own with Dennis Gerber and Chip Payne. Of course, as my Botswana professional hunter's license had long expired, I was not technically in charge. It's rather like riding a bicycle, however—one doesn't forget. In any case, I decided to take Robert Ramajaga in tow so we were at least legal, but I would do the hunting.

We found a series of fresh lion tracks and followed them for perhaps as far as ten miles, eventually forcing them out into a *vlei,* or flood plain, from the riverine heavy stuff and I had a clear look at them. The male was very big, not all that much in the mane department, but an eminently shootable Leo. But it was only four days out, and we all thought we'd come across something from Barnum and Bailey. So, as if he were standing on a pool table, I passed him up.

Idiot.

As you can see in the tapes, there was also a crippled lioness that boded no goodwill. As we followed them through the heavy cover, she kept hanging back, and several times I thought I would have to take her before she took me. Crippled lionesses are not known for their senses of humor.

In any case, I still hoped for a really big chap. Yet, the gimped female worried me. I don't know precisely how many lions I've shot or had to shoot, but I can guarantee you in writing that she would have been trouble. So, like the fool I am, I passed the lion up; videos all set, a scenario like a fifties production, and lions practically in your hair.

Frankly, I was reasonably sure I was about to get killed. We left them and went on to buffalo.

Nice alternative.

Cape buffalo have a definitely negative attitude toward those who try to shoot them. I can't imagine why this might be, but having spent considerable time under professional medical care, I can assure you that it is so.

Ken Wilson and Rick Morgan got an excellent sequence of Ken, with Jeff Rann, taking a good bull with a particularly fine boss. The problem was the same old one: too early. Too much foliage to be able to see the game. You can almost literally get into the middle of the huge herds typical of the Chobe area, yet you can't see the horns because they're feeding, heads down and out of sight.

Finally, after about a thousand miles of following—or so it seemed—I got a shot at a good bull, wider than Ken's but not with that really tremendous boss. I had hunted the same area the year before, when you could almost shake the buffalo out of the trees. You could darn near say, "Here, hold my beer a second. I'm going to collect a buffalo. Back in five minutes. . . ." Brother, not with the grass up. Things got up-close and personal.

One of the things that most impressed me was the incredible staying power of the video cameramen. On the afternoon I happened to put a .375 Silvertip into intimate contact with a buffalo, Dennis Gerber had *run* more than eight miles with a forty-four-pound video camera and nicad belt, filming most of the way. It's quite a spectacular sequence and, although not an ad, well worth your seeing.

I had an interesting experience the following day when I was called over by White, a Masarwa bushman and the chief skinner. He showed me the heart of that buff, and it was drilled right through the geometric center. It's on tape and there's no fake about it. That bull went more than two hundred yards before falling, and then it needed a second shot.

The lions seemed to have gotten a better offer elsewhere. We had our buffalo tape and figured on heading down to the magnificent three-acre island of Etsatsa, which is situated at the head of the main channel of the Okavango Delta, where I had had such wonderful fishing the year before. The rain, most unfortunately, had fouled up the tigerfish, bream, and African pike, so as I flailed the water for three days, Ken went after the legendary sitatunga, the aquatic antelope that will stay for hours with just its nostrils showing above the surface.

Ken did it right, from a *makoro,* a sliver of shallowly dug wood, which, in such civilized parts of the world as the remote reaches of the Amazon or New Guinea, would be called a canoe. Put six feet five inches of producer into such an apparatus, and you're defying all the laws of gravity and balance. Although there had already been eight safaris through the Okavango Swamps that year in search of sitatunga, not one was successful. But what does Wilson pull off? A 230-yard, one-shot kill on a sitatunga on the first day, that's what. Okay, it wasn't in the record book, but it was mature and handsome to a fault. I couldn't believe it, having been a professional hunter in the Okavango Swamps, but Ron Blackbeard set it up just perfectly.

The fishing being strictly for the avians, we decided to head for the Kalahari Desert, which is about as far as you can get from anywhere without getting close to something. As they say, you can only go halfway into the forest without starting to come out.

We were halfway.

If you can get farther away than Matseteng, Botswana, then I haven't heard about it recently.

But the hunting was fabulous. I knew the eastern Kalahari from professional days, but was unfamiliar with this part of the desert, which is actually a water-independent ecology to which the animals have adapted well. Ken, who was hunting the non-dangerous game, took, on tape, an assortment of desert game such as red hartebeest, a phenomenal gemsbok, springbok, and wildebeest.

He also got his lion. On tape.

Gordon and I were out, mostly lying to each other as is our wont, when we came across a magnificent set of pussy pads going across the road, accompanied by, as Gordon would put it, "the most deadly of the species." Female.

We loaded our rifles, Gordon's .500 Wilkes closing after a most satisfying double *tonk,* and my Mauser custom as smooth as a ruby. Not twenty yards off the road was the immaculately fresh kill of one hell of a good gemsbok bull. As I had taken the tremendous lion with Gordon the year before, we decided to leave this chap to Ken and Ron Blackbeard. Seeing that the lions had not fed at all, we knew they were fresh off the carcass, waiting to come back.

Right.

We decided to tie a piece of toilet paper to a tree near the kill and hoped like mad that Ken and Ron would come back for lunch. At half-past eleven they did, sweaty, tired, and discouraged.

No lion spoor. They'd gone the other way. We were delighted to tell them of what we'd found, the carcass of a fresh gemsbok bull that had backed into a thorn tree and put up a helluva fight before being pulled down despite its strong, lancelike horns.

I had had sandwiches made up for them so they could easily roll while it was still hot at midday, when we hoped to find the lions sleeping.

As Rick Morgan faithfully taped, they found the male in a very heavy clump of cover and Ken shot it in the chest with a .375 H&H Magnum, then again, almost in the same hole, smack in the chest. Still, it took three more good shots to put it down. That the female didn't charge was just good luck. That we got the whole kill scene on tape was even better luck and grand kudos to Rick Morgan, who never wavered.

Taping or filming a hunt under real field conditions with dangerous game is for sure not for amateurs. You're not talking about half-tame animals that most people see in parks. The photographer is really taking his life in his hands, as these tapes clearly show, and runs a huge risk of death or maiming. As a breed, I found them indomitable, resourceful, and courageous beyond belief.

Gentlemen, may you live forever through what you have created under real conditions in one of the most dangerous of environments.

GUNPOWDER COCKTAILS?

GUNS & AMMO — APRIL 1980

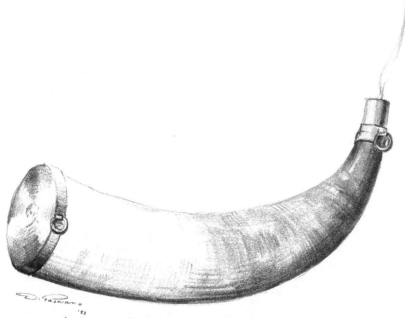

Antique powder horn smoking with—who knows what?

AUTHOR'S INTRODUCTION

A finer friend or better editor I never had than Howard French, former editor of Guns & Ammo. *Yet I was able to terrorize him with the submission of this piece, which was only published almost four years after he received it.*

Of course, no gun magazine will print material that could be harmful to the reader. In fact, all contracts for pending books from any American publisher, including St. Martin's Press, Inc., have a clause that no material offered might be harmful to a reader. Thus, I here append this assurance to you, the reader, that gunpowder of any type and alcohol of any type in ANY mixture may have dangerous or fatal consequences. This piece was run as humor ONLY. Any result of mixing ANY explosive or progressive burning material with alcohol or any flammable material is DANGEROUS and is in no way suggested or implied by this reprint from Guns & Ammo *or by the publisher, St. Martin's Press, Inc., or, indeed, by me, the author, including the original source,* Guns & Ammo, *with whose permission this material is reprinted here.*

Let us not forget that the American sense of humor and the intelligence to recognize humor and parody are backbones of our culture. Mark Twain proved that worldwide, as have many satirists over the history of our humor. The law has indeed dulled the edge of the preposterous, but let it not slaughter our sense of the outrageous.

Read on . . .

It might have never fallen into place if it hadn't been for the Bicentennial, now almost four years past. Although not a fife-toting, mouth-foaming certified founder by hereditary proxy of my country, I *had* been intrigued by the fascinating chunks of Americana dredged up by a raft of historians with nothing better to do than determine that Washington's teeth were probably beech instead of thirty-two-line-to-the-inch, hand-checkered fancy American walnut, or that Paul Revere had the whole works backwards at best. With a fondness for the educational television channels (about the only places I may be absolutely certain not to run across Jerry Lewis, despite the risk of an audio-visual brush with Cleveland Amory or Alice Herrington), the continued electronic exhortation to get stuck into a Bicentennial Project finally took root in my mind, most likely through sheer repetition. My duty clear to strike at least a glancing blow for those undaunted generations of Saturday-Night-Special-packing frontiersmen (a project determined in part by process of elimination; tri-colored bird houses make me bilious) I began my research into uncovering a pet theory: alcohol and gunpowder, indeed, *do* mix, and in actuality represent a great, lost heritage of the modern hunter and shooter.

The first thing I started noticing after beginning my investigation was that our literature and folklore are crawling with clues, far too many to be accidental. Perhaps the first tip-off was the recurring reference to "grape shot." Why not "apple shot" or "kumquat shot?" I asked myself through many sleepless nights. Other lurking facts slunk into my mind. Isn't it suspicious that we still speak of a "shot" of whiskey? Or that both booze and black powder are measured in "drams"? Even smokeless powder is reckoned in "grains," the very stuff alcohol is distilled from. As if that weren't enough, how can we deny the latent meaning implied by reference to a person as "loaded"? And isn't *blasted* the past participle ablative pluperfect of "loaded"?

Perhaps one of the clinchers is the proud Revolutionary adage, usually recorded in taverns of the day, warning Continental soldiers to "keep their powder dry." Was this a reference to conditions of humidity or, as is more likely the fact, a warning not to overdo the vermouth? And when our freezing troops at Valley Forge spoke of a "rammer," were they concerned with ramming home their musket balls or with another quick martini before mess, in itself a glowing description of Continental Army cuisine? Other letters, carefully preserved from a series of wars, bear frequent reference to our troops "being in a fortified condition." Hmmm. Slip of the tongue, or were they trying to tell us something? Was there any connection between a hangfire and a hangover? And if there is any question of possible innuendo, what of the blatant naming of a later rifle first the Peabody-Martini and then the Martini-Henry? Suspicious to a conclusion. . . .

Even masked references to the compatibility of gunpowder and alcohol, interestingly called, at the time, "firewater," have become scarce since the Compromise of 1850, concerning which there still existed dark rumors of an under-the-table deal with Carrie Nation. Tales of a secret pact between Seagrams and Union Metallic Cartridge, circa 1847, still surface. At any rate, it is clear that the mixology of booze and propellants has been a carefully edited and expunged subject for the past 150 years. Still, as my bit to celebrate the second century of progress, I have devoted the last three years (between treatments, of course) to the development of what I like to think of as a revived form of internal ballistics.

For the sake of the novice, who may not even have tried a skin pop of Hercules No. 2400, I had best explain that there are many types of powders; just powders, good powders, and great, vintage powders. Each type or brand is well suited for a particular occasion. Recently, it has been considered snobbish to insist upon one class of powders for red meat and game and another for fish or fowl, but I suspect that this is merely a ploy on the part of Hodgdons and Winchester to keep people buying powder without confusing them. I might add that it follows, ipso facto, that, this being the corporate policy of several manufacturers, there must be many American sportsmen who are closet powder-lovers. If, however, you have not discovered the fascination of powder-and-alcohol combinations, a short rundown may prove helpful. Let's start with the vintages.

Du Pont No. 1 Rifle Smokeless: One of the very best all-around choices and especially palatable with bourbon or blends. Best years were 1919, 1921, and 1922.

Of course, 1903 was surely the finest of all, but unless recorked prior to 1948, surviving canisters have "gone off." Texture is pleasantly irregular, with a moderate bouquet between a 3031 and an IMR 17½—that is to say, brave, pungent, and slightly nutty. May be considered piquant. May be taken as an aperitif straight from a .577 Nitro case with a float of six drops of Hoppe's Number Nine—shaken, not stirred, of course.

Du Pont RSQ (Resque): This superbly smooth yet tangy egg-shaped powder is the basis of many excellent ladies' drinks. Texture is silky; bouquet is delicate, although there may be some sediment. May be taken dry as snuff, provided the user is not a smoker. The heavy rainfalls of 1910 make this the best vintage year.

HiVel No. 6: An old favorite among insiders, this very mild, tube-type grain was never available to the public, hence its rarity. The best years were 1935 and 1937, 1936 having been too dry for the produce of that year to allow the mellow, back-of-the-tongue sensation so preferred by connoisseurs. An especially fine choice best complemented by aguardiente, mustard gas, or, in a pinch, tequila. Some favor the addition of a wedge of lemon to prevent blistering, but any expert who really knows his powders will shun this as simple, shabby theatrics.

1908 Hercules Stag: A medium-strength powder developed for medium-sized cases such as shot glasses and belted demitasse cups, hence its close resemblance to a good blend of coffee grounds and hamster droppings. Will not tell on the breath and goes quite smoothly in company with a half-can of strained Sterno, eight ounces of absinthe, and two ounces of aged deer lure. Ice is optional.

Black Powders: Certainly, even the sketchiest guide to vintage powders could not ignore the greatest, most flexible additive of all. Really nothing more than a 75-15-10 mixture of charcoal, sulfur, and saltpeter, the black powders are still the backbone of any fine collector's celler. Available from Fg all the way down to "meal," a few drams of an appropriate size can give any cocktail a kick you wouldn't believe. Black powder is also rich in minerals and supplies the daily required dosage of Vitamin L. CAUTION: Mouth should be rinsed with soap and warm water after a black powder cocktail, or pitting and rusting of the dental fillings may result.

Despite the excellence of the really great vintage powders, which may require a lifetime of diligence and luck to assemble into a complete cellar, it must be emphasized that there are many "green" or new powders, readily available at your local dealer, that nicely complement the stock of most bars. In fact, although somewhat traditional on such matters, I must admit that some of the robust young California sphericals, available at embarrassingly low prices, are as good as any of the imported French powders on the market. Remember, do not buy by label alone. Actually, I couldn't deny that 300 grains of Du Pont IMR 4350 goes as nicely with a mint julep as the old No. 1 Smokeless. Not only that, but you won't care who wins the Derby, anyway.

In the true American Spirit, exemplified by the grinding, unrewarding empirical process. I have finally developed a short guide to what I have found to be compatible ingredients that can be assembled (if you are not expected at work during the following week, hold Blue Cross/Blue Shield, and have a wife who has just begun an extended cruise on a bathysphere) in your very own home! I hope that you will find them as taste-tantalizing, budgetary, and nutritious as have I.

The development of these traditional heart-warmers has been a great deal of fun and a source of deep personal satisfaction to me. After all, what less could a patriot do for his country? I'd like to give you some more recipes, but I hear them coming. Probably time for them to take me for my bath again.

THE PEABODY MARTINI

In a clean horse bucket, add the following
ingredients:

3 qts. 100-proof vodka
½ lb. Hodgdon 870
Juice of one eggplant
6 oz. Coleman lantern fuel
4 doz. medium ice cubes

Stir well until blended with a wooden canoe paddle,
preferably unvarnished. A kayak paddle may be
substituted, but I take no responsibility for the
metal tips. When the mixture has settled and ceased
to either bubble or smoke, top with 150 grains of
either Bullseye or Unique as a float in the manner of
nutmeg. Remove what may be left of the canoe
(kayak) paddle and pour into heavy glasses. If
bothered by occasional irregularity, seborrhea,
ringworm, or gallstones, you may find this has an
interesting reaction. Serves two—for quite a while.

CAPPY'S CORDITE CALMER

Into an 88-mm shell casing, preferably unloaded,
add:

5 lbs. finely chopped cordite. DO NOT USE
BLENDER.
1 qt. laudanum or 36 tables Miltown or Librium
(Librium is generally my choice, although there are
those who prefer the more tart Miltown.)
2 qts. aquavit
1 dash oregano

Whites of five iguana eggs, well whipped
3 lbs. black olive pits
1 virgin (if available)
1½ lbs. lukewarm blueing salts

Shake carefully—very carefully—and pour strained over frozen cubes of nitro solvent. Garnish with rhubarb. CAUTION: Carefully dispose of any leftover olive pits, as they are toxic to hogs. Serves 16 sportsmen or two gun writers.

HANGFIRE

Into a pretested hydrofluoric acid carboy mix:

1⅝ gallons compass suspension alcohol, well aged
2 qts. lacquer thinner
2 pints vanilla extract
½ pint Vitalis
1 lb. Hercules HiVel No. 2, carefully blended to consistency with ½ lb. Winchester AA12S
5 peyote buttons, scalloped and sautéed in Zerex until crisp
1 pinch FFFg or Red Dot to taste

Stir with duck-plucking machine for ten minutes at "Grackle" setting. On some models, this may be indicated by the position cryptically labeled "GR." Chill with Freon. May be drunk through any good-quality stainless steel straw.